Dear Viraj,

Economics a good major. Hope you do well!

E

Party Life

Eric Li

Party Life

Chinese Governance and the World Beyond Liberalism

Foreword by Graham Allison

Eric Li
Chengwei Capital
Shanghai, China

ISBN 978-981-99-4521-4   ISBN 978-981-99-4522-1 (eBook)
https://doi.org/10.1007/978-981-99-4522-1

© The Editor(s) (if applicable) and The Author(s), under exclusive license to Springer Nature Singapore Pte Ltd. 2023

This work is subject to copyright. All rights are solely and exclusively licensed by the Publisher, whether the whole or part of the material is concerned, specifically the rights of reprinting, reuse of illustrations, recitation, broadcasting, reproduction on microfilms or in any other physical way, and transmission or information storage and retrieval, electronic adaptation, computer software, or by similar or dissimilar methodology now known or hereafter developed.

The use of general descriptive names, registered names, trademarks, service marks, etc. in this publication does not imply, even in the absence of a specific statement, that such names are exempt from the relevant protective laws and regulations and therefore free for general use.

The publisher, the authors, and the editors are safe to assume that the advice and information in this book are believed to be true and accurate at the date of publication. Neither the publisher nor the authors or the editors give a warranty, expressed or implied, with respect to the material contained herein or for any errors or omissions that may have been made. The publisher remains neutral with regard to jurisdictional claims in published maps and institutional affiliations.

This Palgrave Macmillan imprint is published by the registered company Springer Nature Singapore Pte Ltd.
The registered company address is: 152 Beach Road, #21-01/04 Gateway East, Singapore 189721, Singapore

Paper in this product is recyclable.

FOREWORD

Eric Li has a well-deserved reputation as an insightful analyst, pugnacious provocateur, and engaging author who enjoys vigorous debate. In this book-length brief on Xi Jinping's Party-led China, his objective is to challenge American and Western readers by making the case for China. Specifically, his central claim is that in the twenty-first century competition between China and the United States, Xi's Party-led autocracy (Li would dispute this characterization) will outperform Western democracies in delivering what citizens care about most.

Li himself is a remarkable combination of Chinese, American, and international. A native Chinese who graduated from high school in China, he earned his bachelor's degree at Berkeley followed by an M.B.A. at Stanford. As fluent in English as he is in his native tongue, he is as comfortable in the most exclusive elite circles in America as he is in his hometown of Shanghai. With a day job managing the multi-billion dollar venture capital firm that he founded in addition to the popular Chinese media platform, Guancha.cn, he is also an intellectual with a Ph.D. in political science from Fudan University who reads widely and enjoys debating Bentham or Aristotle. And while he has not played any role in the Party or in China's government, he is familiar with many of those who are now in leading positions. While he never presumes to represent China's officialdom, he frequently offers a more candid version of the thinking in the first circle. Thus, he is a frequent contributor to

Western publications, including *The New York Times*, *Foreign Affairs*, *The Washington Post*, and *The Economist*.

Readers of this book will find themselves coming away with second thoughts about five key questions:

1. **How could a Party-led autocracy possibly outperform America's democracy?** Li argues that because members of the Party vanguard put patriotism above their own private, personal interests, they are committed to pragmatism rather than to ideological principles like those currently splintering America's democracy; that China teaches its citizens to value the well-being of their society over their own selfish individual demands; that the Party selects leaders through a process that values meritocracy over racial or ethnic identity; and that its ultimate test of success is not the proceduralism of Western democracies, but performance.

2. **Why must Xi Jinping be understood not as a traditional autocrat or "dictator," to quote Biden, but in Li's term, as a "Party man?"** Why do the differences between Xi and other strong leaders or autocrats like Putin or Erdoğan today or czars and kings from previous eras matter?

    In a nutshell, his proposition is that Xi's commitment to sustaining Party rule is a twenty-first-century version of Chinese emperors' commitment to maintaining their dynasties. Without recognizing that difference, Li argues, it is impossible to understand the key choices Xi has made or to be prepared for the choices he will make on the road ahead. From Li's perspective, Xi is a "revolutionary" Chinese leader who took over a country in crisis facing the existential challenges of corruption, environmental degradation, and economic inequality. Since assuming power a decade ago, he has carefully and competently guided China through the difficult adjustments needed to ensure Party rule outlasts his own.

3. **What is Xi's grand vision for China?** In Li's summary, Xi's vision is to build a country that by the middle of this century will allow the Chinese people to have a per capita income comparable to that of the developed West. As he writes: "Marxist ideals in socialist institutions combined with traditional Chinese values will frame the nation's moral character. Economic and social institutions will be modernized to effectively use capital and entrepreneurial initiatives

in order to drive technological innovations and economic development. The resulting prosperity will be equitably shared by all in an olive-shaped society with no one being below the poverty line. Socialism will be the political compass of Chinese society that places the collective—family, community, and nation—above the individual, but leaves enough room for the latter to flourish."

In short, Xi wants to make China great again; borrowing a phrase from former Singapore Prime Minister Lee Kuan Yew, to make it "the biggest player in the history of the world."

4. **Why does Xi's China reject the Western "liberal international order?"** Li argues that "the atomized individual with divinely endowed rights is corroding community everywhere. Private interests, in the form of oligarchic capital, have become Frankensteins whose avarice is infinite." As Chinese culture has done over the centuries, Xi's China puts the interests of the society ahead of those of the individual.

In doing so, in contrast to the "ideology of liberalism," it offers an alternative that protects the "primacy of culture and the sovereignty of nations" and respects the right of each country to choose its own "development path." The contours of this vision are becoming clearer in China's three Global Initiatives: the Global Development Initiative, Global Security Initiative, and Global Civilization Initiative. Together, they offer a vision of a new international order—with distinct Chinese characteristics.

5. **How can the United States and China avoid the greatest collision of all time?** If Thucydides were asked about what's happening in relations between the United States and China today, what would he say? That was the question put to me in January at the World Economic Forum in Davos. I responded that he would say this is a classic Thucydidean rivalry in which the two parties are right on script, each competing to show which can best exemplify the role of the classic rising and ruling power—leaving him on the edge of his seat anticipating the grandest collision of all time.

Li argues that the way to avoid this trap is to create "a world safe for pluralism." Echoing the words of former US President John F. Kennedy in the most important foreign policy address of his career, delivered 60 years ago this year where he declared the United States and Soviet Union must "build a world safe for diversity," Li argues that this does not require retreating from ruthless competition between regimes with antithetical values and interests. But it does require both finding ways to constrain their competition, compromise, and even cooperate.

Today, the United States and China are locked in conditions defined by two contradictory imperatives: to compete in the greatest rivalry of all time, and to cooperate for each to ensure its own survival. If the United States and China are to avoid Thucydides's Trap, the leaders of both nations must find a way to build a world safe enough to allow the competition between America's liberty-centered democracy and China's Party-led autocracy to continue peacefully long enough for one to triumph—or maybe even to find a way for competitors to share the same small globe. To do this, Americans will have to deepen our understanding of the way the world looks through Chinese eyes. Eric Li's *Party Life* offers an engaging contribution to that end.

Cambridge, MA, USA   Graham Allison

Graham Allison is Douglas Dillon Professor of Government at the Harvard Kennedy School and the author of *Destined for War: Can America and China Escape Thucydides's Trap?*

Acknowledgments

I am of course solely responsible for the content presented and the opinions expressed in this book. However, this manuscript would not have come into existence without significant contributions from many individuals. My two research assistants, William Qiang and Ren Jie devoted countless hours to the research of relevant materials. Kathryn Salem edited many parts and helped make my articulation more succinct. My editor Jacob Dreyer at Palgrave Macmillan helped with his expertise and support that brought this project to conclusion. I am deeply indebted to them.

Many scholars gave me important advice, among them professors Zhang Weiwei and Daniel Bell whose work on Chinese politics and philosophy were invaluable resources to me as I worked on this book. My doctoral advisor Ni Shixiong was for so many years a source of intellectual mentorship that accompanied my studies of the subject. Professors Graham Allison and Michael McFaul were kind enough to read the manuscript and provided me with American perspectives that were both historical and current.

Kishore Mahbubani and George Yeo are two Asian thinkers and practitioners of politics with whom I have had numerous discussions from which I have drawn insights and inspiration. I would also like to thank Nathan Gardels, the editor who first published me in the West more than a decade ago and continued to do so over the years. He gave me confidence that I could propose ideas that might be controversial to my intended audience but still be constructive.

I am both a student of politics and an investment professional. This dual-track career has given me vantage points that are useful in my analysis of the subject at hand. I would like to thank many friends in the business world who are also thoughtful leaders on global issues for providing me with case materials. My investor and mentor Len Baker has for three decades been a close intellectual partner, and the ideas we have shared are present in this book and many of my writings.

I also owe my gratitude to my business partners, Sha Ye, Kang Pei, Richard Gu, Lu Yihao, Shen Jie, and Gu Mengte for their support as I devote time and energy to pursue this public discourse.

The content in this book can be seen as an advocacy for the Chinese worldview and are indeed critical of America in many ways. I realize this would cause resentment. Yet, there have been many Americans, some are mentioned above, who have supported and engaged with my work although they have disagreed with my ideas. I owe them my deepest gratitude and respect.

PRAISE FOR PARTY LIFE

"Eric Li makes the case for the Chinese system with flair and intellectual agility. Some in the West will be angered by his views. They should read him nonetheless."
—Gideon Rachman, *Chief Foreign Affairs Commentator for the* Financial Times

"The biggest story of our time is the return of China, the world's oldest continuous civilization. Yet, despite its legendary universities, think tanks, and professional pundits, the West has completely misunderstood this story. Eric Li has done both the West and the Rest a huge favour by taking a deep dive into the sources of this great misunderstanding. This book is a must-read for all who are looking for an antidote to the massively distorted depictions of China in the Western media."
—Kishore Mahbubani, *a Distinguished Fellow at NUS, author of* Has China Won?

"Eric Li makes a very articulate argument that the Chinese model of economic and political governance is superior to the liberal democracy model of the West. While I disagree with this view his book should be read by everyone interested in understanding China and the reasons behind its impressive development and economic success."
—Nouriel Roubini *is Professor Emeritus at the Stern School of Business, New York University*

Contents

1	Prologue	1
2	From Euphoria to Disillusionment	7
	The Sudden Collapse	7
	Long March of Historical Determinism	9
	One Man Against the Empire	12
	The Moment of Euphoria	13
	The Great Conversion	15
	"Hotel Liberalism"—Check-Out Time	19
	The Final Struggle	25
3	The Chinese Miracle	35
	Deng Xiaoping—China's Anti-Gorbachev	35
	Around the World in Forty Years	37
	The People's Republic of Innovation	40
	The Belt and Road Initiative—Silk Road, 2.0	45
	An Age of Pragmatism	47
	An Age of Vision	49
4	The Rise of China and America's Evolving Response—From Universal Liberalism to America First	55
	Christopher Bounced	55
	Cold Warriors vs. Panda Huggers	58
	We are Pivoting	61
	Quasi-Containment	63

	The Quick Failure of Quasi-Containment	64
	From Trump to Biden	65
	China's "Long Telegram" Strategy	67
5	**Modernization Without Modernity—How It All Came About**	73
	Modernization, Not Modernity	73
	Trial by Errors in the "Century of Humiliation"	77
	Party First, Then State	80
	From Emperor to Party Secretary; from Mandarins to Cadres	84
	Three Phases of the Chinese Party-State and the New Era	88
	State Building vs. Continuous Revolution	88
	The State Builders	89
	The New Era	91
	June 4, 1989	93
6	**Chinese Governance—Who Shall Rule?**	113
	Clinton and Jiang	114
	Bush and Hu	119
	Obama and Xi, Plus Trump	120
	Meritocratic Governance: It's the Org Department!	123
	Good Emperor, Bad Emperor	126
7	**How to Rule**	133
	Experimental Governance: You Are Special, Try It!	134
	Te Qu, from Special to Normal	134
	Experiments in Healthcare	135
	The Test of Taxes, Ying Gai Zeng	138
	The World's Largest Governance Lab	141
	Entrepreneurial Governance: Mayors as CEOs	141
	A Market Place of Governance	143
	Strategic Governance: Planning Makes Perfect	145
	The Visible Hand of the Five-Year Plan	147
8	**China Today—Myths and Realities**	155
	Corruption—Saints or Thieves	157
	Censorship and Free Speech	162
	The Age of "Cyber Utopianism"	162
	The Reckoning	163
	The Chinese Riposte	164
	The Accident That Could Have Stopped China	167

    Revolution (Almost) in the Air—Wumai and Celebrity   169
    On the Rule of Law   172
        The Liberal Myth of Rule of Law   173
        Chinese Rule of Law   179
        On the Covid Pandemic   184

9   **China, the Liberal International Order, and the Future of Globalization**   197
    The Myth of Liberal Globalism   202
    Cold War II   207
    A World Safe for Diversity   210
    Globalism's Death and Globalization's Renewal   212
    A Message to the Populist-Nationalists   215
    A Message to the Liberal Globalists   216
    Globalization's Renewal   219

10 **Epilogue: Xi Jinping and *Tian Xia***   229
    An Interim Report Card   229
    Capital in the Chinese Century   233
    The Economic Transformation   237
    A New Ideological Era   239
    Tian Xia—*a Prospectus*   243

Index   253

List of Figures

Fig. 3.1	GDP Growth of BRICS countries (*Source* World Bank)	38
Fig. 3.2	GDP per capita, BRICS countries, 1979–2017 (*Source* World Bank)	39
Fig. 3.3	Population in poverty: $1.9 poverty line, 1981–2014 (*Source* World Bank)	40
Fig. 7.1	Experimental regulation in China, 1979–2006	136

LIST OF TABLES

Table 3.1	GDP of BRICS countries and the United States: A relative comparison	38
Table 3.2	Record holder of historical development rate	39
Table 7.1	China's policy experiment during YGZ reform	140
Table 7.2	Proportion of quantified indicators of different types in each five-year plan (6th five-year plan period to 13th five-year plan period)	149
Table 8.1	Air pollution prevention and control action plan ("Ten Measures")	171

CHAPTER 1

Prologue

The year was 1995. China had just embarked upon its second wave of economic reforms heralded by Deng Xiaoping's "Southern Tour." Part of that transformation, declared Premier Zhu Rongji (the man credited with bringing China into the WTO) would be high-speed rail.[1] At the time, China's rail network barely stretched 65,000 kilometers—something India had achieved in 1929![2]

Nearly three decades on, the largest high-speed rail network ever known to man is propelling China past the United States as the world's largest economy.[3] It is also extending China's economic power far beyond its borders. Rail links from the country's western interior, Sichuan, have opened a new Silk Road—known as the Belt and Road Initiative—that traverses through Central Asia to Europe. Meanwhile, links from the southern city of Kunming connect China to hundreds of millions of people in Southeast Asia.

Across the Himalayas in India, a lack of infrastructure has been holding back development in the world's largest liberal democracy; its rail network has added a mere 160 kilometers a year for decades. It took a staggering 70 years to connect the nation's tracks to Kashmir.[4] Narendra Modi, running for prime minister in 2014, made simple promises while stumping through the world's largest election. His campaign slogan: I want to give every Indian a toilet![5] Interestingly, as Mr. Modi has begun to succeed in delivering faster growth in India, he is being labeled by many Western opinion leaders as "illiberal" and authoritarian.[6]

© The Author(s), under exclusive license to Springer Nature Singapore Pte Ltd. 2023
E. Li, *Party Life*, https://doi.org/10.1007/978-981-99-4522-1_1

Across the Pacific, the United States—the world's oldest liberal democracy—has spent tens of billions of dollars, but the nation's high-speed rail ambitions are hopelessly stalled. "Within 25 years, our goal is to give 80 percent of Americans access to high-speed rail," U.S. President Barack Obama said in his 2011 State of the Union address.[7] But how? California Governor Jerry Brown's project to link the northern and southern parts of his state was mired in 200-plus lawsuits and eventually collapsed.[8] In the crowded New York to Washington corridor, high-speed rail has proved politically and legally untenable. To raise the current average speed of 80 miles per hour to 220 on just that one route, it would take an astonishing $150 billion and 26 years—if it ever happens.[9]

In a private telephone conversation between then U.S. President Donald Trump and former President Jimmy Carter in May 2019, Trump worried out loud that China was getting ahead of the United States in so many ways. In contrast to the United States, which has spent trillions on constant wars, Carter says he told the president "China has not been in combat with anybody… and they spend on things that are good for the Chinese people."[10]

China's reemergence as a great power has been the most significant development since the Enlightenment, not only because of China's scale, but also because it is happening in the twilight of modern liberalism as an ideological paradigm for the world. Many have characterized the competition between America and China as a clash between liberalism and authoritarianism. This is a misperception. The difference is between universalism and pluralism. While many in the West are still hanging onto the universal outlook of liberalism, China is opening a way to a pluralistic future.

The United States and China view their political systems in fundamentally different ways: Whereas America sees liberal democratic government, defined by predetermined procedures, as an end to which all countries must aspire, China sees its current form of government (or any political system for that matter) as a means to achieving larger national ends. It believes that nations should be allowed the ability to pursue their own development paths.

Whereas the modern Western view, derived from Greek thought, is formulated with ideology and abstraction, the Chinese outlook is pragmatic and contextual. It of course is derived from China's own two-thousand-year-old tradition: Confucianism. In China, political institutions are not to be built from first principles, but are rooted in the actual needs and goals of societies and the particular cultural circumstances of the time.

Although the People's Republic has made missteps, some catastrophic, its overall success cannot be denied: In the past 70-plus years, the one-party state went from failed—wracked by famine, foreign invasions, and civil strife—to thriving. In the past 40 years, China transformed itself from a poor centrally planned agricultural country into the world's largest industrial economy. And it is extraordinarily interconnected with rest of the world.

At the same time, the nature of its political system is fundamentally anathema to the political and moral principles that undergird the dominant paradigm of Western liberalism. How can the world live with this combination of interdependence and divergence? This is the political puzzle of our time.

At the end of the Cold War, almost the entire world came to take for granted that the prescription of liberal politics and market (neoliberal) economics was the path to success. And the world was inextricably moving toward a globalized order based on liberal values. Yet, today, a vast number of countries, both developed and developing, are besieged by political paralysis and economic malaise. Globalization has essentially been stopped and turned back by populist-nationalist forces around the world, especially in America and Europe.

China stands apart from all that—a significant anomaly to the prevailing paradigm as defined and explained by Thomas Kuhn,[11] and its case is worthy of study. The significance of China's development is not that it provides the world with an alternative model to emulate, but that it demonstrates that successful alternatives exist. China's example shows an overburdened West that its costly efforts to spread its own political system around the world are unnecessary—perhaps futile. Furthermore, the China case reveals a much-needed opportunity to restart globalization in a more constructive and inclusive way.

Unfortunately, the United States does not seem to be paying attention. Intense rivalry between the country and China, and among the newly assertive nations from Russia to Europe, are placing the world in danger. The Ancien Régime of the liberal order is collapsing, but new ideas to replace it have yet to truly emerge. A return to the rule of the jungle may be next, with humanity left staring into the abyss.

If the incumbent superpower, the United States, and the Western world, could see China's rise as a natural development to be accommodated instead of a threat to be confronted—and if an increasingly assertive China could recognize its success as part of the legacy of Western modernity and its reemergence as an opportunity to reform the existing world order peacefully—the twenty-first century can escape the fate of the preceding one.

Notes

1. Zhu regarded railway transportation as a bottleneck of China's economic growth in 1990s. During his premiership, railway construction and high-speed rail planning were prioritized in his agenda. See:

    Zhu, Rongji. *Zhu Rongji Meets The Press. [朱镕基答记者问]*. People's Publishing House, 2009, pp. 180–181.

    Zhu, Rongji. *Zhu Rongji on the Record: The Road to Reform 1991–1997*. Brookings Institution Press, 2013, pp. 54, 122, 142–151.

2. The total length of railway network in China was 64,900 kilometers, according to National Bureau of Statistics. Data retrieved from: http://data.stats.gov.cn.

    By 1929, the overall length of Indian railway network had grown to 66,000 kilometers. See: "Timeline: 165 Years of History on Indian Railways." *Railway Technology*. 12 Jun. 2018; and Railway Department, Government of India. Report by the Railway Board on Indian Railways for 1929–1930, Vol. I, 1930.

    https://dspace.gipe.ac.in/xmlui/bitstream/handle/10973/18188/GIPE-016761-Contents.pdf.

3. The operating length of China's high-speed railway network had exceeded 40,000 km by the end of 2021. See: "China's High-Speed Railway Network Exceeds 40,000 km." *China Daily*. 2 Jan. 2022.

4. "Has the Indian Railways Evolved Rapidly Since Independence?" *Hindustan Times*. 25 Feb. 2016.

5. Nair, Rupam Jain. "Modi Aims to Shake Up Sanitation with Clean India Drive." *Reuters*. 2 Oct. 2014.

6. Biswas, Soutik. "'Electoral Autocracy': The Downgrading of India's Democracy." *BBC*. 16 Mar. 2021; Jasanoff, Maya.

"Narendra Modi Is Not Who America Thinks He Is." *The New York Times.* 22 Jun. 2023.
7. Obama, Barack. "Remarks by the President in State of Union Address." 25 Jan. 2011. Retrieved from: https://obamawhitehouse.archives.gov/the-press-office/2011/01/25/remarks-president-state-union-address
8. Varghese, Romy. "California Scraps Plan to Build High-Speed Railroad Between Los Angeles and San Francisco." *Time.* 12 Feb. 2019.
9. Nixon, Ron. "$11 Billion Later, High-Speed Rail Is Inching Along." *The New York Times.* 6 Aug. 2014.
10. Suggs, Ernie. "President Jimmy Carter Returns to Hometown Church." *The Atlanta Journal-Constitution.* 9 Jun. 2019.
11. Kuhn, Thomas S. *The Structure of Scientific Revolutions.* Vol. 111. University of Chicago Press: Chicago, 1970.

CHAPTER 2

From Euphoria to Disillusionment

This book is about China in the twenty-first century. Its sheer size and continuous growth will make it a major force in the world. The United States, for economic, ideological, and geopolitical reasons, is making significant efforts to try to contain its rise. As such, China's present and future, and how the world relates to it, have become the most consequential development of our time.

Sometimes it is easier to see what something is by understanding what it is not. From the late stages of the Cold War to the globalization that followed, China said no to two prevailing models put before it and was very much expected by much of the world to follow. The first was the Soviet reform model undertaken by the USSR; and the second was the liberal model led by the United States.

To better foresee where all this is going, it is important to understand where it has come from. In this context, I would argue that no single event was of more critical influence than the end of the Cold War. This is where I would like to begin.

THE SUDDEN COLLAPSE

No one predicted how fast it would happen. In December 1991, only 18 months after the Berlin Wall came crashing down, the mighty Soviet Union disintegrated. The leader of the "free world," U.S. President George H. W. Bush, watched in shock— and indeed dismay—as a feisty

© The Author(s), under exclusive license to Springer Nature
Singapore Pte Ltd. 2023
E. Li, *Party Life*, https://doi.org/10.1007/978-981-99-4522-1_2

upstart, Boris Yeltsin, publicly called on his former mentor, the beleaguered and pathetic President Mikhail Gorbachev, to put an end to the mighty Soviet Union. Later that month, the Bush administration accepted with some reluctance that Gorbachev had lost the fight.[1] "This was a system," British Foreign Secretary Douglas Hurd remarked with irony, "under which we've lived quite happily for forty years."[2]

What is perhaps most remarkable about this story is that the West's Cold Warriors were caught by complete surprise. They knew full well that they had not won. Rather, the Soviets had lost it. As Cold War historian Vladislav Zubok put it, the Soviets had "committed suicide."[3]

Of course, the man who had contemplated this outcome was George Kennan, the great American strategist and architect of the West's Cold War containment policy, which was premised on the assumption that the Soviet Union would collapse under the weight of its own myriad internal contradictions. The West, he believed, should therefore not aggressively confront the union. Instead, it should check Soviet expansion until the system crumbled on its own. In other words, it should facilitate a Soviet defeat from within.[4]

The events of 1991, when the seeds of dysfunction that were sewn in the Soviet Union's political constitution finally bore fruit, were very much in line with Kennan's strategic predictions. Still, the speed, scale, and timing of the collapse was the result of strategic missteps and historic accidents.

By the late twentieth century, the regime's centrally planned economy had fallen far behind the West's market economies. Misallocations of resources had led to the underdevelopment of the consumer sector. Under Leonid Brezhnev (and the heavy burden of alcoholism, absenteeism, and corruption) the Soviet economy had stagnated. After a failed grain harvest in 1979—and despite significant state investment in agriculture—formal food rationing had been introduced in several major cities.[5]

By 1980, the Soviet standard of living was notably inferior to that in the developed countries of the West. That year, passenger car production in the United States had reached 6.4 million, almost five times the 1.3 million produced by Soviet factories (and that for a population of just over 227 million in the United States compared to around 262 million in the Soviet Union).[6] Everyday consumer products—refrigerators, washing machines, radios and televisions, and tape recorders—were available to American consumers in greater quantity (and perhaps quality) than to

Soviet workers, who subsisted on a diet with less beef, pork, chicken, eggs, and vegetable oil than their American counterparts.[7] As real economic achievements declined, ideology assumed preeminence over economics. It was simply much easier to pretend that the system worked than to try to fix it.[8]

Long March of Historical Determinism

Underlying the malaise was the exhaustion of the usefulness of Soviet communism as an ideology. As the forefather of communist revolutions everywhere, the Soviet version was, at its core, a universal metanarrative—whose "functors, its great hero, its great dangers, its great voyages, its great goal" were increasingly incoherent and alienated from the Soviet reality, as the French philosopher Jean-François Lyotard proclaimed in his book, *The Postmodern Condition*.[9] Soviet communism's claims were universal because its basic units—classes—were above cultural conditions. As defined by Karl Marx, socioeconomic status transcended all other cultural differentiations, including religion and race.[10]

Soviet communism was also deterministic, an idea that originated with the German philosopher Frederich Hegel. According to Hegel, the end-state of human development was predetermined, and larger forces would necessarily drive all human societies toward that end.[11] This process was called progress, which, as described by famed political scientist Francis Fukuyama, arose "not from the steady development of reason, but through the blind interplay of the passions that lead men to conflict, revolution and war." It proceeded, he continued, "through a continual process of conflict, wherein systems of thought as well as political systems collide and fall apart from their own internal contradictions. They are then replaced by less contradictory and therefore higher ones, which give rise to new and different contradictions—the so-called dialectic."[12]

Marx elaborated on Hegel's theory by naming class struggle as the force and communism as the end-state. In Marx's rendition of the Hegelian dialectic, class conflicts drive human society from one stage of development to the next. In the beginning, there was primitive society, which had no class distinctions. The first class system was a slave society, and its primary tension was between slave owners and slaves. The outcome of that struggle ended slavery and society progressed to the next stage, which was feudal society. There, the primary contradiction was between landowners and peasants. And again, that class struggle took us to the next stage, capitalist society. The struggle between the capitalist class and the workers would take us through an interim stage called socialism and then, ultimately, to communist society.[13] Hegel and Marx both accepted that primitive social structures would give way to more complex ones, and they both held out the possibility, or even inevitability, of an end of history; where the two men differed was on history's end-state. Hegel claimed victory for the modern liberal state. Marx believed that the liberal state still had not resolved class conflict and would eventually yield to a global communist utopia.[14]

Ideologies that are based on universal claims and historic determinism often fall victim to dogmatic rigidity. Because the end is predetermined, such ideologies tend to reject wholesale the possibility that differences in circumstances may simply reflect varied social consensuses rather than disparate positions along the path of progress. By the end of the twentieth century, Soviet communism was deep in that state of dogmatism. Propaganda became the currency of the Brezhnev years, and countless hours and billions of rubles were wasted on grandiose schemes to reinforce the Soviet narrative.[15]

Soviet agricultural policy was deeply affected by ideological dogmatism. Soviet leaders avoided the "agriculture first" strategy that worked so well in China. Instead, they largely focused on heavy industry, the most difficult sector to reform. The inefficiency of the agro-industrial complex—subsidized by unwieldy state investments and price subsidies—and the inability to declare bankruptcy, left the Soviet state unable to finance the much-needed economic reforms that could have sustained domestic legitimacy.[16] Even still, Gorbachev "the reformer" was unwilling to abandon the Stalinist emphasis on central control and heavy industry. He was, as Marshall Goldman described, "unwilling to break out of his ideological cocoon."[17] China, of course, went through a similar period of ideological extremism in the form of the Cultural Revolution.

Soviet communism's claims of universalism had another unintended consequence that facilitated the system's ultimate collapse. The ideology stood in opposition to one of the most potent political forces of the modern world: the nation-state. The Soviet Union was a supranational state that was supposed to transcend national differences. Perhaps no one personified this characteristic more than Joseph Stalin, who was himself a Georgian. Yet the idea of the nation-state outlived Soviet communism. Even in the early period of the Cold War, nationalism was simmering in different parts of the Soviet system and several rebellions were put down, violently in many cases. Yugoslavia, led by Josip Tito, was the earliest to challenge Stalin on the national question. Tito accepted national differences within communism, and for his revisionism, Yugoslavia was ignominiously ejected from the broader communist movement in 1948.[18] Yugoslavia's punishment was light compared to what eventually befell Poland and Hungary for their own acts of defiance.

Stalin's death in 1953 and Nikita Khrushev's subsequent 1956 "de-Stalinization" movement unwittingly reignited the embers of nationalism within the Soviet bloc. By October 1956, the Polish United Workers Party had removed Stalinists from key posts and, to represent the face of national Polish communism, had elected as first secretary Wladislaw Gomulka.[19] Later that month, in solidarity with the reformers in Poland, university students in Budapest organized to demand economic and political reforms under the banner of Hungarian nationalism.[20]

That legendary Hungarian uprising ended in tragedy, with the Soviets rolling in the tanks and quashing all dissent. But by the later stages of the Cold War, the universalist Soviet structure could no longer contain the nationalist aspirations of many of the union's inhabitants. The West tends to characterize the resistance movements within the Soviet Union as democratic crusades. That might be true, but only in part. The role of nationalism in the eventual fall of the Soviet Union cannot be underestimated. It is part of the reason that the fall of the union brought about 15 new nation-states[21] with the subsequent breakup of Yugoslavia birthing another seven.[22] It was "a great tragedy of the twentieth century," Russian President Vladimir Putin has famously maintained. Overnight, after the collapse of the Soviet Union, "25 million Russians ... suddenly found themselves abroad."[23] That says it all.

The inherent contradictions in the Soviet Union's deterministic and universalist ideology may have doomed it from the start. But the system's collapse was speeded by strategic blunders and historic accidents. The gravest was the 1979 invasion of Afghanistan, which soon became a quagmire that exhausted the resources and resolve of a superpower. From the initial invasion through 1986, the Soviets committed between 9.5 and 15 billion rubles (or $12.5–$19.8 billion) in 1986 dollars and approximately 120,000 troops—tens of thousands of whom died—to the fight.[24] The disaster discredited the Red Army; it was no longer seen as the party's invincible enforcer. That, in turn, emboldened the independence movements in the non-Russian republics, which viewed the war as a Russian battle for Russian interests being fought by non-Russians. It also emboldened Russians at home; dissatisfied war veterans fashioned new civil organizations that weakened the political authority of the Communist Party.[25] The war fomented social unrest, diverted energy from Gorbachev's pressing political reforms, and increased dissatisfaction with a political hierarchy that failed to end the war.[26]

Even the most ardent historical determinists who believed that the "evil empire" was destined for failure would not reject the notion that Gorbachev's ascendency played a decisive role in the timing and speed of the downfall. Both critics and admirers seem to agree with the historian Vladislav Zubok's assessment that he "did more than anyone else to end the Cold War"; that Gorbachev was "an involuntary, unconscious liquidator of the Soviet Union"; that the systematic dismantling of the Soviet Union was "not an organic Soviet and Russian development. Rather it was a contribution to history linked to Gorbachev's individuality."[27]

One Man Against the Empire

By many historic accounts, Gorbachev's assumption of the highest office of the Soviet Union was almost accidental. His rise was facilitated by the death of Brezhnev and the ensuing two years of weakening Soviet political and economic power under Yuri Andropov and then Konstantin Chernenko. The demise of the sclerotic Chernenko in March 1985 left the party divided; the younger Gorbachev and his primary rival, Viktor Grishin, each had the support of half of the ten full Politburo members. Luckily for Gorbachev, two of Grishin's supporters were away from Moscow that March. Only one of Gorbachev's was away, and besides, he had secured backing of the most important vote: Yegor Ligachev, who was head of the organization department.

At the deciding central committee plenum, the other candidates all withdrew from consideration, and Gorbachev was unanimously elected.[28] Despite Gorbachev's reformist aspirations, his methods were decidedly authoritarian, and he moved quickly to force his erstwhile political rivals into retirement. Having suppressed the Old Guard, Gorbachev had free reign to radicalize public opinion. In short, Gorbachev put himself on a collision course with his power base, the party *apparatchik*, and later with the broader Soviet people.

When Gorbachev became General Secretary of the Communist Party of the Soviet Union, the economy was already in trouble. Gorbachev believed that, in order to fix its economic ills, the Soviet Union needed drastic political reforms, namely the adoption of some Western ideals about political openness and competition. The decision to implement sweeping political changes—*perestroika* and *glasnost*—before market-based economic reforms was Gorbachev's alone. Ligachev, the number two in Gorbachev's Kremlin and his early political ally, and other party members strenuously opposed the reforms when they started to erode party power and undermine the stability of the Soviet system. Instead of heeding their desperate warnings, though, Gorbachev sidelined Ligachev and used procedural maneuvers to sign away the party's monopoly on power.[29] The problem for Gorbachev was that his political programs didn't work. The economy never recovered and the union crumbled.

Over the border in China, something radically different was happening. In the late 1970s, the catastrophic Cultural Revolution placed the country in an even graver situation than that of the Soviet Union. Yet, at the same point in history, China, chose to do almost the opposite of Russia. The Chinese Communist Party kept its tight grip on power while steadfastly engineering a transition from a centrally planned economy to a market economy. Had Gorbachev not become the head of the Soviet Union and had the Soviets pursued a similar path to Beijing, the world today might be a very different place indeed.

The Moment of Euphoria

Even before the winter of 1991, when it all came crashing down in Moscow, the leaders of the Western world were sober about the strategic implications of a potential Soviet collapse. In his August 1991 visit to Kiev, President George H. W. Bush recommended that Ukrainians remain in the Soviet Union. As the British historian Tony Judt put it, Bush also cautioned against the kind of "self-congratulatory narrative" that had already "entered the American public record." Indeed, it was worth remembering that "Washington did not 'bring down' Communism—Communism imploded on its own accord."[30] Kennan, the now octogenarian statesman, warned once more against treating Soviet deterioration as a vindication of Western liberal democracy.[31]

Still, in the hectic early days after the union's demise, intellectuals and politicians reached their conclusion: The Cold War was an epic struggle that ended with the victory of liberal democracy and defeat of Soviet communism. From that moment forward, the world would move inexorably toward liberal democracy in every corner of the earth. Capitalism would unify the world's economies into a single global market. And at the heart of it all, the inherently rational individual would reign supreme. Very soon, the world's six billion individuals would make choices in the voting booth and in the checkout line that would produce good governments and economic prosperity. Those who once struggled against communism had won their preordained victory, as Fukuyama declared in *The End of History and the Last Man*, and now "they will create for themselves a stable democratic society...and one day they too will all have dishwashers and VCRs and private automobiles." In short, the newly freed would become the last men of democratic societies, and they would live out the rest of their days in bourgeois comfort.[32]

The End of History became the dominant narrative of the time, but Fukuyama himself was more circumspect about his conclusion. He recognized that his was not a normative case. Liberal democracy was not the best; rather it was the least bad. "We cannot take the collapse of communism as proof that no future challenges to democracy are possible, or that democracy will not one day suffer the same fate," he wrote.[33] He saw that increasing ethnic conflicts and territorial disputes in Europe could derail the liberal project in those nations.[34] It might not have been a surprise to him when his so-called caravan of wagon trains never arrived at their common destination. But it was to his audience, which adopted his triumphalism and cast the rest by the wayside of thundering wagon wheels.

In the decade after the fall of the Soviet Union, the singular narrative of Western victory and Soviet defeat dominated the world's political, economic, social, and academic institutions. It was termed the Washington Consensus. Later in the 1990s, John Williamson, the World Bank executive who coined the phrase for the doctrine of free-market development, was shocked to see his program—originally a framework to understand Latin America's troubled development—being applied in places as diverse as Indonesia and Kazakhstan.[35] His idea had mutated into a distinctively ideological agenda.

Fundamental to the Washington Consensus as articulated by Anthony Lake, then national security advisor to U.S. President Bill Clinton, was to increase American prosperity and to update American security arrangements by "promot[ing] democracy abroad." The United States' core ideological concepts of liberal democracy and market economics would be exported as part of its new strategy of "enlargement." It would succeed the Cold War doctrine of containment and included strengthening existing liberal states; fostering and consolidating new liberal democracies and market economies; countering the aggression (and supporting the liberalization) of states hostile to markets and ballot boxes; and pursuing a human rights-driven humanitarian agenda. And this time around, America would be the sole hegemon, and its "faith that individuals are equally created, with a God-given right to life, liberty, and the pursuit of happiness" would be the gospel, reflecting values that were both "American and universal."[36]

Lake's assessment of the United States' interests and geopolitical strategy would form the bedrock of an all-encompassing intellectual framework for the almost evangelical process that came to dominate the agenda of globalization: the ever-expanding integration of a global marketplace for goods, services, labor, and capital leading to the continuous and irreversible enlargement of liberalism around the world. The political and military dimensions of the process underwrote color revolutions in many developing countries, American foreign misadventures in Iraq and Afghanistan, and the development and enlargement of both the European Union and NATO.

THE GREAT CONVERSION

The quarter century since 1991 saw the unfolding of an unprecedented phenomenon: A massive number of countries rushed to remake themselves to conform to the messianic message of the "good society" framed by the Washington Consensus. This great conversion touched just about every corner of the earth. Non-governmental organizations (NGOs), mostly American, have taken it upon themselves to institutionalize what might be thought of as certification regimes for this process—a way for the world to know what countries qualify as liberal democracies and free-market economies. The priesthood for the church of the Washington Consensus thus baptizes the newly converted and rewards them for their progress in conforming to standards. Freedom House and the Heritage Foundation (which works with the *Wall Street Journal*) are among the most successful groups in the priesthood.

It is rather telling that Freedom House became a standard setter. During the Cold War, the organization's mission was to fight Soviet communism. Its original raison d'être erased after 1991, the organization changed its focus to spreading liberalism around the world. Freedom House's flagship product, a yearly report called *Freedom in the World*, is composed of numerical ratings of every country in the world's progress toward liberal democracy. Between 1990 and 2014, number of countries that could be classified as "free" went from 76 to an astonishing 125.[37]

Freedom House's representatives regularly testify before the U.S. Congress, brief high-level U.S. officials, and propagate the group's ideology at conferences, in op-eds, and through media appearances.[38] In 2004, *Freedom in the World* was even selected as a formal source in the determination of a country's eligibility for the Millennium Challenge Corporation (MCC), a bilateral U.S. foreign aid agency established by Congress and designed to provide additional aid to poor countries that, among other criteria, achieve certain liberal standards including freedom of information, civil liberties, and political rights.[39]

On the economic front, the Heritage Foundation and the *Wall Street Journal*'s joint indices, the Index of Economic Freedom and the Trade Freedom Indicator, emerged as the authority on adherence to the Washington Consensus' essentially neoliberal economic doctrine of small government and unhindered markets. The MCC likewise uses the Trade Freedom Indicator from the Heritage Foundation to determine which candidate countries will receive the corporation's performance-based aid. According to that index, the number of "free," "mostly free," and "moderately free economies" went from 46 in 1995 to 90 in 2014.[40]

At the outset of the great conversion, there was a widespread sense of euphoria. It was as if a magical formula had been discovered that, once applied, could bring prosperity to all. Clinton called it "a moment of miracles" and committed the United States to expanding "market-based democracies" across the world.[41] More than a quarter century into this great conversion, though, the Washington Consensus' report card was mixed at best. The large number of countries that went through the process came in three basic types, and they met rather divergent fates.

The first group consisted of Eastern European nations. Many of them were quickly integrated into the West after the fall of the Berlin Wall. They had always had extensive cultural links to Western Europe and had been kept in the Eastern bloc more or less by force. As soon as the Cold War was over, many rushed into the West's arms, integrating their economies and societies into Europe. By and large, they have adopted liberal politics and market economies, and their standards of living were approaching those in developed nations. A large number of the 19 countries in this category joined the European Union, and several of them are in the eurozone, NATO, or both.[42] Poland and the Czech Republic are among the most successful.

However, the countries in this tranche face significant political and economic challenges, including growing disillusionment with the state of their politics. Hungary has, in recent years, begun to express reservations about its excessive Westernization. Pew Global surveys conducted in 2009 show that enthusiasm for democracy and capitalism was waning throughout the region. In Hungary, there was "clear frustration with the current state of democracy." More than three quarters of the population believed that democracy wasn't working, and nine in ten people believed that both the country was on the wrong track and that the economy was in bad shape.[43] This had led to the rise of Viktor Orban and the current self-proclaimed system of "illiberal democracy." Interestingly, Hungary's various performance metrics actually improved under this new regime.[44]

Ukraine, on the other hand, was in even worse shape—and that predated the recent conflicts with Russia—and remains so.

The prevailing mood in some of the surveyed countries is that, although the end of communism was a good thing, some things were better under the old regime. Standards of living were higher, and public morality and law and order were taken more seriously. No one advocates a return to the past, but the prevailing nostalgia doesn't say much about the present state of affairs.

The second group that went through the Washington Consensus process was made up of places that attained developed world living standards under authoritarian, or even dictatorial, political systems during the Cold War and liberalized after they got rich. South Korea and Taiwan are the most prominent examples. Both were essentially governed by autocratic regimes while being close American allies.[45] And both successfully industrialized and became advanced economies with high living standards.

On June 29, 1987, when the June Democratic Uprising pushed the ruling military regime to hold elections, South Korea began to liberalize. Taiwan followed suit on July 15, 1987, when the president announced the end of martial law. But their fortunes soon diverged. South Korea, with robust democratic politics, became an industrial powerhouse and one of the world's most vibrant and innovative societies. It leads in information technology and is globally recognized for its innovation prowess.[46] Taiwan, on the other hand, has spiraled downward ever since its first presidential election in 1996. Partisan politics and a polarized public have precluded any consensus on Taiwan's future. Economic growth has plummeted from a high of over ten percent in the high-flying 1980s to a whimpering 0.4% in 2015. Income inequality is rising, infrastructure investment lagging, and the quality of higher education dropping.[47] Not without reason, the public is deeply pessimistic about the future.

The third group of post-Cold War democracies was the vastest—and perhaps the most interesting. Those were the nearly 100 developing countries that converted their political systems to liberal democracies in the decades during and after the Cold War, a trend that the political scientist Samuel Huntington termed the "Third Wave."[48] Some of these countries were military dictatorships; others were newly emergent from civil wars. Some of their political and social structures were fundamentally changed by Soviet and American Cold War policies; some were relatively untouched. This group encompassed a broad range of regional, cultural, and religious affiliations, but the countries included in it have ended up in a similar place: facing a general sense of disillusionment with liberalism.

For example, the post-Soviet Central Asian states[49] all adopted liberal constitutions after 1991, but nearly all of them have since twisted into strange amalgamations of dictatorship, authoritarian government, and populist democracy. Meanwhile, the developing countries in Southeast Asia and Africa that adopted Western-style liberal institutions have mostly stalled out. The Islamic world, for its part, has seen successive waves of liberalization beginning with Iran's Green Revolution and ending, for now, with the Arab Spring. The outcomes have ranged from theocratic republic (Iran) to illiberal democracy (Turkey), military dictatorship (Egypt) to total state failure (Syria). Latin American states in this category seem to have fared somewhat better, but even the apparent successes—including Brazil, Chile, and Mexico—have made halting economic and social progress at best. Whatever the region, the countries in this group have watched virtually every measurable aspect of their national health deteriorate since liberalization.[50] None has found the "good governance" that Anthony Lake once promised.[51]

Of course, beyond these three groups of countries, there was the case of Russia itself. Westerners see Putin as a recalcitrant autocrat and lament his sustained popularity with the Russian public. What they ignore is that the era after the fall of the Soviet Union and before the rise of Putin was, by just about every measure, an unmitigated disaster for the Russian people. In those ten years, Russian GDP dropped by a third. Output in some branches of engineering and consumer industries was barely 40% of the Soviet level. Agricultural production declined sharply. A substantial portion of the Russian people was reduced to poverty and virtual beggary. Life expectancy dropped from 68 in 1991 to an astonishing 59 in the year 2000 (That figure is now back up to above 70).[52]

After the Soviet collapse, the Russian Federation swallowed the Washington Consensus nearly whole—from the liberalization of politics and the separation of powers to the liberalization of markets and the freeing of the press. As Moscow was overrun with neoliberal Western advisors, however, the country fell under the control of one of the greediest oligarchies in the world, and the Russian people suffered.[53] Ironically, Russia, which the West has condemned as sliding backward, now has a governing leadership that has maintained popular support for 20-plus years—even during the current difficult military conflict in Ukraine[54,55] in contrast to the dismal ratings of most Western governments.

Future theorists will surely devote much scholarship to the question of why liberal regimes failed to deliver on its promises. A more pressing concern, though, is that most of the new converts seem to have no paths out of the mess that are both viable and executable. It turns out that once a country has signed on to liberal regimes, it is very difficult or even impossible to change course.[56] Stagnation, or worse, becomes the norm.

The speed of failures of liberal democracies has continued to accelerate. Around half of democratic governments globally are experiencing a decline in various aspects, such as erosion of credible election results, restrictions on online freedoms and rights, and youth disillusionment with political parties.[57] One out of every six liberal democracies that has existed during the past decade has failed.[58]

"Hotel Liberalism"—Check-Out Time

According to an old Chinese saying, "all banquets end."

The liberal feast that began in 1991 seems to be just about over, and some of the guests are throwing up. Larry Diamond, a leading scholar in the field, lamented in 2014 that democracy was heading into a worldwide recession.[59] Nearly ten years later, the picture looks even worse.[60] According to Freedom House, since 2005, global freedom (as defined by them) has been in decline for 15 consecutive years.[61]

Diamond has pointed out that the democratic recession is most intense among developing countries. From Russia to Iraq, Nigeria to Bangladesh,

Venezuela to Thailand, liberal democracy has been in retreat if not blown apart altogether. In Europe, political movements against liberal institutions have been gaining momentum in just about every major country. And Diamond, announcing the democratic recession in 2014, probably never fathomed the force that would later sweep his own country in the form of the nation's 45th President Donald Trump.

Writing in the Atlantic just before the 2016 American election, Diamond quoted the late Yale political scientist Juan Linz in describing the actions of U.S. politicians as "go(ing) beyond the limits of peaceful, legitimate … politics in a democracy." In a paragraph that began with Hitler, Diamond warned: "for more than half a century, Americans have blithely assumed that democracy is so rooted in their norms and institutions that nothing like that could happen here. …. it can." [62] Four years later at the 2020 U.S. election by which Trump was replaced by the traditional liberal Biden, Diamond's assessment of the state of American democracy, and by extension the global condition for liberalism, actually worsened. He now called it a "crisis level."[63]

What went wrong?

Well, it turns out that political bubbles, like economic ones, can pop. At the heart of the great conversion was an assumption that we had discovered an easy formula for political legitimacy, economic prosperity, and social justice. This formula is best defined by the term "liberal democracy." Following this formula became a moral imperative, an act of faith. That's why Clinton, on his state visit to China in 1998, publicly lectured Chinese President Jiang Zemin about getting "on the right side of history."[64] But the faith in liberal democracy turned out to be blind— a "confidence trap" as the political scientist David Runciman has called it—and the assumption that liberal democracy comes hardwired with the ability to overcome all difficulties proved mistaken.[65] Here comes the bubble: liberal regimes are by definition democratic and, therefore, is the only good form of political governance.

The error is all the more striking given that liberal democracy as a dominant political paradigm has had a very short history. Liberal ideas were seeded during the Enlightenment, but as an actual institutional practice, democracy's modern liberal incarnation hasn't lasted long at all. As it is now commonly defined and promoted around the world, it has only been around 96 years or so in the United States.[66]

In 1992, at the end of the cold war and beginning of a golden era for liberal democracy's universalization, the political theorist Lord

Bhikhu Parekh wrote in his much-cited essay, "The Cultural Particularity of Liberal Democracy," that "liberal democracy is liberalized democracy: that is, democracy defined and structured within the limits set by liberalism." And he further pointed out that, in this combination, liberalism was the dominant partner and democracy was subjugated.[67]

At the onset of the modern era, around the turn of the eighteenth century, liberal ideas injected much-needed popular accountability into dysfunctional political systems run by powerful aristocrats—think England—or pampered monarchs—think France. Yet, as more democratic measures were grafted onto the system, the West, with its intellectuals and media, has mis-conceptualized this development. They created an exclusive link between liberalism and democracy that made liberal democracy not only the dominant but also the only form of democracy. This is false both historically and conceptually. They brushed aside the fact that democracy had been a dirty word throughout the first 200 years of modern liberal history.[68]

Indeed, the liberal thinkers who gave birth to the European Enlightenment mostly viewed democracy with contempt. In his book *Representative Government*, John Stuart Mill both touted universal suffrage as a basic requirement for democratic governance and advocated depriving uneducated and non-productive members of society from the ballot, "at the discretion of a public officer," and assigning greater weight to opinions of some in national affairs.[69] Even Montesquieu, famous for his theory on separation of powers, recognized in his 1748 work *The Spirit of Laws* that democracy was associated with equality, not with liberty, and could be seen as a threat to the liberty he sought to protect.[70]

Around the same time, the American Federalists were busying themselves clarifying that they were establishing a republic, not a democracy, and designing myriad bells and whistles to constrain the popular will.[71] They even envisioned their new constitution for the American republic as a break from the preceding Articles of Confederation, which they deemed to be infested with excessive public participation. They sought to establish a powerful federal government in Washington so that decisions could be made by the wiser elites far away from the reach of the nation's populace.[72] James Madison, a leading federalist, even hated the idea of political parties until he was forced by political realities to form his own.[73]

Writing a generation later, Alexis de Tocqueville revealed his own mixed feelings about the practice of democracy. In *Democracy in America*, he explained that the system was conducive to equality but was likely to threaten liberty. Majority rule, he wrote, came with an intolerance of diverse opinion, which could lead to a tyranny harsher than monarchy. In it, "the body is left free and the soul is enslaved...an existence incomparably worse than death."[74]

This is the conceptual and practical history that demonstrates why, as in the United States, most modern liberal political institutions in the rest of the West were designed as much to check the will of the people as to enable it.[75]

No doubt, as I wrote in the past, liberal democracy had enormous successes, notably in the second half of the twentieth century. During that period, liberal democratic countries delivered unprecedented prosperity to their people—so much so that many countries, including China, sought to emulate the West's practices, such as market economics.[76]

But now, it seems clear that liberalism is failing its junior partner, democracy. In the United States, the most powerful liberal democracy of our time and its standard-bearer, vested interests block any meaningful reform through the manipulation of electoral and the legislative processes. Nobel-winning economist Michael Spence once said that American democracy evolved from "one propertied man, one vote; to one man, one vote; to one person, one vote; trending to one dollar, one vote."[77] At the same time, the United States has seen its industrial base hollowed out, its infrastructure fall into disrepair, and its median income stagnate and decline—even as those at the very top accumulate vast wealth. According to a 2020 study by University of California-Berkeley economists Emmanuel Saez and Gabriel Zucman, the top one percent of American households possessed 38% of the nation's wealth in 2018.[78] Saez and Zucman also showed that the benefits of the economic recovery from the 2008 financial crisis accrued unevenly. Among the top 0.1%, real wealth per family rose 7.9% per year between 2009 and 2012. For the bottom 90%, that figure declined 0.6% per year.[79]

No wonder that, according to *NBC News* polling data, in 2023, an astonishing 71% of Americans believed that their country was headed in the wrong track.[80] For the first time since the Great Depression, a majority of Americans fear that future generations will be worse off. And confidence in American political institutions keeps hitting new lows. Approval rates for the presidency have been below 50% for a long time,[81] and for Congress they are in the low teens.[82] In 2010, the approval rate for the Supreme Court even drifted below 50% for the first time ever,[83] then sliding to a record-low 40% in 2021.[84] Everyone seems to agree that reform is necessary, but nothing material is forthcoming.

Across the Atlantic, Europe faces similar problems. In the wake of Brexit, the European project, one of the most ambitious liberal institutional experiments in history, is running aground. Liberal institutions across the continent appear impotent in the face of the problems afflicting them. A refugee crisis involving a few million people paralyzed a union that was 900 million strong. Some of the wealthiest liberal democracies in the world cannot coordinate their fiscal policies to make their common currency, the euro, viable. In some very rich European nations, youth unemployment is close to 50%. Yet labor reforms are stalled—as is everything else.

Perhaps nothing came close to showing that the "emperor" of liberal democracy had no clothes on than the dismal performance by liberal regimes around the world in dealing with the Covid-19 pandemic. In its attempt to counter a rising China, the Biden Administration called a global gathering of liberal democracies in December 2021. One hundred and ten countries and regions were invited. A review showed that these 111 places (with the United States. included) consisted of around 56% of the world's population but, by February 2022, had cumulative Covid-19 deaths of 4.2 million, which was 82% of the world's total. More glaringly, the three countries with the highest deaths at the time were the host country the United States (900,000), which boasted of being the oldest democracy, Brazil (700,000) and India (500,000) which relished being the largest democracy.[85]

It would not be overstating matters to suggest that dysfunctional governance is afflicting a vast majority of liberal democracies, rich and poor, across the globe. Yet Western politicians are still aggressively promoting liberal democracy abroad, sometimes by force. Even some Western thinkers have recognized the problem. Samuel Huntington, for one, studied the phenomenon of political decay, which happens when political institutions are unable to adapt to changing environments, including shifts in technology and economic models.[86] He found that once the degradation starts, it is hard to reverse. The economist Mancur Olson saw liberal democracy as already sinking into that state of ossification. As interest groups continue to accumulate power, he wrote, they become "distributive coalitions" that are able to capture democratic politics to make the system serve their interests at the expense of the collective. The latter, even though it is aware of this state of affairs, is nevertheless too paralyzed to do anything about it.[87] Democratic self-correction, at this terminal stage, is impossible.

In January 2013, the journalist Fareed Zakaria asked on the cover of *Foreign Affairs* "Can America Be Fixed?" Prompted by the then-impending fiscal cliff, a combination of tax increases and across-the-board spending cuts that were to soon come into effect in the United States, Zakaria's article illustrated the disconnect between Washington's focus on levying and cutting taxes and the long-term challenge of retooling the country's economy, society, and government for the twenty-first century. He echoed the urgent calls by many for fiscal, entitlement, infrastructure, immigration, and education reforms and came to the sobering conclusion that "the current system works better as a mechanism for campaign fundraising than it does as an instrument for financial oversight." That's a direct consequence of a status quo in which existing policies benefit vested interests.[88]

A year later, in an article in the same journal, Fukuyama characterized American political governance as suffering from "vetocracy"—too many interest groups that are strong enough to "veto" much-needed reforms but are unable to coordinate collective action. Fukuyama concludes that there is no viable solution to vetocracy, since American democracy is premised on a benign view of interest groups working collectively and in the public interest. But in reality, such special interests often serve the wealthiest segments of society, and operate against the interests of the unorganized, the poor, poorly educated, and socially marginalized—and now even the vast middle class. The process is self-reinforcing, and Fukuyama forecasted the continued decay of American politics, until an external shock—in the form of war or revolution (the violent kind)—disrupted the vicious cycle.[89]

On a deeper level, the concept of democracy has become bogged down by two faulty assumptions. One is that liberalism is necessarily democratic and democracy is necessarily liberal. In fact, there is neither a logical link between the two concepts nor any empirical evidence to support the necessity of their union. Some have even pointed out much evidence that the short history during which democracy has been liberal in the modern West was a historic accident, not a magical formula.[90] As Zakaria pointed out in his breakout work *The Future of Freedom*, electoral democracies are just as capable of producing illiberal outcomes as liberal ones.[91] He was, at the time, referring to developing countries. These days, he might as well have been writing about the West. The failure of liberal regimes to deliver democratic outcomes is leading to calls within the West for "illiberal" approaches. Both populist movements from the right and socialist activism from the left can be seen as such attempts.[92]

The second assumption is that liberal democracy causes good governance—the magic formula syndrome.[93] As a result, liberal democracy has become an aspiration for all those who don't have it. But once implemented, in most instances after extraordinary upheavals and destruction, disappointments and backlash have followed. Western powers, in their zeal to universalize their political system, have come to forget their own violent history. And their belief that better alternatives cannot possibly exist is preventing them from confronting the myriad dysfunctions in their own political institutions.

People have been trained to see liberal democracy as an end rather than a means for effective political governance, which has contributed to its current state of ossification. As liberal democratic institutions lose their ability to self-correct, discontent and anger build among the populace. In a vast number of developed democracies, a struggle between ossification and populism rules the day—and there seems to be no way out. Not unlike the Soviet Union in the last century, the modern West and its understudies in the developing world are trapped in Hotel Liberalism—an ideological prison from which they cannot leave.

The Final Struggle

To break out of the Hotel Liberalism prison, it seems that the people in many advanced democracies have resorted to attempting to overthrow their liberal institutions by means of democratic elections.

Many have characterized the current struggle within liberal democratic institutions as one between the liberal and the democratic. The United States elected in 2016, through democratic means and following the footsteps of both Russia and the Philippines, a president who was decidedly illiberal. Even as a former president, Trump continues to hold enormous sway with a large portion of the American public. According to the Mounk-Foa study, across numerous advanced liberal states, the percentage of people who say it is "essential" to live in a democracy has plummeted, especially among younger generations.[94] Another survey from Harvard Kennedy School found 52% of young people believe that democracy was either "in trouble" or "failing."[95]

In the most recent World Values Survey, support for democracy has collapsed in the Western world. Among the millennials, fewer than one in three affirmed as a ten, on a scale of one to ten, the essentialness of living under a democracy.[96] Many of them even think there are viable options including military governments. One in six of all ages in the U.S. and Europe wants the army to rule.[97]

It seems that Western elites might consider taking a break from evangelizing around the world on their universal truth and focusing on resolving their existential struggle within.

Notes

1. Rosenthal, Andrew. "Bush Reluctantly Concludes Gorbachev Tried to Cling to Power Too Long." *The New York Times*. 24 Dec. 1991; "The Soviet Coup and Its Aftermath: A Recap." *The New York Times*. 24 Aug. 1991.
2. From the quote, refer to Judt, Tony. *Postwar: A History of Europe since 1945*. Penguin, 2005, p. 639.
3. Zubok, Vladislav M. *A Failed Empire: The Soviet Union in the Cold War from Stalin to Gorbachev*. U of North Carolina, 2007, p. 334.
4. First expressed in his long telegram, Kennan would later anonymously call public attention to this idea in his famous 1947 "X-article," formally titled "The Sources of Soviet Conduct," in *Foreign Affairs* Magazine. Gaddis, John Lewis. *George F. Kennan: An American Life*. Penguin, 2011, pp. 200–275.

    For historical context, refer to the U.S. State Department's Milestones in the History of U.S. Foreign Relations, "Kennan and Containment, 1947".
5. Dowlah, Abu F. *Soviet Political Economy in Transition: From Lenin to Gorbachev*. Greenwood, 1992, pp. 79–85.
6. US Bureau of the Census and State Committee on Statistics of the U.S.S.R. *USA/USSR: Facts and Figures*. 1991, pp. 1–2, 4–7.
7. U.S. Bureau of the Census. *USA/USSR: Facts and Figures*. P. 19.
8. Roxburgh, Angus. The Second Russian Revolution: The Struggle for Power in the Kremlin. BBC, 1991, p. 10.
9. Lyotard, Jean-François. *The Postmodern Condition: A Report on Knowledge*. Trans. Geoff Bennington and Brian Massumi. Manchester UP, 1991, pp. xxiii–xxiv, 37; Gill, Graeme. *Symbolism and Regime Change in Russia*. Cambridge UP, 2013, p. 11.

10. Marx, Karl and Frederick Engels. "Bourgeois and Proletarians". *The Communist Manifesto. 1948.* International, 2016.
11. Hegel, Georg Wilhelm Friedrich. *Phenomenology of Spirit.* Trans. Arnold V. Miller & J.N. Findlay. Oxford, 1977.
12. Fukuyama, Francis. *The End of History and the Last Man.* Free, 1992, p. 60.
13. Marx, Karl and Frederick Engels, *The Communist Manifesto.*
14. Fukuyama, *The End of History*, p. 65.
15. Some of these grandiose schemes included designs to "tame Siberia" or to reverse the flow of rivers to irrigate arid cotton-growing regions of Soviet central Asia. Needless to say, these projects had calamitous environmental effects. For more, refer to: Roxburgh. *The Second Russian Revolution.* p. 10.
16. Brooks, Karen M. "The Law of Cooperatives, Retail Food Prices, and the Farm Financial Crisis in the U.S.S.R." *Staff Paper Series*, P88–29, September 1988, pp. 1–17.
17. Goldman, Marshall I. *What Went Wrong with Perestroika.* Norton, 1991, pp. 95.
18. Huage, Hilde K. Creating a Socialist Yugoslavia: Tito, Communist Leadership and the National Question. I.B. Tauris, 2012, pp. 1–15, 59–85, 125–137.
19. Judt. *Postwar.* p. 311–12.
20. Lendvai, Paul. One Day That Shook the Communist World: The 1956 Hungarian Uprising and Its Legacy. Princeton UP, 2008, pp. 6–10.
21. Zubok. *A Failed Empire.* p. 342.
22. Judt. *Postwar.* p. 637.
23. Quote from Charlie Rose's 2015 interview with Putin, and published in *Vladimir Putin Direct Speech without Cuts: Russian Strategy for Winning the Geopolitical Game.* World Freedom Foundation, 2015, pp. 117.
24. United States. Central Intelligence Agency, Directorate of Intelligence. *The Costs of Soviet Involvement in Afghanistan: An Intelligence Assessment.* SOV 87–10,007 (CIA Declassification Release), 1987.
25. Reuveny, Rafael, and Aseem Prakash. "The Afghanistan War and the Breakdown of the Soviet Union." *Review of International Studies*, vol. 25, no. 4, 1999, pp. 693–708; Taubman, Philip.

"Soviet Lists Afghan War Toll: 13,310 Dead, 35,478 Wounded." *The New York Times.* 25 May 1988.
26. CIA SOV 87-10,007, The Costs of Soviet Involvement, p. iii.
27. Zubok. *A Failed Empire.* pp. 301–335. For the original sources of these quotes, see also: Brown, Archie. *The Gorbachev Factor.* Oxford UP, 1996, pp. 317; Volkogonov, Dmitry. "Sem Vozhdei: Galereia liderov SSSR." *Novosti*, vol. 2, 1995, pp. 322-23; Guerra, Adriano. *Urss. Perché è crollata. Analisi sulla fine di unimpero.* Editori Riuniti, 2001, pp. 131-60; Brutnents, Karen. *Nesbyvsheesia. Neravnodushnie zametki o perestroika.* Mezhdunarodniie otnosheniia, 2005, pp. 651; Furman, Dmitry. "Fenomen Gorbacheva." *Svobodnaia Misl II (Moscow)*, 1995, pp. 62; Ligachev, Yegor. *Inside Gorbachev's Kremlin.* Westview, 1992, pp. 126, 128.
28. Roxburgh. The Second Russian Revolution. pp. 5–10.
   Zubok. *A Failed Empire.* p. 278; Goldman. *Perestroika.* p. 96.
29. Roxburgh. The Second Russian Revolution. pp. 68–124.
30. Judt. *Postwar.* p. 659.
31. Runciman, David. The Confidence Trap: A History of Democracy in Crisis from World War I to the Present. Princeton UP, 2013, pp. 226–227.
32. Fukuyama, Francis. *The End of History and the Last Man.* Free, 2006, pp. 312.
33. Fukuyama, *The End of History*, pp. 287–88.
34. Fukuyama, *The End of History*, pp. 272–75.
35. Williamson, John. "What Washington Means by Policy Reform." *Latin American Adjustment: How Much Has Happened?* Peterson Institute for International Economics, 2002, pp. 1–10; Ramo, Joshua Cooper. *The Beijing Consensus.* Foreign Policy Centre, 2004, p. 29.
36. Lake, Anthony. "From Containment to Enlargement." Johns Hopkins University, School of Advanced International Studies, Washington, DC. Speech, 21 September 1993.
37. Freedom House. "Number and percentages of electoral democracies, FIW 1989–2016." Data found at: https://www.freedomhouse.org/report-types/freedom-world.
38. "About Freedom in the World." Freedom House. See: https://www.freedomhouse.org/report-types/freedom-world;

"Our History." Freedom House. See: https://www.freedomhouse.org/content/our-history.
39. Tarnoff, Curt. "The Millennium Challenge Corporation." *Congressional Research Service*, 7–5700 PL32427, 2016, pp. 1–34.
40. Tarnoff. "Millennium Challenge Corporation." p. 34; Heritage Foundation. "Explore the Data." Countries with scores higher than 60.0 are counted in the categories "moderately free," "mostly free," and "free." Raw data found at: http://www.heritage.org/index/explore?view=by-region-country-year.
41. Clinton, Bill. "Remarks to the 48th Session of the United Nations General Assembly." U.N. Headquarters, New York, NY, 27 September 1993.
42. They include Poland, Hungary, the Czech Republic, Slovakia, Ukraine, Belarus, Moldova, Romania, Bulgaria, Albania, the six former Yugoslav states of Slovenia, Croatia, Bosnia-Herzegovina, Macedonia, and Serbia and Montenegro, and the Baltic states of Lithuania, Latvia, and Estonia.
43. Pew Research Center. "End of Communism Cheered but Now with More Reservations." *Pew Global Attitudes & Trends*, 2 Nov. 2009. See more: http://www.pewglobal.org/2009/11/02/end-of-communism-cheered-but-now-with-more-reservations/; Pew Research Center. "Confidence in Democracy and Capitalism Wanes in Former Soviet Union." *Pew Global Attitudes & Trends*, 5 Dec. 2011. See more: http://www.pewglobal.org/2011/12/05/confidence-in-democracy-and-capitalism-wanes-in-former-soviet-union/.
44. Kingsley, Patrick, and Novak, Benjamin. "An Economic Miracle in Hungary, or Just a Mirage." *The New York Times*. 3 Apr. 2018.
45. In South Korea, strongman Syngman Rhee ruled between 1948 and 1960, followed by military generals Park Chung-hee and Chun Doo Kwan. Democratic reforms in June 29, 1987 finally ended authoritarian rule. From: Kleiner, Jürgen. *Korea: A Century of Change*. World Scientific, 2001, pp. v–vi.

Taiwan was under martial law for 38 years until Chiang Ching-kuo, son of Generalissimo Chiang Kai-shek, lifted it in July 1987 and moved Taiwan away from an institution present since May 19, 1949 and "one of the longest durations of martial law in the modern era." From: Cheung, Han. "Taiwan in Time: The Precursor to Total Control." *Taipei Times*. 15 May 2016; and,

Chen, Lung-Chu. *The U.S.-Taiwan-China Relationship in International Law and Policy.* Oxford UP, 2016, pp. 27.
46. McGlade, Alan. "Why South Korea Will Be The Next Global Hub For Tech Startups." *Forbes.* 6 Feb. 2014; Coy, Peter. "The Bloomberg Innovation Index." *Bloomberg.* 2015. See more information at: http://www.bloomberg.com/graphics/2015-innovative-countries/
47. Chen, Cheng-wei and Lilian Wu. "Taiwan's Economic Growth in 2015 Lowest in Six Years." *FocusTaiwan.* 29 Jan. 2016; Diamond, Larry and Gi-Wook Shin. *New Challenges for Maturing Democracies in Korea and Taiwan.* Stanford UP, 2014, pp. 216–249; Wei, Katherine. "In Taiwan, Exports Stabilize Despite 16-Month Decline." *The Diplomat.* 10 Jun. 2016; Chen, Hao and Hsin-Hsien Fan. "Education in Taiwan: The Vision and Goals of the 12-Year Curriculum." *Brookings OpEd.* 11 Nov. 2014; and Chu, Yun-Han, Min-Hua Huang, and Jie Lu. "Understanding of Democracy in East Asian Societies." *Asian Barometer*, Working Paper Series: No. 84, 2013, pp. 27–48.
48. Huntington's "Third Wave" consisted of countries that democratized between the 1970s and the end of the Cold War. His set included formal Imperialist and colonist powers like Spain and Portugal that industrialized long before their political conversion. They are not relevant to our analysis here. Refer to the original article: Huntington, Samuel P. "Democracy's Third Wave." *Journal of Democracy*, vol. 2, no. 2, 1991, pp. 12–34.
49. Armenia, Azerbaijan, Georgia, Kazakhstan, Kyrgyzstan, Tajikistan, Turkmenistan, and Uzbekistan.
50. Linz, Juan J., and Stepan, Alfred. Problems of democratic transition and consolidation: Southern Europe, South America, and post-communist Europe. JHU Press, 1996.
51. Lake, Anthony. "Remarks of Anthony Lake: Assistant to the President for National Security Affairs: From Containment to Enlargement." John Hopkins University, Washington, DC, 21, 1993.
52. Gidadhubli, R.G. "From Resignation of Boris Yeltsin: Why Now?" *Economic and Political Weekly*, vol. 35, no. 5, Money, Banking and Finance, 2000, pp. 261; The World Bank. "World Development Indicators: Russian Federation." World DataBank. Retrieved

in 2022 from: http://databank.worldbank.org/data/reports.aspx?source=2&country=RUS.
53. Not only did Yeltsin allow a handful of oligarchs to emerge, he also showed no political will to protect the interest of honest business groups by dealing effectively with criminal acts and mafia elements. Paraphrased from: Gidadhubli, "Resignation of Boris Yeltsin," pp. 261.
54. Ault, Richard and Smith, Steven. "Seven in 10 Russians approve of Putin, says latest poll." *Nottingham Post*. 2 Mar. 2022.
56. Fukuyama, Francis. "America in Decay: The Sources of Political Dysfunction" *Foreign Affairs*. Sept./Oct. 2014.
57. "Global Democracy Weakens in 2022." *The International Institute for Democracy and Electoral Assistance*. 30 Nov. 2022.
58. Diamond, Larry. "When does Populism Become a Threat to Democracy?" 3–4 Nov. 2017. Retrieved from: https://fsi.stanford.edu/global-populisms/docs/global-populisms-conference-memos.
59. Diamond, Larry. "Democracy's Deepening Recession." *The Atlantic*. 2 May. 2014.
60. Diamond, Larry. "Democracy in Decline." *Foreign Affairs*. 13 Jun. 2016.
61. Repucci, Sarah and Slipowitz, Amy. "Freedom in the World 2021: Democracy Under Siege." *Freedom House*. 2021.
62. Diamond, Larry. "It Could Happen Here." The Atlantic. 19 Oct. 2016.
63. Diamond, Larry. "The Global Crisis of Democracy." *The Wall Street Journal*. 17 May 2019.
64. "Clinton Defends China Trip, Engagement Policy." *CNN AllPolitics*. 11 Jun. 1998. For details, see: www.cnn.com/ALLPOLITICS/1998/06/11/clinton.china/
65. Runciman, David. *The Confidence Trap: A History of Democracy in Crisis from World War I to the Present*. Princeton, UP, 2013.
66. Institutional democracy is now commonly defined, and promoted around the world, as a political system of one-person-one-vote with multiple parties competing for power, with occasional referendums. If we accept this definition, American democracy is but 96 years old on a liberal count—when women were allowed to vote under

the 19th Amendment to the U.S. Constitution, and more conservatively only around 50 years old with the passage of the Voting Rights Act of 1965.
67. "Eric Li on the Failure of Liberal Democracy and the Rise of China's Way." *The Economist*. 8 Dec. 2021.
68. Dunn, John. *Breaking Democracy's Spell*. Yale, UP, 2014, p. 14.
69. Mill, John Stuart. "Of the Extension of the Suffrage." *Considerations on Representative Government*. Parker, Son and Bourn, 1861, pp. 159–167.
70. Hansen, Mogens Herman. *The Tradition of Ancient Greek Democracy and Its Importance for Modern Democracy*. Royal Danish Academy of Science and Letters, 2005, pp. 25.
71. Berggruen, Nicolas, and Nathan Gardels. Intelligent Governance for the 21st Century: A Middle Way between West and East. Polity, 2013, pp. 58–61.
72. Federalist 70 penned by Alexander Hamilton argued for a unitary executive as the main ingredient for both energy and safety. Hamilton, a close advisor to George Washington, played an important role in brokering the Compromise of 1790, which through the Residence and Assumption Acts gave Washington the authority to select the exact site for the future capital. Read more from: Hamilton, Alexander, James Madison, and John Jay. "Federalist 70." *The Federalist Papers: A Collection of Essays Written in Favour of the New Constitution as Agreed upon by the Federal Convention, September 17, 1787*. Coventry House, 2015, pp. 343–349.
73. Hamilton, Alexander, James Madison, and John Jay. "Federalist 10." The Federalist Papers: A Collection of Essays Written in Favour of the New Constitution as Agreed upon by the Federal Convention, September 17, 1787. Coventry House, 2015, pp. 47.
74. De Tocqueville, Alexis. *Democracy in America*.
75. Foner, Eric. *Tom Paine and Revolutionary America*. Oxford, UP, 1976, pp. 90.
76. "Eric Li on the Failure of Liberal Democracy and the Rise of China's Way." *The Economist*. 8 Dec. 2021.
77. Kristof, Nicholas. "Occupy the Agenda." *The New York Times*. 19 Nov. 2011.

78. Saez, Emmanuel, and Gabriel Zucman. "The rise of income and wealth inequality in America: Evidence from distributional macroeconomic accounts." *Journal of Economic Perspectives*, vol. 34, no. 4, 2020, pp. 3–26.
79. Saez, Emmanuel, and Gabriel Zucman. "Wealth Inequality in the United States since 1913: Evidence from Capitalized Income Tax Data." *The Quarterly Journal of Economics*, vol. 131, no. 2, 2016, pp. 519–578.
80. Todd, Chuck et al. "Poll finds 71% of Americans Believe Country is on Wrong Track." NBC News. 30 Jan. 2023.
81. "Presidential Approval Ratings—Barack Obama." *Gallup*. Retrieved from: http://www.gallup.com/poll/116479/barack-obama-presidential-job-approval.aspx.
82. "Congress and the Public." *Gallup*. Retrieved from: http://www.gallup.com/poll/1600/congress-public.aspx.
83. "Supreme Court." *Gallup*. Retrieved from: http://www.gallup.com/poll/4732/supreme-court.aspx.
84. Jones, Jeffrey M. "Approval of U.S. Supreme Court Down to 40%, a New Low." *Gallup*. 23 Sept. 2021.
85. "Eric Li on the Failure of Liberal Democracy and the Rise of China's Way." *The Economist*. 8 Dec. 2021.
86. Huntington, Samuel P. *Political Order in Changing Societies*. Yale, UP, 2006.
87. Olson, Mancur. *The Rise and Decline of Nations: Economic Growth, Stagflation, and Social Rigidities*. Yale, UP, 1982.
88. Zakaria, Fareed. "Can America Be Fixed: The New Crisis of Democracy" *Foreign Affairs*. Jan./Feb. 2013.
89. Fukuyama, "America in Decay.".
90. Dunn, Breaking Democracy's Spell, pp. 17–21.
91. Zakaria, Fareed. The Future of Freedom: Illiberal Democracy at Home and Abroad. W.W. Norton, 2003.
92. "Eric Li on the Failure of Liberal Democracy and the Rise of China's Way." *The Economist*. 8 Dec. 2021.
93. Dunn, *Breaking Democracy's Spell*, pp. 9–10, 23–29.
94. Taub, Amanda. "How Stable Are Democracies? 'Warning Signs Are Flashing Red.'" *The New York Times*. 29 Nov. 2016; Foa, Roberto Stefan, and Y. Mounk. "The Democratic Disconnect." *Journal of Democracy* 27.3, 2016. pp. 5–17.

95. *Harvard IOP Youth Poll.* 1 Dec. 2021. Retrieved from: https://iop.harvard.edu/youth-poll/fall-2021-harvard-youth-poll.
96. "World Value Survey." *Institute for Comparative Survey Research.* Retrieved from: http://www.worldvaluessurvey.org.
97. Gray, Alex. "The Troubling Charts That Show Young People Losing Faith in Democracy." *World Economic Forum.* 1 Dec, 2016.

CHAPTER 3

The Chinese Miracle

Zooming back to the late years of the Cold War, just as the Soviet Union was headlong into its political reforms, China took on a divergent path.

DENG XIAOPING—CHINA'S ANTI-GORBACHEV

It is safe to say that the world's largest developing economy has beaten all expectations. Indeed, few would deny that Chinese leader Deng Xiaoping's reforms, launched in 1979, were one of the most successful state initiatives in modern history.

Former U.S. Treasury Secretary Hank Paulson marveled at China's miraculous progress in his memoir *Dealing with China*:

"China's rise to economic superpower surely ranks among the most extraordinary stories in history. In barely three decades, this once backward, insular country has moved hundreds of millions of people out of poverty while turning itself into the world's second-biggest economy. I can think of no other country that has grown so much so quickly."[1]

Three fundamental features of Deng's reforms were key to setting China apart. Remember that, when Deng became the country's paramount leader in the fall of 1979, Beijing and Moscow faced similar challenges that were inherent to a centrally planned economy. They also shared an objective: to transition toward a market economy. Gorbachev determined that the prerequisite of economic reform was Western-style

© The Author(s), under exclusive license to Springer Nature Singapore Pte Ltd. 2023
E. Li, *Party Life*, https://doi.org/10.1007/978-981-99-4522-1_3

political liberalization, what came to be called *perestroika* and *glasnost*.[2] Deng, on the contrary, saw it as an economic problem not a political one. He decided to use the party's political authority to design and implement economic reforms, which became the government's single-minded focus.[3] During Deng's tenure and those of his two successors, Jiang Zemin and Hu Jintao, meanwhile, Western-style liberalization was consistently and decisively rejected. As veteran China watcher Orville Schell observed, Deng borrowed just about everything from the more advanced West except its liberal political model.[4] Perhaps that is exactly why China has been so successful!

Other than advocating a market orientation, another important feature of Deng's reforms was his emphasis on rebuilding the state. After the Cold War, in the former Soviet Union and in many other liberalizing countries, liberalization meant the dismantling of existing state structures, which were seen as ideologically tainted by the former regimes. The Chinese, however, saw the state as the machinery with which market reforms and economic development could be carried out. So, as many other countries impetuously tore down their state structures, the party went into overdrive to first rebuild institutions that had been destroyed during the Cultural Revolution and then to elaborate on them. In retrospect, it is clear that the resulting abundance of state capacity was the foundation upon which many of China's economic successes were built. It allowed the government to lay new railways, build bridges and dams, attempt bold market experiments, and guarantee social stability.

Finally, and perhaps most important and most surprising at the time, Deng strengthened the party's power within the state. As communist parties lost legitimacy around the world, China's went in the opposite direction. In 1982, three years into the Deng era, the country revised its constitution to enshrine the party's political centrality. To be sure, the party ceded its role as central planner of all aspects of the economy, and thereby unleashed dynamic market forces. And the party was no longer the omnipotent presence in all aspects of Chinese life that it was in the preceding 30 years under Mao.

Still, in one critical dimension—political governance—the party's position and capacity have been dramatically strengthened. And this trend is continuing. In the 40 years since Deng came to power, the party had fully transformed itself from a revolutionary force into a highly complex governing institution. It developed organizational structures that cover all aspects of political governance—economic policy, infrastructure, social policy, and so on—and it uses sophisticated methods to select and promote government officials.

The American political scientist Francis Fukuyama has characterized the Deng era as the party's rebuilding of the traditional Chinese state, which was the oldest and most developed in history.[5] But the transformation went much further than that; in essence, in those years, the party was being infused with the state. By now, the party *is* China's political system.

Around the World in Forty Years

In the 40-plus years after Deng launched his reform program, China smashed just about every single world record in development. In 1979, its GDP of $178 billion (current dollars) equaled less than seven percent of the U.S. figure. In recent years, the country has become an economic colossus with a GDP of $17.7 trillion, over 75% of the U.S. total.[6] In purchasing power parity terms, according to the IMF, as of 2010, China's economy had already outgrown the United States' to become the largest in the world.[7]

Even the much-touted BRICS nations—a group of emerging economies, including Brazil, Russia, India, China, and South Africa—would not have been nearly as remarkable without China. While the other four countries grew their economies (on average) to more than quadruple their original sizes in the 18 years since 2000 (when the term "BRICS" was coined), China's economy grew, over the same duration, by an order of magnitude. In the same period, China added $12.4 trillion to its GDP, which was around twice the total added national product of the other four countries combined (Table 3.1 and Fig. 3.1).

China's economic achievements look even more impressive when compared against the historical records of leading industrial nations—the United Kingdom, the United States, and Japan, at the time when they were experiencing periods of breakneck growth. Even at the heights of their biggest economic booms, these nations never achieved China's growth levels.[8] For example: at the height of its powers within the 150 year-span of the first and second industrial revolutions, the United Kingdom doubled its real GDP per capita only twice. The United States fared better—in the 74 years of rapid growth following the Great Depression, real GDP per capita doubled three times. Japan, once feted to overtake the United States as the world's largest economy, matched

Table 3.1 GDP of BRICS countries and the United States: A relative comparison

	2000		2018			
	GDP (USD, Bn)	GDP % of World	GDP (USD, Bn)	GDP % of World	Incr. GDP (USD, Bn)	Growth Multiple
United States	10,252	30.5%	20,494	23.9%	10,242	2.0×
Brazil	655	2.0%	1,868	2.2%	1,213	2.9×
Russia	260	0.8%	1,658	1.9%	1,398	6.4×
India	468	1.4%	2,726	3.2%	2,258	5.8×
China	1,211	3.6%	13,608	15.9%	12,397	11.2 ×
South Africa	1,364	0.4%	3,663	0.4%	2,299	2.7×

Source World Bank

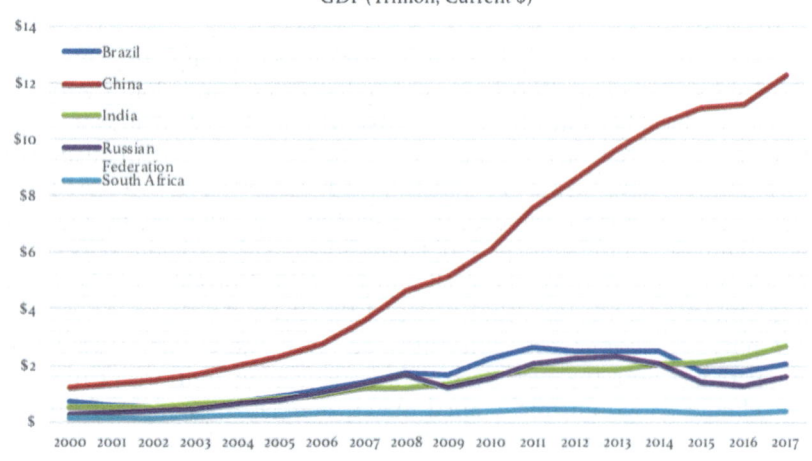

Fig. 3.1 GDP Growth of BRICS countries (*Source* World Bank)

the American feat in 28 years—before succumbing to sustained general economic stagnation (Table 3.2 and Fig. 3.2).

Table 3.2 Record holder of historical development rate

Country	Economic Period	Duration	# of Doubling of Real GDP per Capita
United Kingdom	Industrial Revolution	1780–1910 (150 years)	2
United States	Post Great Depression	1931–2005 (74 years)	3
Japan	Post World War II	1945–1973 (28 years)	3
China	Post Economic Reform	1980–2015 (35 years)	5

Source[9] 2001 Global Economics Paper No: 66 by Goldman Sachs, HIS Database, World Bank

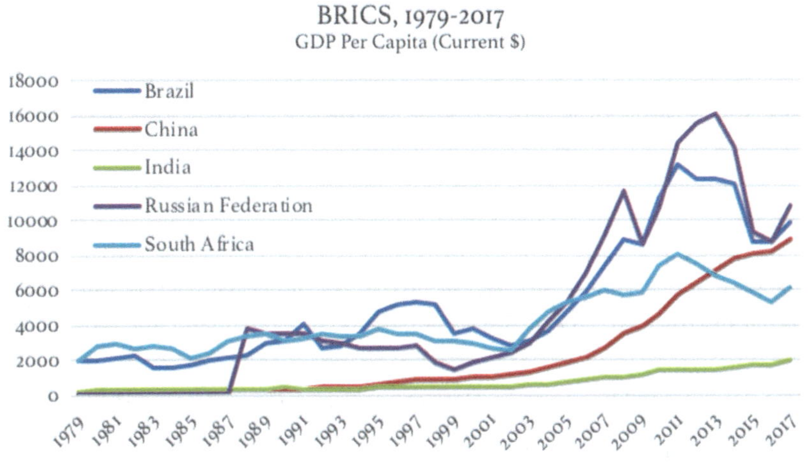

Fig. 3.2 GDP per capita, BRICS countries, 1979–2017 (*Source* World Bank)

China's astonishing economic growth also did more to alleviate suffering. After the Industrial Revolution, the United States and Western Europe took 300 years to lift 700 million people out of poverty.[10] According to the World Bank, China did so for more than 800 million people in just 30 years. In the same period, China's progress accounted for 72% of the total reduction in poverty around the world.[11] In fact, absent China, the number of people emerging from poverty would have been less than the overall population increase. Furthermore, China's rapid

Population in Poverty: $1.9 Poverty Line, 1981-2014 (Million)

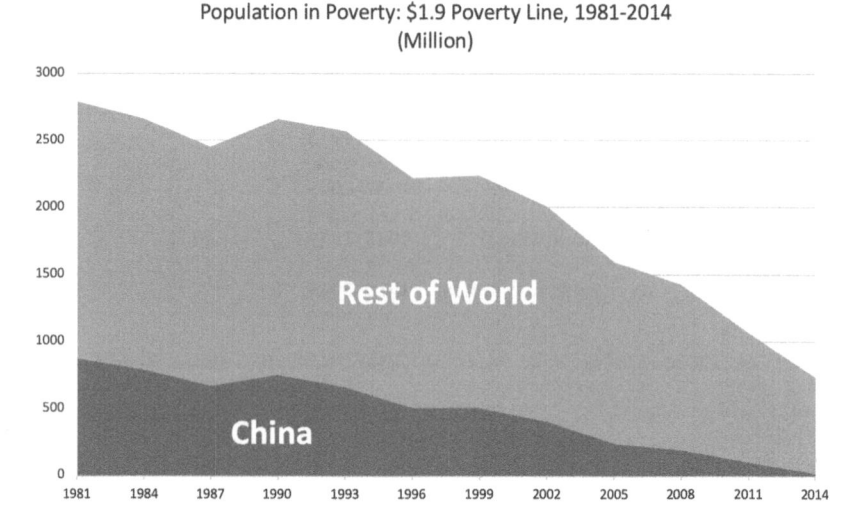

Fig. 3.3 Population in poverty: $1.9 poverty line, 1981–2014 (*Source* World Bank)

economic clip and successful government interventions, for example with urban subsidies and rural pension programs, were critical in helping the world halve extreme poverty in 2010, an important UN millennium development goal[12] (Fig. 3.3).

THE PEOPLE'S REPUBLIC OF INNOVATION

The nature and magnitude of China's economic miracle has neither been historical nor contemporary equal, and it has surprised at every turn. At its onset, observers were skeptical of the country's ability to expand beyond what could be driven by cheap labor and low-cost manufacturing. Yet such skepticism has quickly proved unfounded as China's online and digital sectors have become major forces in their own right. By market capitalization, its Internet companies are among the world's largest and most valuable. Some even rival established American firms. In the 2018 Global Top 100 companies ranking by the professional services firm PricewaterhouseCoopers, China's two Internet titans, Tencent (valued at $496 billion) and Alibaba (valued at $470 billion), were ranked as high as five and seven in terms of market cap (More about China's Big Techs later).

They came in alongside Alphabet (ranked 2) and Amazon (ranked 4) and ahead of Facebook (8), Intel (21), and IBM (56).[13] There are also very large private companies, such as ByteDance which owns Douyin—known outside of China as TikTok, that have dominant positions in the global internet space.

China today leads the world in e-commerce, mobile technologies, and digital applications. Behind the Great Firewall, entrepreneurs have erected digital agoras to sell domestic and imported wares. A cheap smartphone is the cost of admittance. Taobao, a popular online consumer-to-consumer platform by tech giant Alibaba, is one of China's most trafficked marketplaces. Within 24 hours on November 11, 2018 (China's "Singles Day" shopping extravaganza), the platform closed a record $30.8 billion in sales. That figure was more than double the total sales (online and in-store) in the United States for Black Friday and Cyber Monday in 2018.[14] Chinese consumers' appetite extends well beyond holiday deals: in 2018, the total value of all goods sold through Alibaba's e-commerce channels Taobao and Tmall was a hefty $853 billion. By comparison, the figure for Amazon was $277 billion.[15]

WeChat is the first world's first all-purpose "super app" and Tencent's crown jewel. It has an active user base of a billion (and growing)[16]—it offers a dizzying array of on-demand services, from social media to mobile payments; from ride-hailing to online dating; from scheduling doctor appointments to purchasing high-speed rail tickets.[17] WeChat has reshaped Chinese business culture—one scan of a QR code and contact is made: fine paper replaced by digital business cards. It also attracts brands and advertisers. Hollywood has even jumped in on the action. Celebrities like Taylor Swift, Adam Lambert, Kendall Jenner, and Maggie Q were all early adopters and used it to engage with Chinese fans and steer them toward new content and luxury merchandise.[18]

WeChat has already edged out competitors from the lucrative trillion dollar mobile messaging market. The most prominent of its challengers included Alibaba's Laiwang and Kuairu's Bullet Messaging apps—they were long since sacrificed on the altar of a globally more competitive Chinese tech ecosystem.

Silicon Valley has turned to China for inspiration. Popular messaging services Snapchat, Kik, and Facebook Messenger have all used technologies first popularized in the Chinese market. Before Tinder, there was Momo; and before Venmo, Alipay.[19] App by app, feature by feature,

China has shed its reputation as a knockoff economy, and consequentially, has undermined the argument that government censorship inhibits innovation.[20]

China's technological surge fueled the country's breakneck GDP growth and has put millions of people to work. A McKinsey study estimated that the Internet sector could contribute up to 22% of China's GDP growth through 2025, or a potential 14 trillion renminbi ($2.3 trillion).[21] Wealth creation and job creation, in the Chinese case, go hand in hand. A 2018 survey found that the e-commerce sector employed 42.5 million people in China, with one in 18 Chinese workers employed by e-commerce or related industries.[22]

Some estimate that Alibaba's e-commerce platforms led to the creation of 40.8 million jobs in 2018.[23] No doubt, other internet platforms create much the same. The newly created jobs reinforce growth by cultivating a vibrant middle-income class of consumers and unleashing dynamism in the economy. The same cannot be said of Silicon Valley. Oxford economists Thor Berger and Carl Benedikt Frey have fretted that the unfettered valuations have not produced new employment. Labor-saving technologies developed in the Valley are actually cannibalizing jobs.[24] The decoupling of wealth and job creation has manifested many social, economic, and political consequences—which are still unfolding in the United States. Meanwhile, China is speeding ahead.

While China's giant consumer internet companies are the most visible to the world, China's technological advances have gone, and are continuing to go, far beyond that. China has upgraded (significantly) its industrial hardware and this will prove even more consequential in the long term. Many Chinese companies started as low-cost producers and have moved up the value-added ladder—closing in on their American, German, and Japanese competitors. AAC Technologies Holdings is one early example. Formerly AAC Acoustic Technologies, the company began its journey as a mass producer of transducers, and then as a mass producer of multifunctional receivers, high-quality speakers, and ECM microphones. Now it manufactures and distributes miniaturized acoustic components—and which have greatly benefitted from rising demand in mobile smartphones around the world.[1]

---

[1] Chengwei Capital, where I am a founder and managing partner, was an early investor in the company.

Now, a new wave of industrial upgrade is changing China's economic landscape and that of the global supply chain. It touches on multiple areas: telecommunication infrastructure, manufacturing, artificial intelligence, and electric vehicles.

Huawei is the paragon of this trend. The Chinese multinational, a global leader in information and communications technology, once imported telephone exchange switches from Hong Kong. Over the short span of 25 years, Huawei achieved significant success as China's largest innovator, one of the world's top-three patent applicants, and a top-quality supplier of products and technology solutions to more than one-third of the world's population.[25] Then as now, Huawei invested heavily in research and development, first in transmitter and telecommunication network technology, later in Internet and mobile technologies, and now in 5G networks and the design of microprocessors. So much so that the company is now a major battlefield in the economic war between the United States and China. The United States has been leading a global campaign to convince its allies to boycott Huawei technologies in their 5G networks, ostensibly for security reasons. But many countries, including America's allies such as Britain and Germany, find it difficult to implement the best 5G networks without using Huawei's equipment. A U.S. senator has gone so far as to suggest legislating to annul Huawei's IP for fear of being technologically dominated.[26] How could anyone have believed this merely 10 years ago that the world's leading innovation power, America, would fear a Chinese telecom company's technological dominance to this degree?

The answer is simple.

When Beijing started its market reforms more than 40 years ago, it is fair to say that the country's inventory of intellectual property was near zero. Cheap labor and ideas that were copied (and sometimes stolen from abroad) fueled the country's subsequent growth. But as the country's economy has matured, China quickly turned into an IP super power. In 2011, it surpassed both the United States and Japan as the world's top patent filer, after the Chinese government set an ambitious 15-year plan to raise R&D spending to 2.5% of GDP.[27] The result: China now invests more than $254 billion in research annually, second only to the United States. Much of that is in high-impact fields such as big data and gene science[28] and it has paid off.

In 2015, for example, China became the first country to file over a million patent applications in a single year, reflecting, in the words of the World Intellectual Property Organization, "extraordinary" levels of innovation. For context, Chinese innovators filed more patents than their American and Japanese peers combined.[29] Some have argued that the sudden influx of funding has had downsides, such as fraud, corruption, and a couple of high-profile scandals. But on the whole, China (and the world) have come out ahead. For instance, China's investment in science has underwritten the costs of training a growing number of researchers and engineers that contribute more and higher quality publications to expand human knowledge: in 1995, the country was ranked 14 in published science and engineering papers. By 2018, it has overtaken the United States as world's largest producer of science publications.[30] The world should not be surprised if, in the not-too-distant future, China begins to collect Nobel Prizes in science as regularly as it does gold medals at the Olympics.[31]

The Huawei case signals a change in the existing paradigm of China as factory to the world to a lighter, cleaner, technology-driven, sustainable paradigm. The country's development progress did come at the expense of the environment—today China still faces enormous legacy challenges as it seeks to balance meeting the demands of its people and its manufacturing companies with environmental concerns. The government realizes that future growth will be premised on higher value growth. In September 2016, the central government ratified the Paris climate accord—a watershed moment in China's commitment to environmental protection—ahead of a G-20 summit. The decision likely resulted from Beijing's increased awareness and consideration for environmental concerns. And it also reflected a new willingness to explore a new economic structure based on emerging technologies. China's deep investment in green technology may give it leadership at the international level, especially now that the United States has decided to pull out of the Paris Agreement.[32] And its development of 5G and artificial intelligence is paving the ground for a new economy suitable for the twenty-first century.

China is also translating its material gains into the realm of the aesthetic—and has resoundingly disproved the notion that unfettered freedom of speech is a prerequisite to artistic creativity. Public speech is regulated under censorship rules, yet the country has become one of the most vibrant sources of artistic expression in the world. Indeed, a majority of China's successful contemporary artists are products of the state art education system and graduated from the likes of the Central Academy of Art in Beijing and the Chinese Academy of Art in Hangzhou. Thanks to them, the days of kitsch, Mao-era broad posters are gone. Chinese contemporary art has elevated the country into one of the world's top-three largest auction markets around the world—and vying with the United States for first place. In 2016, Artprice, the world's leading art market data and analytics firm, valued the volatile Chinese art market at around $2 billion and bested the United States for the first time in five years in auction turnover. That was despite the dampened Chinese market due to the ferocious anti-corruption drive and the economic slowdown, among other factors.[33] Eleven Chinese artists[34] are ranked among Artprice's 2018 Top 50 Contemporary Artists and five of them count among the most elite cohort of living artists that command more than half a million dollars per piece of art.[35]

THE BELT AND ROAD INITIATIVE—SILK ROAD, 2.0

China's dramatic economic expansion has shifted eastward the world's locus of power. In 1979, the year the country opened its economy, its trade accounted for less than one percent of the international total. Now at 13.8% of the total, it is the largest trading nation on the planet, now and at any time in history.[36] China's resurgence on the world stage has sent enormous shockwaves into the economic, political, and social life of a vast number of countries in the world.

In part, China's rise was made possible by the slowdown of American manufacturing and the outsourcing of American jobs to lower cost production centers. Yet it is important to note that the decline in American manufacturing predated China's opening. By the 1980s, U.S. companies had already started to whittle away at the American industrial base.[37] Corporations seeking higher profit margins from low productivity labor in East and Southeast Asia had taken advantage of trade liberalization to move operations offshore.[38] China's opening serendipitously aligned with the second wave of this process, which carried the country's economic development forward. In turn, as industrial economies slowed, China became the world's economic engine.

Chinese savings and cheap goods have long sustained American consumption binges. The two powers' "codependent relationship," a phrase coined by former Morgan Stanley Chief Economist Stephen Roach, is well documented.[39] Less remarked is that China's raw material needs have spurred global growth in resource-rich economies and in developing markets around the world. In fact, countries rich in minerals and metals, such as Australia; rich in oil and natural gas, such as Indonesia, Russia, and Saudi Arabia; and rich in timber and other natural resources, such as Brazil have all profited greatly from Chinese demand. Australia, in particular, was well served. One reason the Australian economy came through the 2008 financial crisis relatively unscathed, for example, was Chinese demand. Of course, China's sheer size is a double-edged sword for raw materials suppliers. The country's own recent deceleration has created challenges for those that grew by supplying raw materials to China.

On the other side of the balance sheet, developing markets across Africa, the Middle East, South America, and Southeast Asia have benefited from the supply of affordable goods flowing from Chinese factories. In particular, Indonesian consumers and manufacturers have reaped the rewards of integrating markets and supply chains with China, which provides a quarter of its imports, including smartphones, food products, intermediary goods, and capital.[40] Chinese brands such as OPPO and Lenovo are increasingly connecting Indonesians to the world via popular sites such as Facebook and Twitter.[41] In Mali, Chinese motorcycles enable poor consumers to establish greater control over their time, resulting in noticeable improvements in quality of life.[42]

In the span of 40 years, China has become the Atlas upon whose shoulders the world economy rests. Any significant decrease in its GDP growth risks global recession.[43]

It is within this larger dynamic that China initiated the Belt and Road Initiative (BRI). Some have characterized the BRI as the most ambitious state-led international development project since the Marshall Plan. It is actually bigger. China is seeking to revitalize the ancient Silk Road into a modern network connecting developed and developing economies. BRI has established six international economic corridors spanning over 70 countries. It covers one-third of the global GDP and over 60% of the world's population.

China is using its formidable capacity and know-how and capital to build a network of highway systems, deep-water ports, and railroads. This network will physically link China, the Eurasian landmass, and all the way to Western Europe. In the other direction, a Maritime Silk Road will loop China with all of the Southeast Asian economies. Several mega projects have already been launched, such as Temburong Bridge in Brunei, Piraeus Port in Greece, and the Jakarta-Bandung high-speed rail in Indonesia. Such projects usually come with comprehensive infrastructure upgrades, which bring new jobs and economic growth to these locales. Take Gwadar Port in Pakistan, for example: its current schemes include a coal-fired power plant, wind farms, multiple industrial parks, and a freshwater treatment facility that will help address chronic water shortages.[44]

During the first five years of the initiative, China has set up 82 overseas economic and trade cooperation zones and invested $28.9 billion. The entire BRI enterprise is expected to last through 2049 with total investments estimated to reach into the trillions in U.S. dollars. When completed, BRI could boost significantly global trade and uplift tens of millions of people out of poverty.[45] Just one generation into the future, BRI might change the economic map of the earth with China centered at its continental locus. These developments could be enormously consequential for generations of people living in countries along its routes. This is as big as, if not bigger than, the United States's role in reshaping the world economic order post-WWII.

In tandem with China's growing commercial interests, the nation's military power has also grown in recent years. What was once merely a "people's army"—a ragtag outfit of peasants and workers with a minimal nuclear deterrent force designed to defend against foreign invasions—is now a modern force to be reckoned with. It projects power with the largest nuclear submarine force in the world, advanced satellite technologies, aircraft carriers, and carrier killers. The People's Liberation Army is now patrolling the air and the seas around disputed islands, building large artificial islands in the South China Sea in defiance of America's will, and acting as the largest contributor to the United Nations peacekeeping forces.

An Age of Pragmatism

In 1978, as Deng prepared to launch his reform program, he took one of his first overseas trips. It was to Singapore, one of the staunchest anticommunist regimes in the Asia–Pacific during the Cold War.[46] Deng chose Singapore because he was interested in learning how in one generation and under authoritarian one-party rule, the city-state had transformed itself from a poor, forgotten backwater into one of the world's most modern, prosperous, and stable states. By 2015, the Chinese government had sent over 50,000 officials to Singapore for governance training.[47]

During the Deng era, China's development has been guided by a simple idea: pragmatism first, ideology second. That path was not necessarily an easy one to pick. Even after Deng ended the Cultural Revolution, the country was still gripped by the ideological fervor of the preceding decade. The late 1970s saw an intense debate among party elites and within the wider society. China could either continue to adhere to a dogmatic version of Marxist-Leninist ideology or seek a new path of economic and social development. Many senior party leaders, although victims of the Cultural Revolution themselves, saw market reforms as a threat to the party and to China's socialism. There were also significant portions of the Chinese population that feared the dislocation that would certainly result from market economics.[48]

But Deng's idea won the day.

And so, on May 11, 1978, the *Guangming Daily*, a major party mouthpiece, published an editorial entitled "Practice is the Sole Criterion for Testing Truth."[49] It represented nothing short of a historic breakthrough in party doctrine: the abandonment of ideology first.

Seen through this prism, everything the Chinese party-state has done since is of one piece. Market reforms to facilitate economic development, birthrate control to manage the size of the population, constitutionally enshrining the party's political leadership to safeguard stability, and restraint in foreign policy to ensure a peaceful external environment were all driven by enduring pragmatism—a pragmatism that was cemented by Deng's successor, Jiang, who stipulated that private entrepreneurs were eligible to join the party, and Hu, who began to moderate the headlong pursuit of economic development at almost any cost, which had dramatically increased the gap between the rich and the poor, with his program of harmonious society—China's current labor protection law was enacted on his watch.

As Deng quipped: "white cat or black cat, the one that catches mice is a good cat." And just as China was getting comfortable catching mice, the United States placed all its bets on one feline. Now it is suffering the consequences.

An Age of Vision

With Xi Jinping's ascendancy to the core leadership position of the CCP in 2012, the Deng era has been drawing to a close. Some have lamented that Xi's seeming tightening of political control at home and a more forward posture abroad as going backward from Deng's reform era. This is a fundamental misreading of reality and a misguided projection of the future. Xi's "new era" is precisely what China needs at this moment to move the country's development onto a new paradigm.

Forty years of reforms have achieved unprecedented economic success. But it also brought about severe problems. The wealth gap has widened and, as a result, inequality threatens the long-term integrity of Chinese society. Environmental degradation resulting from untrammeled commercial activities is poisoning the living conditions for generations to come. A more comprehensive development model is urgently needed. Systemic inertia and vested interests have been preventing the much-needed paradigm shift. Xi's strong leadership came just in time. At the 19th party congress in 2017, the party central committee spelled out its drastic reform agenda: eradication of absolute poverty, restructuring of the economy, and repair of the environment.[50] If successful, this would be proof that the Chinese party-state, even after 70 years, remains adaptive and vital.

Notes

1. Paulson, Henry M. *Dealing with China: An Insider Unmasks the New Economic Superpower*, Twelve, 2015, pp. xi.
2. Roxburgh, Angus. *The Second Russian Revolution: The Struggle for Power in the Kremlin*. BBC, 1991, pp. 49–89.
3. Vogel, Ezra F. *Deng Xiaoping and the Transformation of China*. Belknap of Harvard UP, 2011, pp. 377–393.
4. Schell, Orville, and John Delury. *Wealth and Power: China's Long March to the Twenty-first Century*. Random House, 2013, pp. 260–261.
5. Fukuyama, Francis. *The Origins of Political Order: From Prehuman Times to the French Revolution*. Farrar, Straus, and Giroux, 2011, pp. 19, 21, 92–93; Fukuyama, Francis. *Political Order and Political Decay: From the Industrial Revolution to the Globalization of Democracy*. Farrar, Straus, and Giroux, 2014, pp. 373–374.

6. Data retrieved from: https://data.worldbank.org/indicator/NY. GDP.MKTP.CD?locations=CN-US.
7. Subramanian, Arvind. "Is China Already Number One? New GDP Estimates." *Realtime Economic Issues Watch.* Peterson Institute for International Economics, 11 Jan. 2011.
8. Shi, Zhengfu. *Supernormal Growth. [超常增长].* Shanghai People's Publishing House. p. 11.
9. Updated from: Tedjarati, Shane. "Thriving in the Global Economy.".
10. In fact, not until 150 years later, in 1970—when an estimated 2.2 billion people lived in extreme poverty—did efforts tackling poverty outpace population growth. By 2015, international poverty alleviation efforts finally more than halved that number to 705 million. Refer to: Roser, Max and Esteban Ortiz-Ospina. "Global Extreme Poverty." OurWorldInData.org. 27 Mar. 2017. Retrieved from: https://ourworldindata.org/extreme-poverty/; the original study: Bourguignon, François and Christian Morrisson. "Inequality Among World Citizens: 1820–1992." The American Economic Review, vol. 92, no. 4, 2002, pp. 727–744.
11. Weisbrot, Mark. "President Obama Inadvertently Gives High Praise to China in UN Speech." *The Hill.* 29 Sept. 2016. *Republished by the Center for Economic and Policy Research.* Data retrieved from: https://databank.worldbank.org/reports.aspx?source=poverty-and-equity-database.
12. Ross, John. "China's Gigantic Role in Reducing World Poverty." China.org.cn, 31 Oct. 2013.
    Stuart, Elizabeth. "China Has Almost Wiped Out Urban Poverty. Now It Must Tackle Inequality." *The Guardian.* 19 Aug. 2015.
    "China Sets Example For World To Tackle Extreme Poverty." China.org.cn, 3 Oct. 2016; The Millennium Development Goals Report 2014. UNDP, 07 Jul. 2014.
13. PricewaterhouseCooper. Global Top 100 Companies by market capitalization: 31 March 2018 update. 2018.
14. Kharpal, Arjun. "Alibaba sets new Singles Day record with more than $30.8 billion in sales in 24 hours." *CNBC,* 11 Nov. 2018; Cheng, Andria. "Black Friday, Cyber Monday Sales Hit Another High, But It's Not Time To Celebrate Yet." *Forbes.* 26 Nov. 2018.

15. "Alibaba Group Announces March Quarter 2018 Results and Full Fiscal Year 2018 Results." Alibaba. 4 May 2018; "Amazon Gross Merchandise Volume $277 Billion in 2018." *Marketplace Pulse*. 12 Apr. 2019.
16. Deng, Iris. "Tencent's WeChat hits 1 billion milestone as Lunar New Year boosts monthly active users." *South China Morning Post*. 5 Mar 2018.
17. Lawrence, Dune. "Life in the People's Republic of WeChat." *BloombergBusinessweek*, 9 Jun. 2016.
18. Millward, Steven. "Hollywood Celebrities Get Chatty with Chinese Fans on WeChat." *TechInAsia*, 11 Feb. 2013; Rapp, Jessica. "Fan Bingbing, Angelababy, and Taylor Swift Among Top Stars Boosting Luxury Brands on WeChat." *Jing Daily*, 28 Aug. 2016.
19. Mozur, Paul. "China, Not Silicon Valley, Is Cutting Edge in Mobile Tech." *The New York Times*, 2 Aug. 2016.
20. Yeung, Edith. "China Internet Report 2019." South China Morning Post/Abacus. 25 July 2019.
21. McKinsey Global Institute. *China's Digital Transformation*. 2014. Meng, Jing. "Internet Sector to Fuel 7% to 22% of China's GDP growth through 2025." *China Daily*, 8 Jan. 2015.
22. "E-commerce in China to create over 48 million jobs in 2018." *People's Daily Online*. 8, Jun. 2018.
23. "Alibaba Ecosystem Helps Generate a Wide Variety of Employment in China." *AliResearch*. 24, Jun. 2019.
24. Kulwin, Noah. "Economists Suggest Silicon Valley Startups Aren't Really Creating Many Jobs." *Recode*, 7 Dec. 2015.
25. Shao, Ken. "History is the key to understanding Huawei." *The Conversation*, 3 Apr. 2012.
26. "Senator Rubio targets Huawei over patents." *Reuters*. 18 Jun. 2019.
27. Plume, Andrew. "Tipping the Balance: The Rise of China as a Science Superpower." *Research Trends*, no. 22, Mar. 2011; Yee, Lee Cyen. "China tops U.S., Japan to become top patent filer." *Reuters*, 21 Dec. 2011.
28. Normile, Dennis. "Surging R&D spending in China narrows gap with United States" *Science*. 10, Oct. 2018; Jimenez, Joseph. "China's Scientific Revolution." *Project Syndicate*, 15 Jul. 2016.
29. Mitchell, Tom. "China smashes world patent record with 1 m filings in a year." *Financial Times*, 24 Nov. 2016; "Global Patent

Applications Rose to 2.9 Million in 2015 on Strong Growth From China; Demand Also Increased for Other Intellectual Property Rights." World Intellectual Property Organization, 23 Nov. 2016.
30. Wu, Nan. "China's rise as a major contributor to science and technology." *Journalist's Resource*, 5 Jan. 2015; Tollefson, Jeff. "China Declared World's Largest Producer of Scientific Articles." *Scientific American*, 23 Jan. 2018.
31. Morelle, Rebecca. "China's Scientific Revolution." *BBC News*, 23 May 2016.
32. Phillips, Tom. "China ratifies Paris climate change agreement ahead of G20." *The Guardian*, 3 Sept. 2016; Spegele, Brian. "China's Legislature Ratifies Paris Agreement on Climate Ahead of G-20 Meeting." *Wall Street Journal*, 2 Sept. 2016; Friedmann, S. Julio. "How Chinese Innovation is Changing Green Technology." Foreign Affairs, 13 Dec. 2011; Meyer, Robinson. "The Indoor Man in the White House." *The Atlantic*. 13 Jan. 2019.
33. Ehrmann, Thierry, editor. *The Contemporary Art Market Report 2015*. "China slows, but remains potent." Artprice.com, 2015; Duray, Dan. "China back on top of global auction sales, Artprice reports." *The Art Newspaper*, 28 Jul. 2016; Kaplan, Isaac. "China Knocked the U.S. Off the Top of the Art Auction Market—Here's How." *Artsy*, 17 Aug. 2016.
34. They include: Chen Yifei, Zhou Chunya, Zhang Xiaogang, Zeng Fanzhi, Liu Wei, Qiu Hanqiao, Yue Minjun, Ai Xuan, Ren Zhong, Liu Ye, and Liu Guang.
35. Ehrmann, Thierry, editor. *The Contemporary Art Market Report 2018*. "Contemporary artists by rank / July 2017 – June 2018." Artprice.com, 2018. For more see: https://www.artprice.com/artprice-reports/the-contemporary-art-market-report-2018/top-500-contemporary-artists/top-500-contemporary-artists-1-to-50/.
36. Barnett, Steven et al. China's Growth and Integration into the World Economy: Prospects and Challenges. Edited by Eswar Prasad, International Monetary Fund, 2004, pp. 1. Retrieved from: https://www.imf.org/external/pubs/ft/op/232/op232.pdf; Glenn, Elias and Pete Sweeney. "China seizes biggest share of global exports in almost 50 years." *Reuters*, 22 Apr. 2016.

37. Slaughter, Matthew J. "Multinational Corporations, Outsourcing, and American Wage Divergence." *National Bureau of Economic Research*, Working Paper 5253, 1995, pp. 1–2.
38. Desilver, Drew. "For most workers, real wages have barely budged for decades." Pew Research Center *FactTank*, 9 Oct. 2014.
39. Roach, Stephen S. Unbalanced: the Codependency of America and China. Yale, UP, 2014.
40. AmBadar & Partners. Goods Producers From China, Japan & Thailand Are Expected To File Their IP Rights' More in Indonesia As A Lot Of Imports Go Into Indonesia. 2016; Yulisman, Linda. "RI is more dependent on Chinese goods." *The Jakarta Post*, 16 Feb. 2012.
41. Purnell, Newly. "The World Leader in Mobile Facebook Access? Indonesia." *Wall Street Journal*. 23 Jan. 2015; "Which Brands Dominate the Smartphone Market in Indonesia?" *Indonesia Investments*, 2 Sept. 2016.
42. "Chinese Motorcycles Flood West Africa." *VOA*, 1 Nov. 2009.
43. Roach, Stephen. "The World Economy Without China." Project Syndicate, 24 Oct. 2016.
44. "Belt and Road projects: Past, present, future." *Chinadaily.com.cn*. 4 Apr. 2019. Frankopan, Peter. *The New Silk Roads: The Present and Future of the World*. Knopf, 2019. pp. 97–99.
45. "Factbox: Belt and Road Initiative in Five Years." *Xinhua*. 26 Aug. 2018; "Success of China's Belt & Road Initiative Depends on Deep Policy Reforms, Study Finds." *The World Bank*. 18 Jun. 2019.
46. Vogel. *Deng Xiaoping*. pp. 226, 280–281, 287–291.
47. Zheng, Yongnian, and Liang Fook Lye. *Singapore-China Relations: 50 Years*. World Scientific, 2015, p. 42.
48. Vogel. *Deng Xiaoping*. pp. 390–391, 400.
49. Vogel. *Deng Xiaoping*. pp. 211; Zhang, Ming'ai. "An Article Influences Chinese History." China.org.cn, 19 Jan. 2008. See full article at: www.china.org.cn/200801/19/content_1240036.htm.
50. "Full text of Xi Jinping's report at 19th CPC National Congress." *Xinhua*. Retrieved from: http://www.chinadaily.com.cn/china/19thcpcnationalcongress/2017-11/04/content_34115212.htm.

CHAPTER 4

The Rise of China and America's Evolving Response—From Universal Liberalism to America First

After China rejected the Soviet model and developed quickly with market reforms, the world very much expected the country to then at least gradually embrace the American model of liberalism. But again, the Chinese party-state said no.

CHRISTOPHER BOUNCED

As Warren Christopher, America's first post-Cold War secretary of state, stepped off his plane in Beijing, a shoving match broke out between the Chinese and American security officers assembled on the tarmac. As far as diplomatic visits go, this one would go down in history as one of the most unceremonious.[1]

It was March 1994, and Christopher had embarked on the highest-level visit to China by an American official since Bill Clinton became president a little over a year prior. He was tasked with auditing China's human rights performance. Five years before, on June 4, 1989, the Chinese party-state had used lethal force in putting down a massive demonstration that had filled Tiananmen Square for weeks. Since then, 15 years of virtual alliance following U.S. President Richard Nixon's opening to China had turned into a deep freeze. No American leader wanted, as Clinton accused President George H. W. Bush of doing, to "coddle dictators."[2]

© The Author(s), under exclusive license to Springer Nature Singapore Pte Ltd. 2023
E. Li, *Party Life*, https://doi.org/10.1007/978-981-99-4522-1_4

It was a time when America was on top of the world. The Cold War had ended. For the first time in modern history, one country was the undisputed and unchallenged leader. Some called it the "unipolar moment," and relished in the promised new opportunities.[3] One theory was that unipolarity and globalization, the increasing interconnectedness driven by the United States, would provide an opening to spread liberal democracy and market capitalism the world over. National Security Adviser Anthony Lake, for one, had his blueprint ready to go.

In contrast, China was at its lowest point since the end of the Cultural Revolution. Its economic reforms and growth had squeaked to a halt as tanks rolled onto Tiananmen Square. The Soviet Union had fallen, and communist regimes around the world were in tatters. Now in the company of only Cuba, North Korea, and Vietnam, the Chinese party-state found itself isolated and vilified. In response to the Tiananmen Square incident, the United States and Europe imposed economic sanctions and arms embargoes, some of which last to this day.[4] China's nascent economic miracle was in trouble; in 1990, its GDP was only 6.1% of that of the United States. The choice facing China's leaders seemed stark, either give up power or risk ending China's economic renaissance before it even could take off.

So, with China seemingly at a crossroads, Christopher, landed in Beijing carrying the biggest stick possible: the threat of taking away the country's Most Favored Nation status (the MFN).

Since 1974, the MFN had allowed China to export its goods to the United States at the same low tariff rates as most other nations. But China's MFN was made renewable on an annual basis.[5] Once a year, the president had to decide whether to extend the MFN for another 365 days or to cancel it, and he had to justify that decision to Congress. The Bush administration dutifully re-upped every year. But when Clinton came to office, the time seemed right to apply a little pressure. On May 28, 1993, in the presence of congressional leaders, Chinese dissidents, and human rights activists, Clinton issued an executive order that required China to make "overall, significant progress" on human rights to obtain the renewal of the MFN in 1994.[6]

With its economy stalled, its regime politically isolated, and a $45 billion trade surplus with the United States at stake (not an insignificant amount for China at that time), what did China do to make the requisite "progress" on human rights as defined by the United States? Nothing. In the months prior to Christopher's visit, American officials repeatedly warned China not to think that it could get away with last-minute cosmetic concessions on America's version of human rights to get MFN renewal. Little did they anticipate that China had no intention of making any cosmetic concessions, let alone substantive ones. On the contrary, to make sure that there would be no misunderstandings, Beijing rounded up scores of dissidents right before Christopher's visit. "China," the Chinese premier told Christopher in person, "will never accept the U.S. human rights concept."[7]

A picture is worth a thousand words. The front page of the *New York Times* revealed a grim-faced Christopher walking briskly out of the Great Hall of the People in the center of Tiananmen Square.[8] A PLA soldier in full uniform stood aside, showing him the door—so to speak.

Secretary of State Warren Christopher after being rebuffed at a meeting yesterday with President Jiang Zemin in Beijing. The American official was flanked by Chinese and United States security men.

On May 26, two months later, a humbled Clinton walked into the White House briefing room and made a clean break from the past. In a brief speech, he announced the permanent de-linking of China's MFN and its human rights record per U.S. standards. The decision paved the way for China's eventual accession to the World Trade Organization.[9]

Many contemporary critics of China now lament that the West was somehow deceived by China into thinking economic integration would bring China onto the path of political liberalization. In his book, *Hundred-Year Marathon: China's Secret Strategy to Replace America*, Michael Pillsbury essentially espoused the view that China conspired to benefit from the U.S.-led globalization while not giving up its political system as it was supposed to.[10] This is a laughable proposition. Even back in 1994, when China was arguably at its weakest and America at its strongest relatively speaking, China was absolutely clear that it would rather forego the MFN than change its political system to America's liking.

Cold Warriors vs. Panda Huggers

In my article for Yale Global in 2013, I divided mainstream Western outlooks on China into two schools of thought. Ever since the 1989 crackdown, when China made its decisive turn away from Western-style liberal democracy, through the Obama era, Western thought about China had been dominated by these two schools.[11] Although they advocated opposite policy prescriptions, they shared a goal of making the world's most populous country a part of a universal order founded on the Western principles of liberal politics and market capitalism.

The first was the "imminent collapse" school. Espoused by cold warriors and many Chinese dissidents, it predicted the wholesale collapse of the country. The one-party system, adherents believed, was inherently incapable of managing intensifying social and economic conflicts as the country went through its wrenching transformation from a poor agrarian economy to an industrialized and urban one. The Western alliance should seek to contain China, just like it did the Soviet Union, and thereby hasten the fall of a threatening power ruled by an illegitimate regime. The author Gordon Chang became the movement's poster child. In 2001, he argued that the modern Chinese state would have five, or perhaps, ten years before it collapsed due to the inefficiency of state-owned enterprises, the lack of an open democratic society, and a ticking time bomb hidden in non-performing loans held by China's four biggest banks.[12] Others joined in with variations on the theme: that the state would collapse from revolution from below or liberal breakthrough from above, from state stagnation or party fragility. The end result, according to the more imaginative accounts, would be China as a fascist state, China under military

4 THE RISE OF CHINA AND AMERICA'S EVOLVING ... 59

rule, and China Balkanized.[13] To point out the obvious, five years, ten years, and now decades have come and gone with no such denouement.

The second group was the "peaceful evolution" school. These are the panda-hugging universalists who believed that China would become just like the West. As the country modernized its economy, it would inevitably accept market capitalism and liberalize its political system, and proponents of this school urged engagement to speed up that evolution. Not surprisingly, virtually all of the American corporate sector, driven by the bottom line, became a strong advocate of this view.

The Clinton administration, after briefly flirting with the imminent collapse school, quickly changed course. China's size and economic potential held too much promise for America's universalist dream in both political and economic dimensions. Clinton quickly became a staunch supporter of the peaceful evolution school, steadfastly expanding trade and other engagements with China. The Chinese, of course, took full advantage.

Ever since that day when Clinton permanently de-linked trade from human rights, the peaceful evolution theory had ruled the day through three consecutive administrations: Clinton, George W. Bush, and Barack Obama. Of course, proponents of the imminent collapse school never stopped agitating for more confrontational approaches toward China, and they have succeeded on various occasions, particularly in the U.S. Congress.

In 1995, the newly appointed House Speaker, Newt Gingrich, publicly challenged One China policy on CBS. During the interview, he called for restoring formal diplomatic ties with Taiwan and asserted that China was "self-deluding" when claiming territorial rights a thousand miles away from the Chinese border.[14]

The investigation on China's security threats also had never stopped in the U.S. Congress. In 1998, a special committee was created by a 409–10 vote of the U.S. House of Representatives and released the document known as the Cox Report, charging China with extensive nuclear espionage. According to a policy assessment by scholars from Stanford University, this report was a "combination of factual errors, misused evidence, incorrect, misleading, or nonexistent citations, and implausible interpretative spins of existing research."[15]

Looking back, however, both schools were wildly off the mark. The cold warriors had had to postpone the effective date of their prediction, year-after-year, for decades. What did they get wrong? It turned out that, far from falling victim of modernization, the party had been leading the process. While keeping a tight grip on politics, the party used trial and error to develop one of the most vibrant market economies in the world. In turn, China's modernization strengthened, rather than weakened, the party's rule.[16]

As embarrassing as it must have been for those who predicted China's collapse, the bitterest disappointment belonged to the universalists, who foresaw with moral certitude China's inevitable liberalization as the certain result of economic development.

But China walked a different path. As the party embarked on dramatic reforms, the country possessed a degree of independence unmatched by most developing nations, thanks to its steadfast refusal to compromise its party-state political system and, of course, its nuclear deterrent. China's ability to control its own destiny allowed it to engage globalization on its own terms. Its one-party system remained intact and even matured and strengthened. Its economic integration with the developed world was carried out in ways that brought maximum benefit to the Chinese people. Market access was granted in exchange for direct investments that created industrial jobs and brought in foreign technology. The government exercised political authority above market forces and led the largest expansion in investment in infrastructure, health, and education in history.

One of the biggest mistakes that observers of China made was the notion that the leader who kicked off the reforms, Deng Xiaoping, belonged to the neoliberal school of thought. In his long diatribe against neoliberalism, the author David Harney even grouped Deng's modernizations in with Reagan-Thatcherism. He argued that because "a large easily exploited and relatively powerless labor force" drove the Chinese growth model, China qualified as a neoliberal economy.[17] But this was a gross over-simplification. Although market reforms did benefit capital in a big way, workers in China's urban and rural areas have also seen massive improvements in quality of life as the country lifted hundreds of millions out of poverty. They escaped the stagnant wage trap that their American and British counterparts have fallen into. In short, Deng was no neoliberal. China engaged the Washington Consensus to extract the maximum benefits for itself. And it got what it wanted.

To be sure, inequality also increased dramatically in this period. China is now in an overdrive to correct this under the leadership of Xi Jinping with the initiative of common prosperity. More on this later.

Now that the imminent collapse prediction has failed and the peaceful evolution dream has evaporated, the United States seems to be struggling to find a new paradigm in its relationship with China. Where it will end up could determine the future of the United States, liberalism as an ideology, and, of course, China.

WE ARE PIVOTING

Though much coverage has been given to the drastic change in U.S. approach to China under President Donald Trump, the change of course really happened under the Obama administration. It was during the Obama years, Americans woke up to a few facts: China was competently run, and it would continue to grow stronger over time. It was not a disciple of the Western school of liberal democracy, and it was not on path to becoming one.

From time to time, Western media still engaged in wishful thinking. The 2012 Bo Xilai scandal, in which the prominent politician was ousted from the party and his wife was given a commuted death sentence for the murder of a Westerner, got blanket coverage. It was euphorically portrayed as a watershed event that could lead to systemic breakdown. The drama came and went, though. Most in the West had come to recognize that the Chinese party-state was not on the brink of disaster.

That emerging recognition lends credence to a new school of thought about China's future: that it is a rising challenger bent on subverting the global system America established and has run. In essence, this new school paints China as a comprehensive adversary to the United States, economically, technologically, geopolitically, militarily, and ideologically. During the Obama years, its proponents were the liberal "pivoteers,"— after the Obama administration's policy called "pivot to Asia." That policy emerged out of two seemingly unrelated trends. First, the global financial crisis of 2008 had crippled Western and other advanced economies. China, meanwhile, weathered the storm and emerged more assured in its own crisis management strategies. The West, wounded by the financial knockout, needed a way to pick itself up.

Second, Obama saw the Middle East as a region to be avoided. The wars there had proved devastating to local economies and costly in American lives. To Obama, Asia represented the future. In a 2011 *Foreign Policy* op-ed, his Secretary of State, Hillary Clinton, wrote that "harnessing Asia's growth and dynamism is central to American economic and strategic interests."[18] Since then, Obama's turn to Asia was enshrined as a central element of U.S. foreign policy.

The pivot was carried out in the context of an overall reevaluation of China by the media, opinion leaders, and think tanks. The new China watchers combined hard realist calculations with U.S. geopolitical interests and a liberal universalist outlook. Their portrayal of China consisted of three overlapping dimensions.

First, China's rise was taken as a multigenerational plan by the Middle Kingdom to challenge American hegemony. The most prominent advocate of this idea was American defense policy advisor Michael Pillsbury—who later became an influential advisor to the Trump White House. His book, *The Hundred-Year Marathon*, was a lamentation that he and other disenchanted "panda huggers" (his term) missed signals hidden in plain sight about China's global expansionist ambitions. China was always aiming at hegemony, Pillsbury argued, and it was a particular shame that the Carter administration was hoodwinked into training thousands of Chinese scientists in American universities, leading to what Pillsbury described as the "the greatest outpouring of American scientific and technological expertise in history."[19] Pillsbury would have the public believe that American universities had nothing but altruistic—if misguided—reasons for accepting tuition-paying students.

Second, came a realist-style prediction of inevitable military conflict between China and the United States—a Thucydides' Trap, in which a rising power strikes fear in a dominant power, which escalates to war. Distinguished Harvard professor Graham Allison first married the ancient Greek metaphor with contemporary China's rise, suggesting that tensions between Beijing and Washington must be managed carefully to avoid direct military confrontation.[20] John Mearsheimer, a leading realist political scientist, also argued that China's surge would invariably result in a return to great-power politics, with the resulting security competition drastically increasing the potential for war.[21]

The third dimension of the pivoteers' portrayal of China was most frequently promoted by the U.S. government and served as the central theme for Obama's policies. It was based on the notion that China represented a threat to the post-Cold War, or even post-WWII, world order that was designed and led by the United States. In this narrative, the United States' primary objective was to implement strategies that effectively check China's ability to alter the fundamental structure and rules of the order. Doing so would involve strengthening the existing U.S. military alliance system in East Asia and South East Asia to counter China's growing military might, denying China a role in designing or leading any major economic system with global reach, and continuing to challenge the legitimacy of China's political system.

QUASI-CONTAINMENT

While retrenching elsewhere, the Obama administration aggressively pursued a quasi-containment strategy against China. As opposed to straight containment, which was the stated policy of the United States during the Cold War, quasi-containment sought to do many of the things that containment would do without publicly calling it containment—in fact, the Obama administration repeatedly disavowed the notion of containment in public. This was because of China's high degree of integration with the rest of the world and the singular importance of the United States–China bilateral relationship with both countries and the world at large made it inoperable to announce a containment strategy against China. In the West Pacific, the United States backed, militarily and politically, every country that had conflicts with China, namely, Japan, the Philippines (under the previous Aquino administration), and Vietnam. Although Washington publicly insisted that it did not take sides in territorial disputes between China and its neighbors, in word and deed, it did just that. It provided strong backing to Japan in the Diaoyu/Senkaku Islands disputes and to the Philippines in the South China Sea disputes. When the Philippines elected a new president who improved relations with China, the United States became even more strident about "defending" the Philippines' interests. Sometimes, U.S. officials were more vocal than the country's own government, to the extent that a member of the Philippine Supreme Court christened Obama "defender of the West Philippine Sea."[22]

In the quasi-containment playbook, economics played only a supporting role. For example, a centerpiece of Obama's pivot strategy was the Trans-Pacific Partnership (TPP). The initiative was led by the United States and included 11 other Pacific Rim nations. As a group, they accounted for nearly $28 trillion in GDP—roughly 40% of the global total—and one-third of world trade. It was to be the largest regional trade pact in history,[23] and it pointedly excluded China. The publicly stated reason was that China did not enforce "high standards" in protecting labor, the environment, and intellectual property.[24] That might be true, but Malaysia, which was included, had been censured for its slash-and-burn practices, and Vietnam, another party to the deal, was well known for lax copyright protection.

The Obama administration expended tremendous amounts of political and diplomatic capital on making the TPP a reality, only to see it jettisoned by President Trump on his first day in office. Critics blasted him for that decision, yet most economists agree that the economic gains from the trade pact would have been marginal at best. In the United States, for example, the trade deal would have generated $131 billion by 2030, or about 0.5% of baseline GDP.[25]

But economics was never the objective. Politics and geopolitics were. In Obama's attempt to cajole a reluctant Congress into giving him so-called fast-track authority to negotiate the TPP, he defined the deal in starkly political terms. "With TPP," Obama stated in his 2016 State of the Union address, "China does not set the rules in that region; we do."[26] Contrast this with Trump, who opposed the deal largely on economic grounds.

While some of the United States' initiatives aimed to reduce China's influence in Asia, others sought to deny the country the ability to play any substantial role in designing or leading new economic institutions with global reach. The clearest example came in 2014 and 2015, when the United States tried—and failed—to stop many countries, including key allies such as Australia, Germany, South Korea, and the United Kingdom—from signing up for the Asian Infrastructure Investment Bank (AIIB), conceived and led by Beijing. Washington saw it as a challenge to the World Bank and the Asian Development Bank, both of which are essentially controlled by the United States and its allies.[27]

THE QUICK FAILURE OF QUASI-CONTAINMENT

Quasi-containment failed quickly, although some in the United States still tried to carry it forward under the Trump "America First" banner. The only reason the Obama administration opted for a partial version to begin with was that full containment—in this case, the full diplomatic encirclement of China and its isolation from the international system—was not executable. China was not the Soviet Union in two fundamental respects. The Soviet-led Eastern bloc was completely economically segregated from the West. China was deeply integrated in the world economy.

In fact, it may be the most integrated ever. Economic sanctions against the Soviet Union only hurt the Soviet Union. Economic war with China would hurt the United States and its allies just as much as it would harm their intended target.[28]

Containing the Soviet Union was costly. Containing China would come at an even higher price. And China's actual threat to the United States is much lower. For one, its recent initiatives to regain a leading strategic position in Asia notwithstanding, China's military and strategic posture is entirely defensive. Its nuclear deterrent of several-hundred warheads is limited relative to the United States' of 7100.[29] It has no intention of a first strike or participating in a harmful arms race. In addition, whereas the Soviet Union did proselytize a narrative that competed with the West's own, and the two powers fought over how to remake the entire world, China speaks more of cooperation. Indeed, far from China trying to remake the world, it is the United States that seems insistent on somehow changing China, and many other parts of the world.

In this regard, the United States is fighting an ideological battle that doesn't exist—and at a time when its own political institutions, and those of its Western allies, are failing. Even so, Washington continues to employ the Cold War approach of challenging China's political legitimacy. And once every election cycle, congresspeople and presidential contenders, Democrats and Republicans alike, climb on their stumps and lambast Chinese goods, Chinese hackers, and the Chinese government. China bashing draws media attention (and dollars), but it never delivers any result other than Chinese irritation.[30] The quasi-containment strategy thus had the United States–Chinese relationship seesawing between a cold war and a cold peace. It carries neither sufficient carrots nor sticks to alter China's orientation to America's liking.[31] And it is doubtful that, given the increasingly high costs and lack of rationale, it is sustainable.

From Trump to Biden

Between Trump's four years and Joe Biden's first two years, the United States, in its attempt to contain China's further growth, has lumped together short-term tactics that did not serve long-term interests and ideological overreach that actually weakens itself. The one thing that is lacking is strategic consistency.

At first, Donald Trump's presidency had the potential to bring a true paradigm shift, upending the post-WWII architecture that the United States designed and led.

Trump put forth a worldview that was totally opposite from that of the Washington Consensus. It transcended right and left, and it certainly transcended the various schools of thought that had guided modern U.S. approaches to China.

First, Trump showed little desire to spread liberalism around the world. In fact, he seemed to loath liberalism in America itself. On the campaign trail, he exhibited a clear distain for liberal interventionism in foreign policy. He called it "a dangerous idea that we could make Western democracies out of countries that had no experience or interest in becoming a Western democracy."[32] Relatedly, although his pro-Russia stance caused much angst among the American political establishments, Trump made no pretense of hiding his affinity, even admiration, for political leaders who were conspicuously anti-liberal, such as Russia's Vladimir Putin, the United Kingdom's Nigel Farage, and the Philippines' Rodrigo Duterte, and even Kim Jong-un of North Korea. Breitbart News and its former leader Steve Bannon, the media outlet that was critical to Trump's success in the United States, actually set up shops in Europe to support various anti-liberal movements.

Aside from moving away from liberalism, under Trump, the United States, for the first time since the Cold War, began to retreat from universalism in its foreign policy outlook and re-emphasized national sovereignty.

On this new paradigm, there was, and still is, a distinct possibility that the United States might give up its attempt to universalize the world in its own image and focus on retaining its own dominant competitive position in the world. To that end, the United States under Trump was perfectly willing to undermine the global system America designed and built in order to take back more power to fight for its own interests. In this worldview, allies such as Europe were free riders weakening America's ability to compete.

Four turbulent years passed between China and the United States during which Trump took on China with gusto. A trade war, a technology war, and a direct political confrontation over the Covid-19 pandemic put the two countries constantly on multiple collision courses.

Biden continued nearly all of Trump's hostile policies and added many of his own, including intensified confrontation in technology, security threats over Taiwan, and constant attempts to rally other nations into alliances against China. A newly formed military alliance with Australia and the United Kingdom in the Pacific called AUKUS is the latest example.

There are risks for serious clashes. In the past, American leaders attempted to play a dual role of guardian of an international system and defender of U.S. national interests. Doing so has brought benefits to the United States, but it has also cost the country dearly. Trump was ready to ditch the first role and pursue bareknuckle competition around the world in his attempt to put "America First." Biden is back to straddling both. If America continues to want to dominate the world in every way, financially, technologically, militarily, and ideologically, and at the same time do what's in its own best interests, it is likely to be exhausted and end up with the worst of both worlds.

China's "Long Telegram" Strategy

If one reads George Kennan's long telegram advising the U.S. government on how to deal with the Soviet Union,[33] one could be surprised by how similar China's current approach to the United States is to Kennan's prescription more than half a century ago. While stating its core interests unambiguously, China is avoiding direct confrontation with the United States When the Speaker of the U.S. House of Representatives visited Taiwan in the spring of 2022, Chinese public opinions were in an uproar. Some even advocated intercepting her plane. Media reports and think tank analysts also warned of potential military conflicts.[34] But China held back.

At the same time, China is deploying its considerable global clout to counterbalance the United States in just about every arena. In the United Nations, China stands its ground on just about every issue it disagrees with the United States. In the South China Sea, China continues its naval presence. In Southeast Asia, Africa, and South America China is making dramatic inroads in political and economic engagements. With the military conflict between Russia and NATO in Ukraine, China hangs in there with its position of neutrality against U.S. pressures. In trade, China fights the U.S. tooth and nail at the WTO on every dispute.[35]

To counter America's attempts to encircle China with its military alliance systems, China is building softer-power networks of partnerships around the globe. Currently, China has three broad levels of bilateral partnerships with other countries and regions: comprehensive strategic partnership, strategic partnership, and regular partnership. At the most recent count, China has formed comprehensive strategic partnerships with 36 countries and regions, strategic partnerships with 30, and regular partnerships with 17.[36] These partnerships are not as hard power as U.S. alliances, but they are more complex and encompass much broader engagements, culturally, economically, and policy coordination.

Then, of course, China is still single-mindedly focused on solving its own problems and developing its economy and society. It may be betting that America cannot keep dominating the world and solving its own enormous internal problems at the same time. To borrow Kennan's idea, let it "collapse under the weight of its own contradictions."[37] It would be ironic if China had studied Kennan's advice to the United States in countering Soviet aggressions and is deploying it with the United States now. Why not? It worked once!

Notes

1. Mann, Jim. "Christopher in Beijing; Mood Tense: Asia: In China for Human Rights Discussions, He Makes No Statement at the Airport and Rejects Banquet Offers. His Arrival is Further Marred by a Shoving Match." *LA Times*. 12 Mar. 1994.
2. Lippman, Thomas W. "Bush Makes Clinton's China Policy an Issue." *The Washington Post*. 20 Aug. 1999.
3. Krauthammer, Charles. "The Unipolar Moment." *Foreign Affairs*. 9 Nov. 1990.
4. Blanchard, Ben. "In Dig at U.S., China Says All U.S. Arms Embargoes Should Go." *Reuters*. 26 May 2016; Harding, Robin. "Japan Fears Brexit Blow to EU Arms Embargo on China." *Financial Times*. 4 Jul. 2016.
5. Dorn, James. "Time to Repeal the Jackson-Vanik Amendment." *Journal of Commerce*. 14 Jul. 1999. Republished online at: https://www.cato.org/publications/commentary/time-repeal-jacksonvanik-amendment.
6. Friedman, Thomas L. et al. "Clinton and China: How Promise Self-Destructed." *New York Times*. 29 May 1994.
7. Sciolino, Elaine. "China Rejects Call From Christopher For Rights Gain." *New York Times*. 13 Mar. 1994.

8. Sciolino, Elaine. "Christopher Ends Beijing Talks Citing Modest Gains." *The New York Times*. 14 Mar. 1994.
9. "Clinton's Call: Avoid Isolating China." *New York Times*. 27 May 1994. For the full press release, refer to: https://clinton6.nara.gov/1994/05/1994-05-26-president-in-press-conference-on-china-mfn-status.html.
10. Pillsbury, Michael. *The Hundred-Year Marathon: China's Secret Strategy to Replace America as the Global Superpower*. St. Martin's Griffin, 2016.
11. Li, Eric X. "Two Schools of Thought on China—Both Wrong." *YaleGlobal*. 19 Nov. 2013.
12. Chang, Gordon. *The Coming Collapse of China*. Random House, 2001.
13. Shambaugh, David. *China's Communist Party: Atrophy and Adaptation*. University of California Press, 2008, pp. 174–178.
14. Kovaleski, Serge F. "Gingrich Backs Ties With Taiwan." *The Washington Post*. 10 Jul. 1995.
15. Johnston, Alastair Iain, et al. *The Cox Committee Report: An Assessment*. Center for International Security and Cooperation, Stanford University, 1999.
16. Li, Eric X. "Two Schools of Thought on China—Both Wrong." *YaleGlobal*. 19 Nov. 2013.
17. Harvey, David. *A Brief History of Neoliberalism*. Oxford UP, 2005, pp. 120–151.
18. Christensen, Thomas J. "Obama and Asia: Confronting the China Challenge." *Foreign Affairs*. Sept./Oct. 2016; Goldberg, Jeffrey. "The Obama Doctrine." *The Atlantic*. Apr. 2016; Clinton, Hillary. "America's Pacific Century." *Foreign Policy*. 11 Oct. 2011.
19. Pillsbury, Michael. *The Hundred-Year Marathon: China's Secret Strategy to Replace America as the Global Superpower*. St. Martin's Griffin, 2016, p. 71.
20. Allison, Graham. "The Thucydides Trap: Are the U.S. and China Headed for War?" *The Atlantic*. 24 Sept. 2015; Mo, Shengkai and Yue Chen. "The U.S.-China 'Thucydides Trap': A View from Beijing." *The National Interest*. 10 Jul. 2016.
21. Mearsheimer, John J. "Can China Rise Peacefully?" *The National Interest*. 25 Oct. 2014.
22. Hedarian, Richard Javad. "Barack Obama's Pivot to Asia in Tatters." *Al Jazeera*. 24 Sept. 2016; Viray, Patricia Lourdes.

"Carpio Wants Obama Named 'Defender of West Philippine Sea'." *Philstar Global*. 9 Sept. 2016.
23. Granville, Kevin. "This Was the Trans-Pacific Partnership." *New York Times*. 11 Nov. 2016.
24. Hsu, Sara. "China and the Trans-Pacific Partnership." *The Diplomat*. 14 Oct. 2015.
25. Meltzer, Joshua P. "The Significance of the Trans-Pacific Partnership for the United States." *Brookings*. 16 May 2012; Petri, Peter A. and Michael G. Plummer. "The Economic Effects of the Trans-Pacific Partnership: New Estimates." *Peterson Institute for International Economics*, Working Paper 16–2, 2016, p. 1.
26. *Remarks of President Barack Obama—State of the Union Address As Delivered*. Office of the Press Secretary, The White House, 13 Jan. 2016. For full transcript: https://www.whitehouse.gov/the-press-office/2016/01/12/remarks-president-barack-obama-%E2%80%93-prepared-delivery-state-union-address.
27. Lipscy, Phillip Y. "Who's Afraid of the AIIB." *Foreign Affairs*. 7 May 2015; Perlez, Jane. "U.S. Opposing China's Answer to World Bank." *New York Times*. 9 Oct. 2014; Gale, Alastair and Rob Taylor. "Decision to Join China-Led Bank Tests South Korea's Ties to U.S." *The Wall Street Journal*. 24 Mar. 2015.
28. Tiezzi, Shannon. "Yes, the US Does Want to Contain China (Sort Of)." *The Diplomat*. 8 Aug. 2015; Browne, Andrew. "Can China Be Contained?" *The Wall Street Journal*. 12 Jun. 2015.
29. Chandran, Nyshka. "The US has 7,100 Nuclear Warheads, China has Just 260. Here's Why." *CNBC*. 31 Oct. 2016.
30. Wagner, Daniel. "With its China Bashing, America Risks Breaking a Profitable Partnership." *South China Morning Post*. 22 Mar. 2016.
31. Ikenson, Dan. "Soured U.S.-China Relationship Approaches Inflection Point." *Forbes*. 29 Jan. 2013.
32. Li, Eric X. "The End of Globalism." *Foreign Affairs*. 9 Dec. 2016.
33. Kennan, George. "The Long Telegram." 1946.
34. See: Hsu, Sara. "US Firms Cannot Ignore the Growing Risks of a Possible China-US Military Conflict." *The Diplomat*. 2 Jul. 2021; "Odds 'Very High' of U.S. Military Conflict with China, top Republican Says." *Reuters*. 30 Jan. 2023.
35. "China, U.S. Spar at WTO Meeting Over Disputes." *Reuters*. 28 Jan. 2023.

36. Li, Quan, and Min Ye. "China's Emerging Partnership Network: What, Who, Where, When and Why." *International Trade, Politics and Development*, vol. 3, no. 2, 2019, pp. 66–81.
37. Tharoor, Ishaan. "The End of Cold War Thinking." *The Washington Post*. 26 Feb. 2021.

CHAPTER 5

Modernization Without Modernity—How It All Came About

Now we know what China rejected. Let us examine the path China has chosen. I would argue that China's success to date is a result of taking a path that worked with its history, tradition, values, and present circumstances. These are distinctly different from the liberal vision propagated by America. And China's choices and experience are becoming increasingly relevant today as a large number of developing countries are seeking new paths for their futures.

As Lee Kuan Yew, the founder of Singapore, once said about East Asia in general:

> Values are formed out of the history and experience of a people. One absorbs these notions through the mother's milk. The values that East Asian culture upholds, such as the primacy of group interests over individual interests, support the total group effort necessary to develop rapidly.[1]

I would like to call this view "modernization without modernity."

MODERNIZATION, NOT MODERNITY[2]

Over the past seven decades since the founding of the People's Republic, China has been able to debunk a foundational myth about development—namely that modernity is the only route to, and is a prerequisite of, modernization. In doing so, its rise may prove the most consequential phenomenon of the modern era.

The distinction between modernization and modernity is subtle but critical. Modernization essentially means industrialization and the material prosperity the process brings about. Modernity, on the other hand, is an ideology. (The ideology of liberalism to be precise.) It is based on a set of ideas, namely, freedom, individualism, inalienable rights, reason, and procedural rule-of-law. Because modernity sprang from supposedly universal values, its proponents presumed that it was universal as well. Meanwhile, they believed that modernization flowed uniquely out of a society's acceptance of those universal values. In the political narrative of the modern West, the concept of democracy has essentially been captured by liberalism; hence liberal democracy has become the hegemonic political ideology of our time.

As the case of China shows, however, it might be modernity that is unique and modernization that is potentially universal.

The direct product of the Enlightenment, modernity was a unique experience of Western culture. The values of modernity, or liberalism, were then infused into the development of political institutions that undergird the modern West. That liberal recipe has been two thousand years in the making.

Modernity's intellectual ancestry traces back to Plato. His ideas about elite rule may seem totally incompatible with the modern concept of liberal democracy; after all, "[tyranny] evolves from democracy," he wrote in *The Republic*, "and from the most extreme form of liberty "tyranny … [and] the most severe and cruel slavery" ensue".[3] In turn, rule by elites was far more stable and preferable; aristocracy was seen to be "good and just."[4] But it was Platonism that gave birth to the idea of abstract truth—that is, a truth a priori—independent of human experience.[5] Ever since, the pursuit of an abstract truth has guided and consumed Western civilization, from Christianity to the Enlightenment, and heavily influenced its cousin Islam. As Nietzsche famously put it, "Christianity is Platonism for the 'people'."[6] Other civilizations were rarely driven by the same zealous pursuit.

The belief in abstract truth manifested itself across religious and political dimensions, especially with the concept of freedom. More than 1500 years ago, the collapse of the Western Roman Empire in 476 AD and the parting of the two strains of Christianity in the first schism created fertile ground for freedom to flourish in the West as a moral virtue. From the political vacuum that ensued, the concept was nurtured and institutionalized by clashes among the feudal lords—each claiming possession of the eternal truth (and the material interests it concomitantly legitimized). In Western Europe, the princes were strong enough to check each other, but none could compel the others into imperial submission. Princely power was weakened, and the balance was sustained by the independent spiritual authority of the Catholic Church. Indeed, for many centuries, the Vatican operated as Western Europe's only transcontinental power: it even organized its own standing army.[7] Centuries of endless wars resulted from this separation of political power. While the development of the idea of freedom might have been almost incidental in the West, freedom, nevertheless, became canonized as a fundamental value of liberalism and modernity.

Even within the Western cultural tradition, the emphasis on freedom only developed in Western Europe. On the other side of the first division of Christianity, the Eastern Church was kept under the authority of an organized and stable Eastern Empire. No meaningful separation of political power emerged there, with cultural and political consequences that last to this day.

Beyond the concept of freedom, religious power that was independent of political authority was also at the root of the development of a version of rule-of-law that is defined by the primacy of procedures. The basic institutions, concepts, and values in the Western legal system derived heavily from codified religious doctrines that checked temporal power through spiritual power.[8] Countries that took different paths of political development—China, Russia, and many others around the world—have found far greater difficulty for such rule-of-law to take hold.

The Protestant Reformation further encouraged the Western concept of universal modernity. In 1517, German theology professor Martin Luther began a revolt against a corrupt Catholic Church. From there, some leaders of the Protestant Reformation, including John Calvin, advocated a version of Christian fundamentalism that then became mainstream.

Early Protestant ideas—such as the individual's complete subservience to God in every aspect of life, the dominance of religious beliefs in community life, and even pre-destination—are anathema to so-called modern values.[9] But the Protestants, in their attempt to circumvent the Catholic Church, which they saw as standing between the believers and

God's true will, inadvertently advanced a worldview that placed the individual at the center, so that a believer could connect with God without the Church. And that, in turn, formed another of the central elements of modernity: individualism. In modern politics and society, the individual, it often seems, has become God himself.[10]

All these religious, cultural, and political ideas developed over centuries in the corner of a small peninsula called Western Europe. They might have stayed there, but for the success of modernization, which developed in parallel to the ideas of modernity and propelled the West to dominate much of the world. Virtually every other society has tried to emulate that success, but to little avail; they mistook what was unique to be universal, and what could be universal to be unique. Herein lies the significance of the modern Chinese experiment. China's success—its modernization—no doubt was influenced enormously by the West. Yet its essence is not and cannot be modernity.

In today's China, political power is not divided between centers of power but is centralized under a single political authority. Meanwhile, the individual remains part of the collective. He or she is by no means the independent and basic unit of society. To be sure, ordinary Chinese people enjoy as wide a range of personal liberties as in the Western world. But those with political aspirations contrary to the state and society's collective objectives are severely constrained, even repressed.

A market economy, adapted from the West, efficiently allocates resources and returns high rates of growth, lifting hundreds of millions out of poverty. Yet, it is pointedly not capitalism—for two reasons. First, the Chinese state maintains a strong determinant role in overall economic strategy, in the design of developmental frameworks, and in the regulation of enterprises. Second, unlike in the West, in China, capital does not have inherent rights that invest it with power beyond or even above political authority. Beijing's authority to redistribute wealth is theoretically unconstrained, and it can prevent capital from entering the socially destructive cycle of infinite accumulation.[11]

China's way of thinking about modernization is clear from the language. The word "modern" is translated into Chinese as *xiandai*—which simply means "the current generation" or "what is new." This is the same meaning as the word modern in its original Latin—*modo* (just now). *Xiandai* does not carry the value-laden connotations of the English word "modern." *Xiandaihua*—modernization—has only material meaning, that is improvement in society and lifestyles brought about by industrialization and technological advancements. *Xiandaihua* has been the guiding objective of the Chinese nation since Zhou Enlai, one of the founding fathers of the People's Republic of China, announced near the end of the tragic Cultural Revolution that China's national aspirations could be summed up in four modernizations: of agriculture, industry, national defense, and science and technology.

The four modernizations by no means added up to modernity, nor were they predicated on it. Concocting a narrative in which they did obscures more than it clarifies. Though China's project of becoming a developed country is still not a forgone conclusion, its success to date is beyond dispute. China's example is too big to ignore, and when we understand how Chinese modernization differs fundamentally from that of the West, it could provide the needed proof that modernity is no longer the only viable route to modernization. So if not a tale of modernity, then, what is China's story?

Trial by Errors in the "Century of Humiliation"

A little more than 200 years ago, in 1793 AD, a fateful event shook the Forbidden City. The great emperor Qianlong reluctantly received the visiting Lord George Macartney representing King George III of the then-emerging British Empire. Macartney presented a seemingly simple idea: Let us trade. To that, Emperor Qianlong replied in an edict:

> Our dynasty's majestic virtue has penetrated unto every country under Heaven, and Kings of all nations have offered their costly tribute by land and sea... Swaying the wide world, I have but one aim in view, namely, to maintain a perfect governance and to fulfil [sic] the duties of the State: strange and costly objects do not interest me.[12]

Qianlong certainly had good reasons for his initial position against trade with Britain. At that moment, Qing China represented 33% of the entire world's GDP and was the mightiest and most prosperous continental power on earth.[13] A stable society built on Confucian values—developed and refined over 2000 years—placed the Middle Kingdom at the seemingly unassailable apex of human civilization. Indeed, to Qianlong, his empire was at the "end of history." Little did he know that Macartney's request for trade was anything but simple. Behind it were Immanuel Kant, John Locke, Jean-Jacques Rousseau, Adam Smith, and

Voltaire, men whose ideas were about to dominate intellectual discourses for centuries to come. Just three years before Qianlong's meeting with Macartney, the French Revolution had upended Europe. And only a few years before that, a brand new republic based on the same ideas was launched in a faraway land. Eventually, it would expand "from sea to shining sea."

For another half century, Qianlong's "shining city upon a hill" persisted. Then history intervened. The newly industrialized modern West raced ahead and brought its might with merciless aggression and destruction upon the ancient giant.

In 1842, Imperial China lost the first Opium War to British trading interests. In the aftermath, it was forced to open its ports to the drug. By 1888, even the British were staggered by the rates of opium addiction among the Chinese population: *The Times of London* reported that an estimated 70% of adult Chinese males partook. By 1937, the disease of addiction had spread to 40 million Chinese or 10% of the entire population; elsewhere in colonial Hong Kong, that figure reached 30%.[14] Although history did not record how many Chinese were drugged to death, or how many families were torn asunder by the ravages of opium, Harvard historian John K. Fairbank went so far as describing the opium trade as "the most long-continued and systematic international crime in modern times."[15]

Insult followed injury. Western powers, blinded by greed, forced on China a series of treaties in which it ceded territories. The weakened Qing dynasty run by Qianlong's descendants reeled from internal strife, instability, and the bloody Taiping Rebellion, which lasted 14 years. The decaying Qing state invited further aggression by Western interests: it lost the second Opium War, watched impotently the infamous sack and pillage of the Old Summer Palace, and bungled its war with the French for control of Southeast Asia. The last irreversible ruin came in 1895 with the defeat in the first Sino-Japanese War (also known as the Jiawu War), in which China lost Taiwan and influence in Korea to Japanese occupation. At the turn of the twentieth century, the once mighty Chinese civilization was on its knees facing imminent extinction.[16]

Once the center of "all under heaven," the near collapse of China's continuous 2000-year-old civilization came so precipitously that almost no one in the Chinese political or intellectual establishment was prepared. The central debate among Chinese elites was how to save the Chinese civilization: Should China resist and risk annihilation or capitulate and essentially turn into one of its enemies?

After the loss of the second Opium War, there was a brief period during which a middle ground was sought. The Chinese Mandarins began a political and economic revival, called the *Yangwu* (or "Self-Strengthening") Movement, to import modern methods of production, warfare, and governance from the West. Headed by the statesman Li Hongzhang, China made several economic and educational reforms, including setting up the country's first "state-owned enterprises" and sending young students to receive engineering, business, and military training in the West.[17] China's defeat in the first Sino-Japanese War, however, was a major setback.[18] Reformers in the political establishment pressed the Manchu court for wider economic, industrial, and administrative changes, which included a failed attempt to emulate Japan and adopt a Western-styled constitutional monarchy while keeping China's traditional cultural essence, social structure, and political institutions intact.[19] Interestingly, an early proponent of that system was a young Mao Zedong.[20]

Alas, for the reformers, the historic baggage of Qianlong's "end of history" appeared too difficult to shake off without fundamental change. That change would happen in the form of the 1911 Xinhai Revolution, led by Chinese elites who saw that gradual imperial reforms were insufficient to arrest the rapid collapse of the Chinese nation. These elites called for the end of China's dynastic system and the adoption of liberal democracy. They would try to establish modern Western, particularly American, political institutions. The new China would be called a republic and a president would replace the emperor. Parliamentary institutions, a senate and a general assembly, would be designed after the U.S. Congress. However, although the Xinhai revolutionaries did manage to overthrow the Qing dynasty, ending China's two-thousand-year dynastic history, at least in form, they found it much more difficult to build a new state.

The newly established Republic of China was unable to gain control of the country's many warlords. And externally, it was just as powerless as the Qing dynasty in the face of Western aggression. That was made abundantly clear in 1919, when the United States and the victorious powers of WWI—of which China was nominally one—reneged on a promise to revert Shandong province, the sacred birthplace of Confucius, back to Chinese sovereignty from its German occupiers. Instead, in secret treaties, the Allied powers recognized Japan's legal rights to the territory.

The Chinese envoy, Gu Weijun,[21] subsequently refused to put his signature on the Treaty of Versailles. Out of this humiliation came the May Fourth Movement, which advocated a complete break from the past.[22] Liang Qichao, a main proponent of constitutional monarchy and one of modern China's most influential early thinkers, called for a total abandonment of Chinese tradition in all aspects of Chinese life, not just in politics, but in culture and society as well.[23] But in addition to the pursuit of modern progress, which was Western in essence, the May Fourth Movement was also driven by nationalist and anti-Western fervor.

During the period just before and after the May Fourth Movement, China tried just about every form of government it could find in the outside world: it made an attempt at constitutional monarchy (1898),[24] a constitutional republic which regressed into absolute monarchy (1912–1916),[25] warlordism and military government (1916–1928),[26] and Nationalist one-party rule, with experiments in fascism (1927–1948).[27]

During this period, every time it seemed like things couldn't get any worse, they got worse. Several generations toiled and bled only to see China sink deeper into the abyss of warlord wars, eight brutal years of Japanese invasion, and civil war, with the people suffering unspeakable horrors.[28] A century and a half after the heady days of Qianlong, China's share of the world's GDP was less than 5% in 1949.[29]

Party First, Then State

In the dark of China's bleakest moment, in July 1921, a group of 12 men[30] secretly met in a small Shanghai townhouse. That meeting, the First National Congress of the Chinese Communist Party (CCP) changed the course of China's history, and indeed, the world's. At the time, the party had only 57 members nationwide. By 1949, merely 28 years later, the party had recruited over 4.4 million members, won the civil war, and founded the People's Republic—a nation with a population of over 540 million.[31]

One cannot truly understand the nature of contemporary China's political system without grasping one crucial fact: China is a party-state. Its unique political present is the result of a complex past. And that past is full of historic circumstances particular to the birth and development of modern China. No modern state, including the Soviet Union, had comparable developments.

Interestingly enough, the CCP was neither the originator of the concept of the party-state, nor its first practitioner. That honor belongs to its predecessor in post-dynastic China and its rival for political power, the Chinese Nationalist Party, or Kuomintang (the KMT).

Those who have been to China's most sacred political space—Tiananmen Square—have likely seen the permanent fixture of Mao Zedong's giant portrait adorning the front of the Gate of Heavenly Peace. From the center of the nation, his deep gaze looks out on the republic that he founded. What many do not know is that, once a year, on the first of October—the national day of the People's Republic—another man's portrait is erected in the middle of the square. He is from an earlier generation, and he remains paramount in the Chinese consciousness. The two great men spend the nation's most important holiday staring at each other intently across the world's largest public square.

That man is Sun Yat-sen, the founding father of modern China.

Sun founded the KMT in 1912.[32] The party unified the patriotic forces behind the 1911 Xinhai Revolution that overthrew the Qing Dynasty and installed Sun in the newly established role of provisional president of the Republic of China.[33] Sun and his followers in the KMT, including his successor Chiang Kai-shek, drew inspiration from the Russian Bolshevik Revolution.[34] Sun admired the success of Soviet communism but thought it inappropriate for China, given its national condition at the time.[35] Chiang, in late 1923, actually declared that the national revolution in China was not only a struggle against warlords but also part of a broader anti-imperialist movement, centered around Moscow, to overthrow world capitalism.[36] Both men believed that the only way to save China from extinction was to build a singular political force with its own army to establish, govern, and defend a new modern Chinese state—the original DNA of the party-state.

After 1923, responding to the Sun-Joffe Declaration,[37] Sun reorganized the KMT in line with Leninist doctrines so that it could better carry out the nationalist revolution. He also institutionalized the party's domination of the state, a political system that Chiang would inherit and expand upon.

Throughout this period, Moscow was the KMT's biggest patron, which it saw as the best vehicle to expand Soviet influence and revolutionary efforts in the East.[38] And whereas the Soviet Union did not believe that the CCP, its nominal satellite in China, had any chance of success and was skeptical about its commitment to Marxist theories of the proletariat revolution, it appreciated that the KMT's focus on the urban classes and the bourgeoisie more neatly fit the Marxist model.

As a result, Soviet leader Joseph Stalin bankrolled the KMT's efforts to establish the party-state of the Republic of China, supplying finances, arms, and military advisors.[39] Moscow helped fund and staff the Whampoa Military Academy, build the party's army, and consolidate Chiang's grip on power[40]—all critical for the launch, in 1926, of the Northern Military Campaign, which aimed to seize power from the warlords and unify China. By comparison, the early CCP received only meager support from Moscow.[41]

Under Sun, one of the central themes of the KMT political platform was *lian'e, rong gong, fuchi nonggong*,[42] better known as the First United Front.[43] A united front meant an alliance between the KMT and the CCP. In 1923, the KMT obtained permission from the Soviet Union to absorb the CCP, technically part of the global Communist Party led by the USSR, into the KMT. Moscow in turn encouraged CCP members to join the KMT, thereby essentially unifying the parties. The merger resulted in CCP members taking a quarter of the KMT Central Committee seats, and Mao himself joined the KMT.

But in 1927, a few years after the death of Sun, Chiang believed the national revolution would soon succeed, and his greatest rival for power was the CCP. He repudiated the merger and violently purged former CCP members, including Mao, from the KMT. The decision was fateful and eventually resulted in the birth of the People's Republic.

In exile in China's southeast, Mao launched a new, uniquely Chinese, revolution. On November 7, 1931, he declared the Chinese Soviet Republic (CSR) in the Jiangxi region,[44] The KMT government had cobbled together numerous warlords who formally pledged allegiance to the Republic of China but retained their own loyal armies and power bases. This loose arrangement provided space for the CCP to organize its own army and build its own territories. Despite the name, the CSR was qualitatively different from the revolutionary design of the Soviet Union. Mao pursued a revolutionary path based on the peasantry in the vast Chinese countryside instead of on the urban proletariat workers.

Ever since 1931, the CCP nearly always had its own state in the form of the *jiefangqu*[45]—"liberated area." The only exception was the Long March period of 1934–1935, when the CCP's Red Army had to pull back in the face of sustained attacks by KMT forces. From its earliest days, the CCP's experimental *jiefangqu* had most of the functions of a full-blown state, and it closely resembled the eventual People's Republic. It had policymaking bodies, it had taxation, it had a bureaucracy, it had a military under the leadership of the party, and it even had a national bank.[46] When the CCP won the civil war against the KMT and established the People's Republic in 1949, therefore, the party was in possession of an almost two-decade old party-state that was ready to be expanded nationwide. By contrast, merely months before the Russian Revolution[47], Lenin and Stalin were still living in exile.[48] There was no state to speak of before the Bolsheviks actually gained control of all of Russia in 1917.[49]

More than the Soviet example, a closer analog to the CCP's party-state revolution was imperial China's cyclical dynastic reshuffling. Both Liu Bang and Zhu Yuanzhang, the founding emperors of the Han and Ming dynasties, for example, began their quests for ultimate power by building political and military bases, mini-states within the old dynasties, before leading rebellions that overthrew the old order and established a new one. Even some of their political initiatives were similar. Both emperors built their legitimacy by redistributing land first within their mini-state territories and, once they became emperors, across their realms. Of course, Mao did exactly that as well. He confiscated farms from feudal landlords in the *jiefangqu* and redistributed them to the majority of landless peasants, thereby building a strong political base for the CCP among the peasantry. And after the establishment of the People's Republic in 1949, nationwide land reform was among Mao's first political initiatives.

Chiang led several failed military campaigns attempting to annihilate the CCP's *jiefangqu*, and succeeded once, which forced the Red Army into the Long March.[50] But in the end, the CCP was able to defend its territories long enough to establish a stable mini-state with its own army. The Japanese invasion and WWII led to a temporary halt to the KMT's military attacks on the CCP, as the two parties created a second united front to fight off the Japanese. That break allowed the CCP to further build its *jiefangqu* and state capabilities.[51]

In almost all other modern nations, the state came first and then the parties materialized to represent the different parts of the society—this is what the word party means. But in modern China, the reverse happened. The party came first, it established the state, and then it laid claim to the representation of all Chinese nationals. The party institution *is* China's political system, and it is complex, elaborate, and opaque to the outside world.

From Emperor to Party Secretary; from Mandarins to Cadres

Off to one side of Tiananmen Square is Xinhuamen, the old imperial gate that now serves as the entrance to the CCP Central Committee compounds. In front of it is a large monument in traditional Chinese imperial style and colors, with a quote from Mao inscribed on it: *Wei Ren Min Fu Wu* ("To Serve the People"). Many see it as an expression of communist egalitarianism. That is appropriate. It is also a symbol of something much older: the *shidafu* tradition.

Perhaps no one played—or plays—a more consequential role in China's long cultural and political development than the *shidafu*, what is commonly known in the West as the Mandarin, or the scholar-official. Idealized by Confucius, further defined by Mencius, and continuously refined by generations of Confucians throughout history, the *shidafu* ethos has been and remains a central part of the moral foundation of Chinese society.

Two essential characteristics are notable. One is meritocratic selection; the other is the fusion of the political and the moral. Whereas the West was ruled by aristocratic power for more than a millennium, China effectively ended its aristocracy during the Han Dynasty (which began in 202 BC) when it adopted Confucianism as the country's official religion. From then on, members of the vast Mandarin class that served the emperor and governed China were selected from the populace without consideration of their lineage. A peasant's son could, by pursuing higher learning, enter the Mandarin class and, through superior service, move up the ranks and potentially attain the highest political office, just below the emperor. In fact, for thousands of years, Imperial China had only one position that was truly hereditary: that of the emperor. Without exception, all other government positions, including the premiership, were filled by Mandarins who entered the political system by imperial exam and moved up through service.[52]

Many have likened Imperial China's political system to that of government by an absolute authority—akin to "absolutism" as understood by modern Western political thought. But this view is mistaken. Although the emperor's position was paramount, his power was severely constrained, both theoretically and practically, by the Mandarins. It was theoretically constrained by the central Confucian doctrine of *li*, which prescribed both formal and informal national customs and ethical codes that managed relations among ordinary people and between the emperor and the Mandarins.[53] This unwritten constitution was the central scaffolding that upheld Imperial China through the dynasties for two thousand years. Westerners may wonder at the stability. Perhaps an analogous example in the West is that of Great Britain. The British parliament rules by custom alone. Legally, the queen or king has always had absolute power.

Practically speaking, because the emperor was the only one with hereditary power on top of a vast state bureaucracy filled with Mandarins, he had no choice but to rely on them to govern.[54] Chinese history is replete with accounts of emperors being constrained by their Mandarins. Thus, during the millennia spanning from ancient times to the modern age, China alone among all major civilizations was governed by officials who were meritocratically selected, and the *shidafu* was its institutional and cultural core.

The other essential characteristic of the *shidafu* ethos is moral. Confucius made it a moral duty for those who achieved higher learning to serve in government in *the Analects*. He said, "one who excels in learning should then devote himself to official service."[55] For thousands of years, government service remained the highest calling for China's intellectual elites. The intelligentsia, which developed in Europe as a separate political and social force independent of political authority, never existed in China and is in many aspects anathema to Confucian morality. In turn, although there were, of course, many stories about emperors in Chinese folklore, the true heroes have been *shidafu*: the likes of Fan Zhongyan, Zhuge Liang, Yue Fei, and Lin Zexu, who toiled and bled in their loyalty to the emperor and service to the people.

If one examines the lives of those who founded the CCP, one would find much evidence of the *shidafu* ethos. Mao was a monarchist in his youth and was deeply schooled in the Chinese classics. He later engaged in bitter rivalry with the party's Soviet wing, which advocated a Soviet-style revolutionary path. Mao insisted on a Chinese one, which involved localizing Marxist theory to include the interests of peasants within the party's early representation.[56] The party's forefathers, such as Chen Duxiu, Li Dazhao, Liu Shaoqi, and Zhou Enlai, all had similar outlooks. Their revolt against Chinese tradition was mostly driven by the belief that these traditions were no longer able to sustain a Chinese civilization that was being decimated by Western powers. The survival of the nation and the need to establish a modern state to preserve Chinese civilization required a radical break with tradition. Right or wrong, that break is now part of China's political DNA. It culminated in the Cultural Revolution, with tragic consequences.

Even so, from the imperial court during the late years of Qing Dynasty to the revolutionary era of modern Chinese nationalism, China's leaders, from both the KMT and CCP, were steeped in the *shidafu* ethos. In this respect, that ideology was fundamentally different from European nationalism, which was a modern invention designed for nation-building.[57] This Chinese nationalism had a moral dimension—a Confucian soul. Liu Shaoqi, President of the People's Republic from 1959 to 1968 devoted his signature work, Gong Chan Dang Ren De Xiu Yang (On the Self-Cultivation of a Communist), to articulating a virtual amalgamation of the communist code of conduct with Confucian ethics.[58]

Shifadu ethic is also part of the reason why, even though other modern ideologies failed in China, Marxism found fertile soil. In the early decades of the twentieth century, the Chinese *shidafu* class was desperate to find a new ideology to replace Confucianism, which they believed had completely decayed. Marxism resonated in two critical respects. Its communist egalitarianism struck a chord with the deeply held *shidafu* ideal of duty to the people and their own meritocratic roots. Marxism was also rather unique in that it was both Western, as it came from Europe, and anti-West, because of its anti-capitalist and anti-imperial revolutionary outlook. Chinese elites saw their nation as a victim of Western capitalist-colonial aggression. And in Marxism, they found a theory that was both modern, which was desperately needed, and identified the correct villain.

Yet, Marxism was not sufficient to build a new China. To establish a modern state in the face of chaos and destruction, the Chinese needed a new means to organize as well. Leninism became the central organizational ideology of the party-state. In it, the country's rulers found an effective and often brutally disciplined political system that had already succeeded in launching a communist revolution and establishing a modern state in a major Western country, Russia. Thus China became what the Sinologist Lucian Pye called a "Confucian Leninist state."[59]

One of the greatest misconceptions about China is that the communist revolution and the CCP's continuing rule are a break with—even oppositional to—the Confucian tradition. Mao's Cultural Revolution, which promoted violent repudiations of Confucianism, is often cited, along with other communist ideological dogmas, as proof. But such explanations go only skin-deep. In fact, the Chinese communists found Marxism, a modern source of moral inspiration, very much in sync with Confucian values. And their adherence to Leninism as the party's fundamental organizational structure was only a tool to revitalize the centuries-old Chinese civilization.[60] Richard Solomon, who was U.S. assistant secretary of state for Asian and Pacific affairs from 1982 to 1992, said it best: "Mao 's conception of political leadership combined a complex reaction against many traditional values even as it drew upon those behavioral patterns and emotional concerns which he deemed essential in gaining popular support."[61]

After the fall of the Berlin Wall, many inside and outside of China predicted that, before long, the Chinese party-state would meet the same fate as the Soviet Union and most other communist countries in the eastern bloc. Their prediction was far off the mark because they saw only the Marxist–Leninist part of the party-state and ignored the Chinese part—the *shidafu*. Indeed, the *shidafu* ethos persists and sustains the party-state to this day.

Consider, for example, China's current leader, Xi Jinping.

At his first public appearance after being named general secretary of the CCP at the 18th party congress in 2012, Xi took the seven members of the newly inaugurated Politburo Standing Committee on a trip to the Chinese National Museum. One of the museum's galleries exhibited in painful detail the humiliation and suffering of China since the middle of the nineteenth century. In front of it, Xi proclaimed the beginning of a great Chinese national renaissance, which he termed "The Chinese Dream." In essence, he was acting as the quintessential *shidafu*. His intentions were made all the clearer when he visited Beijing University, one of China's foremost institutions of higher education, shortly thereafter.[62] During a tour of the library, he lamented on national television that Chinese public schools do not teach enough Chinese classics. And of course, Chinese classics are made up of Confucian texts, which form the spiritual foundation of the *shidafu* ethos.

Xi was right to remind viewers of the importance of the classics. Without them, China would not be where it is today. The most common explanation for the CCP's continued success and popularity is China's economic growth. But performance legitimacy is only part of the story. Deep historical legitimacy is the other part; rather than an "organizational emperorship,"[63] as China scholar Zheng Yongnian once characterized Chinese political establishment, Beijing today is in fact a renewal of the traditional Confucian state governed by a collective *shidafu* class with modern Leninist organizational methodologies. Today's communist officials are reincarnations of the Mandarins who took seriously their moral duty to protect and advance the welfare of the people, and the party-state is their vehicle for doing that work.

Three Phases of the Chinese Party-State and the New Era

The Chinese party-state developed in three broad phases: revolution, during which the party gained power by overthrowing the old order; infusion, when the party became China's political system; and consolidation, which is the ongoing maturation and expansion of the party-state.

State Building vs. Continuous Revolution

The revolutionary period began in 1921 with the founding of the CCP. In the decades that followed, the party used Marxism as its modern revolutionary ideology and Leninism as its organizational structure to execute a fundamentally Chinese nationalist revolution. In 1949, the revolution culminated in Mao's declaration of the People's Republic, but the revolutionary period was not quite over. For nearly three more decades, politics was dominated by a tug-of-war between those party elite who wanted to build a state and those who subscribed to a more stringent version of Marxism and insisted that China continue down the path of realizing a communist society through means of continuous revolution.

At first, Mao was in the state-building camp, and so, soon after his 1949 declaration, he began a process of land reform. Land redistribution, of course, had been central to the party's political platform since the days of the *jiefangqu* decades earlier. And before that, land redistribution had been typical at the beginning of every new dynasty as a nod toward egalitarianism. Then, as each dynasty matured, society would stratify and ossify. Land ownership would become concentrated, contrary to the Confucian doctrine that, "those who till shall have land"[64] in the words of Mencius. When the system reached a breaking point, the old dynasty would be overthrown and a new emperor would redistribute land once more.

The party followed the same playbook. But this time, land redistribution explicitly combined China's traditional Confucian values with the modern ideology of socialism. The land was taken from the landlord class and redistributed to the peasantry. For most practical purposes, the peasants "owned" the redistributed land, in that they kept the gains of production.[65] The program was a major success. Agricultural production increased dramatically and the peasantry became the bedrock of the party's political support. Optimism about the new China reached an all-time high in the early 1950s.[66]

By the middle of the 1950s, however, ideology had begun to overtake reality. Mao became impatient and threw his lot in with the revolutionaries. Traditional land reform gave way to communization: lands were completely publicly owned, with the peasants unable to even keep the gains of their production. By 1958, the Anti-Rightist Campaign had toppled some 800,000 intellectuals in just a few months, and critics considered right-wing were no longer tolerated under this political atmosphere.[67] It was clear that continuous revolution had won out over state building.

The results were disastrous. Initially, from 1952 to 1958, collectivization yielded impressive successes. But in 1959, agricultural production plummeted and continued to decline for three successive years. Grain output plunged 15% from the previous year, dropped another 16% the following year, and remained at the same low level the year after. The sudden shortage of food from crop failures resulted in tens of millions of deaths.[68]

In an attempt to correct its error, the party began to quasi-privatize land in the early 1960s. Initial gains in production indicated that the reform would be a success, but it was interrupted by a new bout of revolutionary fervor that resulted in Mao's 1966 Cultural Revolution. Across Chinese society, other sectors—from basic industry to education to government bureaucracy—traced a similar arc. And so, by the end of the Cultural Revolution in 1976, state building had come to a complete halt, with many sectors of the new state in major deterioration.

The State Builders

A junior founding member of the revolution survived those dark days after being twice purged from office. Biding his time, he accumulated power and support within the party and assumed its leadership upon Mao's death in 1976. That man, of course, was Deng Xiaoping. And he was a state builder.

Most analysts like to describe the Deng era as one of the economic reforms that transformed China into a world power within a generation.

But few have emphasized the underlying political movement that framed his economic reforms and that had far more significant and longer-term consequences. On Deng's watch, the Chinese party-state decisively and irreversibly moved from the revolutionary period to the state-building period.

Deng's first order of business was to rebuild and expand the party institution. In 1979, he proposed the Four Cardinal Principles—uphold socialism, maintain rule by the people, enshrine CCP's leadership, and honor Maoism—as the national political framework for the new era, and these were incorporated into China's constitution in 1982.[69] For three decades, three generations of leaders, Deng, Jiang Zemin, and Hu Jintao, each deepened the institutional infusion of party and state in a revival of the centuries-old Confucian Mandarin system.

Of course, in building a modern state, these leaders did not simply repudiate Mao's ideological bent and take the country in the opposite direction. No doubt Deng's reforms corrected many previous policy mistakes and delivered enormous successes, but the reforms also built on a strong foundation developed in the previous decades. Namely, Mao had centralized political authority to mobilize limited national resources and build the basic industrial and human infrastructure of a modern nation.[70]

On the eve of Deng's reforms in 1979, about 9000 newly built hydroelectric dams powered extensive national and local electric grids. The dams had increased electricity coverage from nearly zero outside of urban areas before the revolution to over 60% even in the poorest far-flung locations by 1979 coverage is now near 100%).[71] Literacy rates had tripled to over 60% (now 96%).[72] Hundreds of millions of people had been immunized against common diseases, over 95% of children at the age of one, and average life expectancy had risen from 36 to 65 (now 76).[73] In fact, before Deng took over, China was already closing in on much richer developed nations on the human development index.[74]

Meanwhile, Mao had given China the gift of national independence, without which no meaningful state-building could have been sustained. After a century of civil conflicts and dismemberments in the hands of foreign aggressors, the establishment and consolidation of the People's Republic under Mao's leadership had firmly placed the nation's destiny in its own hands. With few resources and a young (and in many aspects still unstable) state, Mao beat back the advancing army of the United States in the Korean War and successfully developed China's own nuclear deterrent. It was this national independence that, many years later, enabled

China to engage the post-Cold War wave of globalization on its own terms. By contrast, many other developing countries were drowned in it.

There is no doubt that China had come under destructive spells of ideological fervor at several points during Mao's rule. Certainly, unmitigated disasters, such as the Great Leap Forward and the Cultural Revolution, did set China back. And the Chinese people paid a heavy price for independence. But the People's Republic survived, namely because, far from a wanton ideologue, Mao had his pragmatic streaks, particularly in foreign policy. It was he who led China out of Soviet domination in the late 1950s. For a newborn nation to decisively walk away from its ideological mentor—a mentor at the zenith of its power—was daring. And Mao didn't stop there. At the height of the Cold War, he reached across the ideological divide and built a de facto alliance with the United States to counter the Soviets. This in turn paved the way for China's engagement with the West.

Indeed, all Mao had achieved—with limited resources and under an international embargo—was the necessary groundwork for the country's miraculous takeoff. The post-Mao dividends have been significant and, in all likelihood, will continue for generations to come.

The New Era

The 18th Party Congress, held in 2012, marked the Chinese party-state's entrance into a new era—consolidation. Xi, who ascended to the party's general secretaryship at that congress, is a different kind of leader for a different age. The change was made abundantly clear in November 2013, when the party held it's Third Plenum. Such plenums usually take place a year after a party congress and are generally used to set policy priorities for the next five years. Some are far more consequential than others, and the Third Plenum of 2013 was such a meeting. At the time, most analysts focused on the plenum's wide-ranging economic reform package. But the most consequential developments were political initiatives that could fundamentally alter, and also cement, how the world's largest nation is governed.[75]

When the party established the People's Republic in 1949, it modeled its government on the so-called three carriages from the Soviet Union. In form, three parallel bodies share power: the National People's Congress (NPC), which is a legislature headed by a chairperson; the State Council, which is a cabinet run by a premier; and the CCP Politburo, which oversees the party and is led by the general secretary. In reality, however, the party is paramount. Both the chairperson of the NPC and the premier of the State Council are members of the Politburo Standing Committee.

The pretense of separation created damaging institutional complexity and uncertainty. During the first 30 years under Mao, the "great helmsman," even alternated between leading only the party and asserting direct control over the entire government. And since then, there have been debates about the appropriate degree of integration between the party and the government. Institutional conflicts have been exacerbated by the strong personalities involved, with dire consequences. In the mid-1960s, the political differences between Mao, then leading the party, and Liu Shaoqi, then heading the government, played no small role in igniting the disastrous Cultural Revolution.[76]

The Third Plenum of 2013 initiated a significant departure from the old three carriages model. Since then, the party established a total of six leading groups and committees under the direct authority of the Politburo with the power to design and implement national policies.[77] The bodies have a wide range of inter-ministerial governance functions, which brings greater strategic coordination among the different parts of the national bureaucracy.[78] Xi, who is general secretary of the Central Committee, heads a portfolio of nine of these policymaking bodies.[79] Two particularly important new leading groups are the Central Reform Leading Group and the National Security Committee, which are designed to coordinate national economic and security policies.

Of course, similar groups designed to coordinate activities among permanent government ministries, have been a feature of the party's political structure for decades.[80] The party's Central Finance and Economic Leading Group, for instance, has played a major role in setting China's economic policies for many years. However, the institutionalization of such organs after the Third Plenum has been unprecedented and signals a new phase of consolidation.

Beyond the new committees, perhaps the most significant institutional reengineering brought by the plenum was to one of the most powerful party organs, the Central Disciplinary Inspection Commission (CDIC). As part of the broadest and most intense in the history of the People's Republic (perhaps even in the entire history of China[81]), the institution in the eye of the storm has been centralized and fused with the state law and order apparatus—a most critical fusion of party and state.

Of course, despite these far-reaching changes, Western media outlets mostly ignored the party's political reforms on the grounds that they did not move China further down the path toward multi-party liberal democracy. Yet such views reflect an immature, if not outright harmful, understanding of China.[82] In reality, the new political reforms were carried out, and the Third Plenum of 2013 began a new era of the Chinese party-state. The fusion of party and state in the previous phase will be consolidated, and the party will become a truly mature governing institution, not altogether dissimilar to the centuries-old Mandarin class of the old Chinese dynasties.[83]

But that was only the beginning. At the 19th and 20th party congresses, deep and broad institutional reforms were initiated. Common prosperity and high-quality development became the guiding framework for the country's development. Whether one likes it or not, the decade after the 18th party congress has seen a comprehensive transformation of the country. (More about the Xi era in the epilogue.) Xi's new era is now proving to be the third most significant development phase for the People's Republic, the first two being Mao's and Deng's eras. Judging from the past, such an era lasts 30–40 years and impacts just about every aspect of Chinese society. If this is the case, we are only at the early stages of the Xi Jinping era.

June 4, 1989

No assessment of China's recent history can be meaningful without an account of June 4, 1989.

In the fateful spring of 1989, Beijing was gripped by weeks of mass protests. Unlike previous incidents, which had mainly fielded students and members of the educated class (the so-called *zhishi fenzi*)[84], this one encompassed a wider cross-section of Chinese society—students and intellectuals, as well as workers, civil servants, and ordinary urban dwellers. The scale was also unprecedented. At its height, the demonstrations brought an estimated 1.2 million people onto the streets.[85] They occupied the nation's most sacred public space, the enormous Tiananmen Square. By mid-May, demonstrations had spread to other cities and provinces and had brought the entire nation to a standstill.[86]

Then, it all ended—violently.

In the predawn hours of June 4, the People's Liberation Army moved in to clear the square. Soldiers used live ammunition. There is still no confirmed accounting available, but estimates for the number of dead range from hundreds to several thousand.[87]

It was a significant coming-of-age moment for modern China. And, 30-plus years on, emotions still run high for many of that generation. Around the world, the events are told as a tale of the violent suppression of pro-democracy fighters. But the reality was much more complex.

It was the tenth year of Deng's ground-breaking economic reforms. The first phase of agricultural liberalization produced tremendous benefits for the country, particularly its 830 million strong rural population. The ubiquitous food stamps of the previous decades were largely gone. Market forces were beginning to drive economic growth in the cities as well, leading to substantive improvements in urban life. Consumer electronics, such as television sets and refrigerators, were fast making their way to ordinary families. But major structural issues remained, and the centrally planned economy stood in the way of further market reforms.[88]

Pricing was the most significant issue. In the previous decades, the government-set prices for everything from industrial products to food and clothing. That led to gross misallocation of resources and a lack of productivity. In the early 1980s, the government thus decided on a policy of dual-track pricing. Although government-set prices remained, the state-owned enterprises were mandated to sell a portion of their products at market-determined prices. The policy proved effective. It accomplished the goal of improving productivity and avoided the disruption of moving the entire economy to market pricing in one fell swoop. Had the dual track been allowed to progress, many economists now argue, China would have had a smoother transition to a market economy over the next ten years.[89]

But that was not to be. The team in charge of the economy, led by Premier Zhao Ziyang, became impatient. In 1988, it made the fateful decision to abolish the dual-track system and move almost the entire economy to market pricing. The resulting disruption led to catastrophic double-digit inflation and widespread panic.

Larger social and political forces complicated things further. In the cities, ten years of economic reforms had reengineered China's social structure. Before the reforms, the educated classes—party cadres, civil servants, professionals from state-owned enterprises, and the *zhishi fenzi*—occupied the commanding heights of mainstream urban society. Because Deng's reforms were carried out within the existing socialist structure, they were designed to first release productive forces among the poor. As a result, new classes of uneducated merchants were making many times more money than engineers and professors. Meanwhile, the dual-track pricing policy produced a byproduct: rampant corruption. Private merchants made shady deals with state-owned enterprise managers to split extra profits created by the quota system. Elite dissatisfaction was reaching a boiling point just when policy blunders led to an even more severe economic catastrophe.[90]

In the spring of 1989, people began to take to the streets. In the popular telling of the June Fourth, story, one fact is omitted: the protests were initiated by the political left, which was angry with the inequality and corruption produced by a newly emerging market economy. The first protestors wanted the government to reinstate the socialist egalitarianism of the past. Liberal democratic slogans emerged only later.

The political dimension was even more complicated. Zhao, recently elevated to the position of general secretary of the party, found himself in a precarious position. In addition to being held responsible for the policy blunder of full price-marketization, his immediate family was accused of benefitting from the corruption that came with the dual-track policies. (Zhao's own son was said to be involved.[91]) With Deng remaining as China's paramount leader, Zhao's room for maneuvering was narrow. Apparently, Zhao made what was, in retrospect, a badly advised political move. To shore up his own position and challenge Deng, he signaled his support for the protests.[92] And, seeing that they had a powerful backer in the highest ranks of the party, the protestors became ever more determined to press their case to the end. Meanwhile, Zhao's maneuvering led to a divided and paralyzed Politburo.[93] Instead of devising a political solution to bring the simmering protests to an end, the body looked on as the demonstrations became uncontrollable.

The movement's course was influenced by its larger historic and global context. The Cold War was coming to an end. Gorbachev's glasnost and perestroika were sweeping the Soviet Union. Without the benefit of the lessons that would follow the coming collapse of the USSR, the Chinese public seemed convinced that China's problems were caused by a lack of political reforms. A Western-style political system was perceived as the panacea, and the reticence of the party to launch an immediate political transition became a point of popular resentment. Given such demands, it is not surprising that the June Fourth Movement morphed into an existential threat to the entire People's Republic.

More than thirty years have passed since that tragic June. It is now possible to assess the protests and response in context. Two years after the June Fourth Movement, the mighty Soviet Union collapsed. The end of the Cold War brought about a new phenomenon that would sweep the globe: maidanocracy, or rule of the square. The term "maidan" is, of course, derived from the revolution in central Kiev that overthrew the sitting government of Ukraine.

The end of the Cold War threw many nations around the world into transition. From the former Soviet Union to Southeast Asia, from the Arab world to Hong Kong, *maidanocracy* has gone by many names—the color revolutions, the Arab Spring, and in the case of Hong Kong, the umbrella revolution—but it has changed the lives of millions. Rule by the Square shares similar characteristics across the world: First, it comes amid general popular discontent over the prevailing state of affairs and anxiety about the future. Second, the foot soldiers of such movements are largely well-intentioned people with genuine grievances, but the leaders are activists with strong ideological agendas. They usually aim to overthrow the government or sometimes the entire political system. Third, the press relentlessly cheers on the protests, encouraging a binary divide between democracy, the banner under which the protestors always march, and tyranny.

In the past 30-some years, the track record of *maidanocracy* movements has been dismal. When they fail outright, they are usually put down by force with massive loss of life (think: Syria). When they succeed, they lead to long periods of suffering and destruction (Ukraine, where more than a decade of continuous color revolutions have torn the country apart and now threaten the nation's very survival). And some *maidanocracy* movements seem to run on a treadmill: get on the square to remove a government only to return to the square to remove the next one (see: Egypt). In the meantime, paralysis, chaos, and even violence reign (as in Libya).

The inaugural *maidanocracy* movement was, of course, the one in Beijing in 1989. It failed. The violence was tragic, but it was not nearly as devastating as in many other countries where *maidanocracy* movements resulted in years of internecine conflicts. If the protests had succeeded, the consequences would surely have been far worse. Chinese society was in a highly combustible state. The remnants of mass mobilization from the Cultural Revolution, popular discontent, and the short-term dislocation caused by economic reform would have combined to turn back the nation's tentative progress toward the development of a market economy. Then, stalled economic progress would further deepen popular anger. The vicious cycle would destroy the legitimacy of the entire political system, which could have collapsed leaving a complete power vacuum. Political, commercial, and military forces would have competed to fill that void. A failed state with general chaos and even civil war would have been a likely outcome.

Look no further than Russia to see why. After the euphoria of Gorbachev's reform and Yeltsin's revolution, post-Soviet Russia experienced a sustained period of destruction that caused deep suffering for the Russian people—suffering that in the 1990s decreased life expectancy from 69 to 65, and doubled the suicide rate.[94] Some of the consequences of those turmoils last to the present day. It was the Soviet example that led many who had participated in or sympathized with the June Fourth Movement, to grow disillusioned in such revolutionary upheaval in the years following, which partially explains the absence of any mass Chinese demands for regime change since 1989.

The rest of the explanation lies in what happened at home in China after the catastrophe. Just three years after the tragedy in the square, the party launched a new round of economic reforms that put China on track to become the largest economy in the world in purchasing power parity and the largest trading nation in history. Eight hundred million people were lifted out of poverty. To call China's development "miraculous" is not an exaggeration.

The main drivers of this achievement—political governance and economic policies—are discussed at length in other parts of this book. What is worthy of discussion here is an addendum. Immediately following the horrific and violent outcome in Tiananmen Square, Deng and the party began to enforce a policy of "no debate." The ideological schism that tore the party and the country apart was to be expunged from public discourse. China was to focus single-mindedly on economic development.

Looking back, this approach was wise. Under the circumstances at the time, the ideological conflict and power struggle between Deng and Zhao was politically irreconcilable. To dwell on it would likely have led to large-scale instability. It may be a case worthy of study by other societies undergoing fundamental change, during which time ideology often plays a destructive role. The entire population gets polarized into hardened ideological camps; the state cannot function and no problems can get solved. Even rich societies like the US now cannot sustain such a development, let alone poor and developing ones.

Of course, a byproduct of the "no debate" policy was that a comprehensive narrative of that June's events never emerged. As a result, around the world, the dominant understanding of the movement and, by extension of contemporary China, is the one propagated by dissidents in exile.

As China's political system and society continue to mature, history must be allowed to render a fair judgment. The outlines of that narrative are clear: the June Fourth Movement was driven by a complex set of forces in a country undergoing a change of scale, depth, and speed unprecedented in human history. A vast majority of those who took part in the protests were well-intentioned with legitimate grievances, yet the movement came to be led by those who aimed at overthrowing the entire political system. The movement's young foot soldiers were swept up by ideological fervor fermented by the global trends of the time. The schism at the top of the party leadership (and within society) rendered the government unable to contain the movement at an early stage by responding to the protestors' legitimate concerns. The party's own political infighting allowed the movement to transpire into an existential threat, and the choice became violent suppression or catastrophic chaos. The loss of life was a national tragedy.

As we turn the page, the June Fourth incident, though tragic and catastrophic, would be a mere footnote to a larger and much more consequential narrative for the world. China has demonstrated, for the first time in modern history, that it is possible to achieve modernization, in large scale, without modernity. This precedent could prove invaluable to many nations who are still searching for ways to modernize that are suitable to their own cultural and historic conditions.

Notes

1. Gardels, Nathan. "The Sage of Singapore: Remembering Lee Kuan Yew Through His Own Words." *Noema. 23 Mar. 2015.*
2. This section is adapted from the author's opening remarks at the *Tsinghua Centennial China Model Forum* for the centennial celebration of Tsinghua University, and was translated from Chinese and made available for English print in *The New York Times.* See:

Li, Eric X. "Where the East Parts From the West." *The New York Times*. 27 Apr. 2011.
3. Plato. *Republic VIII*, eds. John M. Cooper and D.S. Hutchinson. Plato: Complete Works, Hackett, 2009, p. 1172.
4. Ibid. p. 1157.
5. Heidegger, Martin. "Plato's Doctrine of Truth." Trans. Thomas Sheehan. In Martin Heidegger, *Pathways*, ed. William McNeill. Cambridge UP, 1998, pp. 155–182.
6. Nietzsche, Friedrich Wilhelm. *Beyond Good and Evil*. Cambridge UP, 2002, p. 4.
7. Palmer, R.R., Joel Colton, and Lloyd Kramer. "The Rise of Europe." *A History of the Modern World: To 1815*. Knopf, 2002, pp. 23–24.
8. Berman, Harold J. *Law and Revolution: The Formation of the Western Legal Tradition*. Harvard UP, 1983, p. 165.
9. Palmer, Colton, and Kramer. "The Protestant Reformation." *History of the Modern World*. pp. 77–84; Hillerbrand, Hans J. *The Protestant Reformation*. Harper Perennial, 2009, pp. ix–xi.
10. Nietzsche announces the individual has supplanted God through a mad man's rants, wherein he comes to the realization that "God is dead ... and we have killed him," and inquires, "Must we ourselves not become gods simply to appear worthy of [the deed]?" From: Nietzsche, Friedrich. "Section 125." *The Gay Science*. Trans. Walter Kaufmann. Vintage Books, 1974, pp. 181–182.
11. In essence, while the Chinese economy deploys market-mechanisms to manage capital, China's political system resists capture by private interests. Consequently, the system is designed to manage the inexorable tendency for capital to accumulate and become concentrated in ever fewer hands, resisting the so-called "principle of infinite accumulation." A brilliantly concise summary of Karl Marx's critique of end-stage capitalism can be found in: Piketty, Thomas. *Capital in the Twenty-First Century*. Trans. Arthur Goldhammer. Belknap of Harvard UP, 2014, pp. 7–11.
12. Excerpt from Emperor Qian Long's Letter to King George III. From: Backhouse, Edmund Trelawny, and John Otway Percy. *Annals and Memoirs of the Court of Peking*. Houghton Mifflin, 1914, pp. 322–331.
13. Traditionally, power and prosperity was closely linked with human population size. China's share of world population in 1820, shortly

after the Macartney Mission, is estimated at 36.6%—with India's a distant second at 20.1%. Refer to: Maddison, Angus. *The World Economy: Historical Statistics.* Development Centre of the Organization for Economic Co-operation and Development, 2003, pp. 258–259.
14. Hanes, W. Travis, and Frank Sanello. The Opium Wars: The Addiction of One Empire and the Corruption of Another. Sourcebooks, 2007, pp. 293–297.
15. Fairbank, John K. "The Creation of the Treaty System." In John K. Fairbank, ed. *The Cambridge History of China vol. 10 Part 1.* Cambridge UP, 1992, p. 213.
16. For a brilliant and scintillating historical overview, refer to: Spence, Jonathan D. *The Search for Modern China.* W.W. Norton, 2013, pp. 139–178, 208–215, 222, 261.
17. Spence. *The Search for Modern China.* pp. 210–212.
18. China's northern fleet—built with extreme care and expense during the early days of the Yangwu Movement—was heavily damaged by Japanese torpedo boats in a battle off the coast of Shandong province. The embarrassing defeat led to the suicides of many senior Chinese military officials, saddled the country with heavy war indemnities (200 million silver taels), and paralyzed the Qing court—causing long lasting economic damage. From: Spence. *The Search for Modern China.* pp. 214–217.
19. Championed by Kang Youwei and Liang Qichao, these constitutional reforms received the endorsement from the young Qing Emperor Guangxu. Unfortunately, the real power behind the throne, his aunt Empress Dowager Cixi disagreed and crushed the so-called "Hundred Days' Reforms." Refer to: Spence. *The Search for Modern China.* pp. 217–218, 220–221.
20. In his early years, Mao considered the Emperor and most officials to be "honest, good, and clever men...[and] only needed the help of Kang Youwei's reforms." From: Snow, Edgar. *Red Star over China.* Grove, 1968, p. 138.
21. Known also as Wellington Koo.
22. Spence. *The Search for Modern China.* pp. 277–278.
23. Before 1911, Liang Qichao (Wade-Gilles: Liang Ch'i-ch'ao) decried the prevailing influence of tradition on his contemporaries in Chinese society. He believed that to liberate his people from the "dead hand of the past," they needed to "wash out the poison

of thousands of years"—which included the thoughts, customs, scripts, and tools of Liang's present day. From: Levenson, Joseph R. *Liang Ch'i Ch'ao And The Mind of Modern China.* Harvard UP, 1953, p. 93.
24. Kwang, Luke S.K. *A Mosaic of the Hundred Days: Personalities, Politics, and Ideas of 1898.* Harvard UP, 1984, pp. 151–201.
25. Fairbank, John K., and Denis C. Twitchett, eds. *The Cambridge History of China: Volume 12, Republican China, 1912–1949.* Cambridge University Press, 1983, pp. 217–255.
26. Ibid., pp. 284–317.
27. Eastman, Lloyd E. "Fascism in Kuomintang China: The Blue Shirts." *The China Quarterly*, vol. 49, 1972, pp. 1–31.
28. The Chinese people, in the words of Rana Mitter, paid a "ghastly price." From 1937 to 1945, 14 million Chinese lives were lost, and over 80 million displaced in massive refugee flight. The country's embryonic modernization was miscarried, and state power, in a state of rot. The Japanese Imperial Army took advantage of Chinese weakness, and invaded Nanjing. Japanese soldiers massacred over 300,000 Chinese when the KMT armies retreated, and in an orgy of rape and pillage, they defiled the erstwhile Chinese capital city. Refer to: Mitter, Rana. *Forgotten Ally: China's World War II, 1937–1945.* Mariner, 2014, pp. 5, 134–140.
29. Maddison, *The World Economy.* p. 259.
30. They were Li Da, Li Hanjun, Zhang Guotao, Liu Renjing, He Shuheng, Dong Biwu, Chen Tanqiu, Wang Jinmei, Deng Enming, Chen Gongbo, Zhou Fohai, and of course the young Mao Zedong. The twelve Chinese representatives elected to the post of General Secretary, Chen Duxiu, who *in absentia* sent Bao Huiseng as a delegate on his behalf. Two Comintern observers were also in attendance, including Henk Sneevliet.
31. Zheng, Shiping. *Party vs. State in Post-1949 China: The Institutional Dilemma.* Cambridge UP, 1997, p. 47.
32. The KMT was founded twice; first, by Sun Yat-sen and Song Jiaoren, as one of many parties in a constitutional parliamentary democracy, and much later, by Sun, as an opposition force to the Beiyang warlord government. It was later reorganized along Leninist principles after he established contact with the Soviets.
33. Sun's tenure was overshadowed by the military power of Yuan Shikai, the ambitious northern warlord to whom he would

later cede the presidency. Defeated, Sun eventually retreated to Guangzhou, where he envisioned a unified republic first under military rule, followed by a period of political tutelage, before transitioning to democracy. Of course, the military and political tutelage would be provided by his KMT. The Chinese party-state was, thus, conceptualized.

34. Taylor, Jay. *The Generalissimo: Chiang Kai-shek and the Struggle for Modern China.* Belknap of Harvard UP, 2011, p. 34.
35. This view was enshrined in the Sun-Joffe Declaration, which was signed in Shanghai on January 26, 1923 and formed the basis for KMT rapprochement with Soviet Russia. Joffe himself concurred with Sun's analysis. See: Pantsov, Alexander. *The Bolsheviks and the Chinese Revolution.* p. 89.
36. Chiang's views were expressed, in written report and speeches to the Comintern Executive Committee, during his visit to the Soviet Union at the head of a delegation to learn ways to improve KMT military, ideological, organizational, propaganda, and party work. Refer to: Yu, Min-ling. "A Reassessment of Chiang Kaishek and the Policy of Alliance with the Soviet Union, 1923–1927." *The Chinese Revolution in the 1920s: Between Triumph and Disaster.* Eds. Mechthild Leutner, Roland Felber, Mikhail L. Titarenko, and Alexander M. Grigoriev. RoutledgeCurzon, 2002, pp. 102–103.
37. Pantsov, Alexander. *The Bolsheviks and the Chinese Revolution.* pp. 57–58.
38. In a January 12, 1923 resolution on CCP-KMT relations, the Comintern Executive Committee determined that the KMT was "the only serious national-revolutionary group in China." Later that year, in a secret resolution, the Executive Committee declared that the CCP would not develop into a mass organization in the near future, and therefore, the CCP must cooperate with the KMT and CCP members must join the KMT. Refer: Pantsov, Alexander. *The Bolsheviks and the Chinese Revolution.* pp. 90–91.
39. By late 1924, the Soviets had provided the KMT army with over 23,000 rifles, along with machine guns, and artillery pieces; 1000 military and political personnel; and subsidies amounting to over 35,000 Chinese yuan a month. From: Taylor, Jay. *The Generalissimo.* p. 47.
40. The Whampoa Military Academy was opened in June 1924 with a Russian gift of 2.7 million Chinese yuan. Chiang personally

selected the first classes of cadets, and over the next twelve months, the academy would train some 2000 new officers. These early graduates, the "Whampoa clique" would become Chiang's inner circle over the next twenty-five years, and also Taylor, Jay. *The Generalissimo.* pp. 45–47.

41. For a detailed account of this history, see: Jin, Yinan. *Misery and Glory. [苦难辉煌]*, 2016.
42. It roughly translates to "ally with Soviet Russia, admit the CCP, and support peasants and workers."
43. Hendrik Sneevliet (Maring) orchestrated this arrangement to suit the needs of both the Comintern and Sun Yat-sen. Initially; he failed to convince the early members of the CCP to enter the agreement voluntarily, and eventually had to rely on the Comintern's authority to obtain their acquiescence. (Bing, Dov. "Sneevliet and the Early Years of the CCP." pp. 679–690).
44. Often referred to in historical sources as the Jiangxi Soviet (Waller, Derek J. *The Kiangsi Soviet Republic: Mao and the National Congresses of 1931 and 1934.* U of California, 1973, p. 23).
45. The term *Jiefangqu* was commonly used during the Second-Sino Japanese war to symbolize Communist Chinese reoccupation of enemy territory. Prior to that, the term *Geming Genjudi* ('Revolutionary Base') was used to describe territory controlled by the CCP. For our purposes, the terms are used interchangeably.
46. The CCP's main policymaking body, the Central Committee, was set to move from Shanghai to the newly established Chinese Soviet Republic in 1932. In the interim, the Central Bureau of the Soviet Areas was created to coordinate the transition, consolidate the soviet areas, and establish a provisional central government. The Red Army, under Mao and Zhu De, was already an established presence in the area. From: Waller, Derek J. *The Kiangsi Soviet Republic.* pp. 22–24.
47. The Russian Revolution was in reality a pair of revolutions: the February Revolution (March 1917), which overthrew the Tsar, and the October Revolution (November 1917), which ushered in the Bolsheviks. Here, the Russian Revolution refers to the latter. The name-date discrepancy in both the February and October Revolutions results from differences between the Julian and Gregorian calendars, with the latter formally adopted after Lenin took the reigns of power.

48. Lenin, living in exile in Zurich, returned onboard the legendary 'sealed train,' which arrived at Finland Station on April 16, 1917 to a cheering crowd of workers. Stalin had returned a month earlier, in mid-March, from his Siberian exile, and was running the *Pravda* newspaper. Refer to: Figes, Orlando. *A People's Tragedy: The Russian Revolution, 1891–1924*. Bodley Head, 2014, pp. 385–386, 388.
49. Meisner, Maurice. *Mao Zedong*. pp. 108–109.
50. Known as "encirclement and extermination" campaigns, they failed to unseat Mao and the communists from Jiangxi four times. In October 1933, the fifth campaign succeeded only after Chiang Kai-shek mobilized nearly a million troops, employed mechanized artillery and an air force of 400 planes, and hired two German generals using a new blockhouse strategy. Facing overwhelming numerical and technological superiority, the bulk of the Red Army retreated and attempted to escape Nationalist encirclement on the Long March. Many would not survive. (Meisner, Maurice. *Mao Zedong*. pp. 66–71).
51. Between the war years of 1937 and 1945, the Red Army transformed from a primitive guerrilla army of 70,000 into a 1-million-strong regular army. Membership within the CCP grew dramatically, to approximately 1.2 million by 1945, and its cadres de facto administered rural areas with populations of almost 100 million. Source: Meisner, Maurice. *Mao Zedong*. p. 83.
52. Deviations from this general principle occurred cyclically in Chinese history—most notably in periods of dynastic decline and weak central government, and in periods under non-Han rule. Local elites preferred an official selection process by "recommendation" over selection by state-based competitive examinations—which had the effect of creating powerful hereditary aristocracies and discrediting the examinations. For in-depth discussion of the merits and limitations of the exam system, refer to: Bell, Daniel A. "On the Selection of Good Leaders in a Political Meritocracy." *The China Model: Political Meritocracy and the Limits of Democracy*. Princeton UP, 2015, pp. 63–89.
53. Ko, Sung Bin. "Confucian Leninist State: The People's Republic of China." *Asian Perspective*, vol. 23, no. 2, 1999, pp. 229–231.
54. Nivison, David S. and Arthur F. Wright, eds. *Confucianism in Action*. Stanford UP, 1969, p. 12.

55. Originates from the Confucian Analects 19.13. "One who excels in learning should then devote himself to official service (学而优则仕)." See: *Confucius. Analects: With Selections from Traditional Commentaries.* trans. Slingerland, Edward. Hackett Publishing, 2003. p. 225. The classic Daxue (or, The Great Learning) linked the ideas of government, self-cultivation, and investigation of things in its exegesis of Confucian philosophy—and with the other three classic texts formed "Four Books" as the basis of the Chinese imperial examination. See: Gardner, Daniel K. *Confucianism: A Very Short Introduction.* Oxford University Press, 2014. pp. 77–85.
56. As a young boy, Mao never received formal schooling, but had two tutors who widened his horizons and awakened a profound interest in classical Chinese texts. Later into his early education, Mao would read the works of Kang Youwei and Liang Qichao and "knew them by heart." Despite this, he was unable to accept Liang's radicalism and considered himself "a monarchist." Refer to: Spence, Jonathan. *Mao.* Viking/Penguin, 1999, p. 6, 10. By late 1938, Mao finally overcame Comintern representative Wang Ming (Chen Shao-yu) and his Soviet returnee supporters to secure his organizational and ideological leadership over party matters at the Sixth Plenum of the CCP Central Committee, which allowed Mao to pursue an independent strategy from Moscow. Refer: Benton, G. "The 'Second Wang Ming Line' (1935–1938)." *The China Quarterly,* no. 61, 1975, p. 61.
57. Alesina, Alberto, Bryony Reich, and Alessandro Riboni. "Nation-Building, Nationalism and Wars." Working Paper, p. 2.
58. Liu drew upon the Confucian virtue of "self-cultivation," while stressing Marxist-Leninist study for cadres. The "new socialist man" needed to consciously strengthen and cultivate himself, and avoid becoming set in his old ways. From: Liu Shaoqi. "How to Be a Good Communist". *Selected Works of Liu Shaoqi, vol 1.* Foreign Languages, 1984, pp. 107–168.
59. Pye, Lucian W. *The Mandarin and the Cadre: China's Political Cultures.* pp. 30–35.
60. Metzger, Thomas A. *Escape from Predicament: Neo-Confucianism and China's Evolving Political Culture.* Columbia UP, pp. 16, 191–235; Metzger, Thomas A. "Continuities between Modern and Premodern China: Some Neglected Methodological and Substantive Issues." *Ideas across Cultures: Essays on Chinese Thought in*

Honor of Benjamin I. Schwartz, ed. Paul A. Cohen and Merle Goldman. Harvard UP, 1990, pp. 263–292.
61. Solomon, Richard H. *Mao's Revolution and Chinese Political Culture*. U of California, 1971, p. xv.
62. Zhang, Pinghui. "Xi Jinping Stresses 'Cultural Heritage' on Youth Day." *South China Morning Post*. 5 May 2014.
63. Zheng, Yongnian. *The Chinese Communist Party as Organizational Emperor: Culture, Reproduction, and Transformation*. Routledge, 2010.
64. Mencius pointed out that the farmers should own the land by saying "those who have their own permanent property (hengchan) have a constant heart". (Mencius, Book I Part A). See Ho, Norman P. "A Confucian Theory of Property." *Tsinghua China Law Review*, vol. 9, 2016, pp. 7–9; and Lau, D. C. *Mencius*. Penguin Classics, 2003, pp. 13–14.
65. Meisner, Maurice. *Mao Zedong*. pp. 119–124.
66. Early on, even as the young republic fought under wartime conditions, the new government was able to effectively adapt its ideology to the economic and political challenges of the day and carry out radical land reform. Between 1950 and 1952, 42% of the country's arable land was redistributed and the party consolidated support among average and poor farmers. In urban areas, many intellectuals, scientists, entrepreneurs, and skilled labor were persuaded to work in the same capacities as they had previously for the construction of the new China. As a consequence, the government was able to revive industry surprisingly quickly. From: Naughton, Barry J. *The Chinese Economy: Transitions and Growth*. MIT Press, 2007, pp. 64–65.
67. Naughton, Barry J. *The Chinese Economy: Transitions and Growth*. MIT Press, 2006, pp. 69–72.
68. A good game theoretical explanation for the disaster can be found in: Lin, Justin Yifu. "Collectivization and China's Agricultural Crisis in 1959–1961." *Journal of Political Economy*, vol. 98, no. 6, 1990, pp. 1228–1252.
69. The Four Cardinal Principles are the four issues for which debate is not allowed in the People's Republic of China. They are: (1) the principle of upholding the socialist path; (2) the principle of upholding the people's democratic dictatorship; (3) the principle of upholding the leadership of the Community Party of China;

and (4) the principle of upholding Mao Zedong Thought and Marxism-Leninism; The words "dictatorship of the proletariat" were replaced with the "people's democratic dictatorship") in the new 1982 constitution, opening up the possibility for a wider section of society to be represented.

70. This is adapted from the author's article in *South China Morning Post*, see: Li, Eric X. "Debunking the Myths of Mao Zedong." *South China Morning Post*. 26 Dec. 2013.
71. Peng, Wuyuan, and Pan, Jiahua. "Rural Electrification in China: History and Institution." *China & World Economy*, vol. 14, no. 1, 2006, pp. 71–84. (In this paper, Peng and Pan cite the number of small hydroelectric stations built to be 90,000. This number differs from the 2015 Ministry of Water Resource reporting that, as of the end of 2014, over 47,000 rural hydropower stations were in operation.) Refer: https://www.scio.gov.cn/xwfbh/gbwxwfbh/xwfbh/slb/Document/1474150/1474150.htm; Bhattacharyya, Subhes C., and Sanusi Ohiare. "The Chinese Electricity Access Model for Rural Electrification: Approach, Experience, and Lessons for Others." b, vol. 49, 2012, pp. 676–687; Bie, Zhaohong, and Lin Yanling. "An Overview of Rural Electrification in China: History, technology, and emerging trends." *IEEE Electrification Magazine*, vol. 3.1, 2015, pp. 36–47; The World Bank. "Access to Electricity (% of Population)." *World DataBank*. Retrieved in 2017 from: https://data.worldbank.org/indicator/eg.elc.accs.zs.
72. Zhang, Tiedao. Literacy Education in China. UNESCO, 2005, Paper commissioned for the EFA Global Monitoring Report 2006, Literacy for Life. p. 3.
73. Kantha, S.S. "Nutrition and Health in China, 1949 to 1989." *Progress in Food & Nutrition Science*, vol. 14, 1990, p. 93.
74. Life expectancy, under-five mortality, and adult male literacy are some indicators that reflected China's significant closing of the gap in the overall human development index. See: Draper, William H. *Human Development Report 1990*. United Nations Development Program, 1990.
75. This is adapted from the author's article in *Foreign Affairs*, see: Li, Eric X. "Party of the Century: How China is Reorganizing for the Future." *Foreign Affairs*. 10 Jan. 2014.
76. Li, Eric X. "Party of the Century: How China is Reorganizing for the Future." *Foreign Affairs*. 10 Jan. 2014.

77. The 18th Third Plenum authorized the creation of four (4) central leading groups—three civilian bodies and one military body. They are the Central Reform Leading Group, the National Security Committee, the Cyberspace Affairs Leading Group, and the Central Leading Group for Military Reform. Two (2) additional groups have been created since: the Central Commission for Integrated Military and Civilian Development, which reports to the Politburo and its Standing Committee of the CCP Central Committee; and the Joint Battle Command of the People's Liberation Army, which answers to the leadership of the Central Military Commission.
78. Johnson, C., Scott Kennedy, and Mingda Qiu. "Xi's Signature Governance Innovation: The Rise of Leading Small Groups." *Center for Strategic and International Studies*, vol. 17, 2017.
79. They include the powerful Foreign Affairs Leading Group, Financial and Economic Affairs Leading Group, and Taiwan Affairs Leading Group in addition to the six aforementioned groups (Central Reform, National Security, Cyberspace Affairs, Military Reform, Integrated Military and Civilian Development, and Joint Battle Command). From: Chan, Minnie. "How Xi Jinping Has Taken On Multiple Roles ... And Amassed Unrivaled Power in China." *South China Morning Post*. 27 Jan. 2017.
80. The earliest "leading groups" were established in 1958 to free the Politburo Standing Committee from the day-to-day affairs and focus on long-term policymaking. From: Huang, Cary. "How Leading Small Groups Help Xi Jinping and Other Party Leaders Exert Power." *South China Morning Post*. 20 Jan. 2014.
81. From 2012 to 2018, China's anti-corruption campaign has swept up some 2 million officials, including 254 "tigers" (those ranking at or above deputy provincial or deputy ministerial level). Those estimates of the number of investigated officials were tallied by ChinaFiles based on press releases and the working reports of the Central Disciplinary Committee. The anti-corruption campaign is explored in depth in Chapter 7. See: "Visualizing China's Anti-Corruption Campaign." *ChinaFile*. Retrieved in 2018 from: http://www.chinafile.com/infographics/visualizing-chinas-anti-corruption-campaign.
82. Li, Eric X. "Party of the Century."
83. Ibid.

84. Here, it is important to distinguish between the modern 'zhishi fenzi' and the traditional Confucian literati. The former behaving more like talking heads on television (the chatterati).
85. A State Security Ministry report (May 17, 1989) estimated that 1.2 million people took to the streets in Beijing after Zhao Ziyang's attempt at dialogue with students failed to bring any change. Source: Zhang, Liang. *The Tiananmen Papers*, ed. Andrew J. Nathan and Perry Link. Public Affairs, 2002, pp. 193–194.
86. On May 17, 1989, twenty-seven provinces reported large-scale demonstrations, of which sixteen involved ten thousand or more demonstrators. For more details on those events, refer to: Zhang, Liang. *The Tiananmen Papers*. pp. 196–199.
87. Most of the tallied deaths occurred in west Beijing between the Muxidi and Liubukou intersections, as the 38th Army attempted to enter the city to maintain order. The high death rate of civilian encounters with the 38th army, and vice versa, can, in part, be accounted for by the fact that bullets had been distributed to lower-ranking officers and rank-and-file soldiers there earlier than most other armies, and that discipline broke down. For a detailed account of the military crackdown, see: Zhao, Dingxin. *The Power of Tiananmen: State-Society Relations and the 1989 Beijing Student Movement*. U of Chicago, 2001, pp. 200–207.

    The exact number of deaths may still be open to debate, and the various estimates are accounted here: Zhang, Liang. *The Tiananmen Papers*. p. 421.

    There is also emerging evidence (from Wikileaks) that in clearing Tiananmen Square, no blood was shed. Refer to: Moore, Malcolm. "Wikileaks: No Bloodshed Inside Tiananmen Square, Cables Claim." *The Telegraph*. 4 Jun. 2011.
88. Zhao, Dingxin. *The Power of Tiananmen*. pp. 42–43, 47–49.
89. China's dual-track reform model, which was once ridiculed as one of the worst efforts, achieved unprecedented success through its gradual reform process; other countries guided by then-mainstream economic theories failed to achieve the desired results. To be sure, reforms faced the challenges of managing profiteering and rent seeking behaviors, but reforms included incentives to boost worker enthusiasm, which ultimately improved productivity. Materials, foreign exchange, financing, and the changing roles of non-state

firms allowed the market to slowly develop and economic development to pick up rapidly. The rapid expansion of trade activity spurred inflation at levels over 15%, something China had experienced little of before 1986. A longer transition period could have provided more time for a smoother transition. Refer to: Lin, Justin Yifu. *Demystifying the Chinese Economy*. Cambridge UP, 2012, pp. 152, 178–186.

90. In the 1980s, Chinese students (and some intellectuals) did not quite understand the double-edged nature of capitalism and market forces—that the market economy could bring prosperity to the country, and also degrade the prestige and privileges that they had enjoyed in traditional societies. High inflation and corruption compounded that angst, as even elite students could not find jobs, or live independently on their scholarships. Refer to: Zhao, Dingxin. *The Power of Tiananmen*. pp. 84–90.

91. To say corruption erupted had a pernicious effect on society is perhaps a great understatement. In 1988, a record-breaking 55,710 cases of economic crime (corruption, bribery, profiteering, smuggling) were tried; and in the first quarter of following year, 560,000 criminal cases were prosecuted (compared with the 540,000 cases for the entire year of 1985). Refer to: Zhang, Liang. *The Tiananmen Papers*. p. 6.

As general secretary, Zhao presided over a state that committed certain policy errors that, to some extent, encouraged the growth of corruption. He did not assign anti-corruption work as a top political priority, allowed public institutions to make money to supplement insufficient budgetary allocations, and encouraged a comfortable or luxurious life style within the party. (He, Zengke. "Corruption and Anti-corruption in Reform China." *Communist and Post-Communist Studies*, vol. 33, 2000, p. 252.) Zhao was aware of rumors that his sons were using his position to pursue a lucrative business in colored televisions—and in a conversation with Yang Shangkun, he proposed an investigation into his children's activities. It is unclear if the matter was followed through. (Zhang, Liang. *The Tiananmen Papers*. p. 124.).

92. In his speech to the delegates of the twenty-second Asian Development Bank Conference, his tone was strikingly different from that of the April 26 *People's Daily* editorial, which had been approved by the Standing Committee and Deng Xiaoping. Refer: Zhao,

Dingxin. *The Power of Tiananmen*. pp. 226; Zhang, Liang. *The Tiananmen Papers*. pp. 71–73.
93. The gamble Zhao Ziyang made is explained by Zhao Dinxin (no relation): Zhao, Dingxin. *The Power of Tiananmen*. pp. 226–234.
94. The World Bank. "Russian Federation: Life Expectancy at Birth, Total (Years), Suicide Mortality Rate (Per 100,000 Population)." *World DataBank*. Retrieved in 2019 from: https://data.worldbank.org/indicator/SP.DYN.LE00.IN?locations=RU; https://data.worldbank.org/indicator/SH.STA.SUIC.P5?locations=RU.

CHAPTER 6

Chinese Governance—Who Shall Rule?

In the following two chapters, I delve into the mechanics of how Chinese governance actually works. These are, by necessity, highly simplified versions of one of the most complex systems in the world. It is more appropriate to treat them like case studies rather than some sort of theoretical framework. To be specific, we study the who and the how of Chinese governance.

From Plato to John Stuart Mill, from Confucius to Marx, from Julius Caesar to Thomas Jefferson, for as long as human civilization has existed, pundits and pols have been vexed by one central question: Who shall rule?

In his *Republic*, Plato painted an ideal polis, one in which an elaborate system bred and cultivated the most moral and capable to be rulers.[1] Mill, for his part, saw the tension between the liberal ideals of the Enlightenment and the reality of an uneducated and ill-informed public.[2] Confucius, meanwhile, banked on the mandate of heaven whereas Marx proposed the proletariat as the most legitimate embodiment of power.[3]

But we need not deal too much with abstractions. Rather, the real-life comparison of modern China and the United States—the world's foremost promoter of liberal democracy[4]—shows much about who should rule.

Clinton and Jiang

Bill Clinton was one of the most skillful politicians in contemporary America and his presidency was arguably the most successful since the end of the Cold War.[5] When he moved into the White House in 1993, however, his resume consisted mainly of being governor of Arkansas for over 12 years (one of his terms a failure), with a short stint as attorney general of the same state and a year in private legal practice. During the years of Clinton's governorship, tiny Arkansas had a population of 2.4 million and average annual GDP of $31.2 billion, or 0.7% of the national total. At the state's helm, Clinton's most notable achievement was enacting education reforms, which boiled down to mandating that the state's 30,000 primary and secondary teachers take a onetime test to demonstrate their fitness to instruct students.[6] From that platform, the gifted debater and glad-hander entered the presidential election of 1992—and won.[7]

In addition to being the most skillful post-Cold War American president, Clinton was also the luckiest. The United States' victory in the Cold War brought his time in office a significant peace dividend—one that historians agree was largely wasted both domestically and internationally.[8] At home, his lack of governing experience was laid bare with his failure to enact healthcare reform legislation, a project that would have to wait another 17 years. Clinton did have significant accomplishments in office such as welfare reform and leaving the economy in strong shape with a budget surplus, but even that was soon to be squandered.

Internationally, Clinton was guilty of misinterpreting America's victory in the Cold War and misjudging the exercise of U.S. power in the world. Imperial overreach began with the Clinton presidency. Lofty rhetoric about "the indispensable nation" and high-minded humanitarian slogans brought America into unnecessary conflicts in Bosnia, Haiti, and Somalia that had nothing to do with the country's national interests and distracted it from real long-term strategic imperatives like Russia, China, and world trade.[9] Furthermore, Clinton's hasty expansion of NATO to Russia's doorstep undermined what goodwill might have once been possible between Russia and the West, the consequences of which can still be felt today and most tragically shown in the current military conflict in Ukraine.[10]

By contrast, it took Clinton's Chinese contemporary and counterpart, Jiang Zemin, 40 years to rise to the top of a complex hierarchy to become general secretary of the Chinese Communist Party. Born into an ordinary family, Jiang joined the party as a 20-year-old undergraduate at Shanghai Jiaotong University in the mid-1940s. He entered into Chinese officialdom through a state-owned enterprise (SOE), one of the three pillars that make up the party organizational structure.[11] After two short stints at the party's lowest organizational level, *ke*, in 1956, he launched to the *chu* level, working for five years in the mid-1950s as a manager of the Changchun First Automobile Works (FAW), a major SOE in the country's industrial heartland of the northeast.

At that time, large SOEs like FAW were much more than businesses. They functioned as cradle-to-grave industrial-social complexes, organizing the lives of tens of thousands of people (employees and their families), often with their own schools, hospitals, housing, and directly managed retirement programs.[12] A manager of an SOE, especially during that period, was responsible for a full range of social and political matters beyond the technical and commercial realms.

When Jiang took over at FAW, it was a particularly difficult time for the business and for China's economy. First Automobile Works had been one of the first major SOEs built after the founding of the People's Republic. Its establishment had been possible thanks to financial and technical aid from the Soviet Union. But in the late 1950s, Sino-Soviet relations deteriorated, and the Soviets withdrew their support. At the same time, the Chinese government launched the disastrous Great Leap Forward.[13] Along with virtually all sectors of the Chinese economy, the automobile factory was given totally unrealistic production goals that had detrimental effects on its operations.

To secure enough electricity to reach the factory's targets, Jiang was given the nearly impossible task of changing its coal-fired electrical plants over to oil in three months. His team managed to complete the task in three and a half months while also ensuring that over 100,000 people had access to heating through the coming winter.[14] Early in his career, in short, Jiang had rather harsh training in managing tough economic and political problems and in-depth exposure to the catastrophic consequences of policy failures in a centrally planned economy.

Jiang's advancement was interrupted, like everyone else's in his generation, by the Cultural Revolution, during which he was sidelined in Wuhan.[15] By the mid-1970s, though, he had secured promotion to the higher *ju* level with a position in the central government in Beijing. He worked first as deputy director of the Bureau of Foreign Affairs,

First Ministry of Machine-Building Industry, and then as vice chairman of two new commissions, Foreign Investment Commission and Import–Export Commission. In that role, he drafted the Guangdong Provincial Special Economic Zone Regulations, which put Jiang at the frontline of Deng Xiaoping's economic reform program. In his report to the National People's Congress on the designs of special economic zones, Jiang proposed policies that would grant local governments the authority to offer tax incentives to attract businesses, permit the transfer of land usage rights, and let foreign-invested companies—and later all private businesses—hire and terminate employees largely at will. As China was just beginning its transition from a strictly centrally planned economy to a market economy, those policies were nothing short of revolutionary.

Guangdong went on to become the pioneering region of the Deng era. Its Shenzhen special economic zone led nationwide experiments in economic development. Guangdong now has a GDP totaling $1.92 trillion, which would rank in the top 10 globally if the provincial economy were that of a country.[16]

For his part, in 1982 at the age of 56, Jiang entered high officialdom as Vice Minister of Electronic Industry. Concurrently, he became a member of the Central Committee. Three years later, Jiang was made mayor of Shanghai, which, with a population of 12 million and a GDP of 47 billion RMB, was one of the largest and most important economic regions of China. Two years after his mayoral appointment, Jiang became the party secretary of Shanghai and entered the Politburo at the age of 61. During his term in Shanghai, Jiang and Zhu Rongji, who succeed him as mayor and who would later become China's legendary premier, eventually grew the city's GDP to 90 billion RMB.[17]

In 1989, Jiang became General Secretary of the Chinese Communist Party. His leadership of China lasted 13 years through 2002 when he retired from the position at the party's 16th Congress. He kept the position of Chairman of the Central Military Commission for an additional two years.

Under his leadership, China went from a robust but still poor developing economy to a global industrial juggernaut. The country's GDP quadrupled from $348 billion to $1.47 trillion and ranked number six worldwide. Trade volume grew six times from $111 billion to $620 billion.[18] Perhaps more importantly, the structure of the Chinese economy went through a fundamental transformation. What was an economy clearly dominated by the state sector in 1989 became two-thirds private sector by 2002.[19]

It wasn't just China's top official whose trajectory was impressive. Jiang's deputy, Zhu, had a similar rise.

By just about all measures, Zhu was China's most aggressive economic reformer in that era, a maverick credited with overcoming tremendous internal resistance to bring China into the WTO. After graduating from Tsinghua University, one of China's preeminent institutions of higher education, with a degree in engineering, Zhu began his career in the early 1950s as the lowest level official in the northeastern industrial heartland. Zhu may be seen as a daring market reformer today, but he started off squarely in the mode of a central planner; the northeastern provinces pioneered China's large-scale industrialization by importing wholesale the Soviet model of top-down economic management. As a young official, Zhu was at the forefront of implementing that strategy. As such, he gained a first-hand understanding of the pitfalls of that system, but at the same time, its effectiveness.

During the Mao era, Zhu was expelled from the party for his outspokenness. He spent years toiling in the countryside and gained in-depth knowledge of Chinese rural life and the agricultural sector. He was reinstated after the Cultural Revolution, and his subsequent rise through the party ranks followed a similar pattern to those of his contemporaries, through many levels of government and from industrial zones to the countryside. In 1988, he became the mayor and then party chief of Shanghai, where he had first served as Jiang's deputy. In 1991, he was promoted to vice premier and governor of the central bank, which effectively made him the economic tsar of the Jiang era. It was a nearly 40-year zigzagging ascent to the top, but he eventually made it.[20] By 1998, he became premier.

Through it all, Zhu's roots in central planning held tight. Zhu was wary of what he saw as the market excesses in the go-go era of the late 1980s and early 1990s. In response, he implemented his famous "16 Measures" to rein in the economy.[21] Those measures included direct command-and-control policies, such as quotas for bank lending and mandatory purchases of state treasury bills. His initiatives were later credited for providing the Chinese economy with a soft landing during its market transition, and they paved the way for sustained growth in the following two decades.

China's modern economic success was as much about deftly wielding the powerful hand of the state as it was about allowing the invisible hand of the market to do its work. Zhu's career is one of the best illustrations of that fact. During his tenure at the top, under President Jiang's leadership and with his full backing, Zhu used government power to effectively restrain run-away inflation while maintaining near double-digit growth. He revamped the entire banking system by restructuring the four major state industrial banks into commercial banks and establishing three new policy banks.[22] He reformed the nation's tax code and increased central government tax receipts 30-fold between 1993 and 2012.[23] The new revenue provided the necessary resources for China's infrastructure-led growth.

Zhu also restructured the entire central government by eliminating 11 ministries (out of 40 total) and reducing central government personnel by 1.15 million. He also shut down a large number of underperforming state-owned enterprises. As part of that process, he managed the reemployment of 26 million laid-off SOE employees.[24] Most notably, he led China into the WTO.

Some of the WTO negotiations began when he was vice premier between 1991 and 1997, but most of it was carried out during his five-year term as premier between 1998 and 2003.[25]

It is not outlandish to suggest that any one of Zhu's initiatives faced more resistance from vested interests, overcame more bureaucratic and societal obstacles, and resulted in more fundamental and lasting changes than the major policy accomplishments of Clinton and all his successors combined. Clinton's welfare reform, George W. Bush's tax cut and Medicare reform, and Barak Obama's healthcare reform and financial reform fell far short of what they promised to do—and what the country needed. By contrast, Jiang and Zhu improved the fates of more than a billion people.

Why the difference? At least in part, it is because people like Jiang and Zhu, before assuming their positions at the top, went through decades of trial by fire at many different levels of government and in many different sectors and locations. By the time they were running the country, they knew how to execute. Their American counterparts did not.

BUSH AND HU

If Jiang Zemin and Zhu Rongji hailed from the epicenter of China's economic miracle, Shanghai, their successor came from a rather different place. Hu Jintao was a product of China's forgotten hinterlands. After graduating from Tsinghua with a degree in hydroelectric engineering and spending a few years practicing as an engineer, Hu began his party career at the deputy *chu* level in Gansu province, China's western interior. He moved up several ranks there from deputy *chu* to *ju*, mostly in infrastructure development positions. In the early 1980s, he returned to the central government in Beijing to serve as the head of the Communist Youth League, a ministerial position. The league was a major training ground for young officials at that time, and leading it gave Hu a unique top-down vantage point from which to study the party's talent pool and management structure.

After four years of training in Beijing, Hu was sent back to China's southwest interior and became party secretary of Guizhou province in 1985. At that time, Guizhou had population of 29 million, a mid-sized province by Chinese standards. Meanwhile, its GDP and income per capita ranked it dead last in China—a mere $144 per year based on the contemporary exchange rate. It was the poorest place in a poor country.[26]

On his first day at work as provincial party secretary, more than 10 million of Guizhou's 29 million citizens were living below the poverty line, and many faced food shortages. Guizhou's territory covered 176,000 square kilometers, but it barely boasted ten kilometers of paved roads and hardly any other infrastructure to speak of. Many years of unsustainable agricultural practices led to major losses of arable land.

Once settled in Guizhou, Hu pioneered several strategies for alleviating poverty. He borrowed the idea of special economic zones, which had been used in coastal regions so effectively to initiate market reform, to create so-called poverty alleviation special experiment zones. One such experiment was to let local governments rebate taxes to businesses in return for equity ownership. In another, credit unions were set up to provide microlending. These policies set the stage for Guizhou's steady and dramatic growth. By 2019, its GDP per capita is more than 40 times its size when Hu took over.[27]

After Guizhou, Hu became party secretary of another very poor region—Tibet. He dealt with tough challenges there, too, and not just economic issues but also a violent ethnic rebellion that broke out in the spring of 1989. He proved tough and declared martial law in the face of a direct challenge to government authority. While ensuring stability with an iron fist, Hu also pushed through economic development measures that put Tibet on a growth trajectory not far behind the rest of the country.

In 1992, Hu was promoted to member of the Politburo Standing Committee, where he served for ten years as the designated successor of Jiang before taking over himself in 2002.

Across the Pacific in the United States, if Clinton's presidency was less than satisfactory considering the extraordinarily favorable conditions he inherited, George W. Bush's was by most measures a disaster. In his biography *Bush*, Jean Edward Smith characterized the 43rd U.S. president as "unprepared for the complexities of governing, with little executive experience and a glaring deficit in his attention span."[28] A short budgetary surplus of 1998–2001 quickly turned back into deficit. Tax cuts further reduced government revenue. Income disparities began to worsen, and the wealth gap has continued to widen to this day.

Domestically, Bush's inexperience and ignorance proved damaging; although signs and warnings abounded, the administration was caught completely off guard by the bursting of the housing bubble in 2007–08, and it showed poor judgment throughout the 2008 financial crisis. "Economies should cycle... If houses get too expensive, people will stop buying them... Let the market function properly," Bush answered when asked about the cost of housing before the financial crisis. "Your kind of question has been asked throughout the history of homebuilding... Things cycle. That's just the way it works."[29] A Chinese premier would never be caught uttering such nonsense.

Things were no better on the foreign policy front. Ill-conceived and badly executed, the Iraq war will go down as one of the greatest examples of political incompetence in the history of political governance. It was what Charles de Talleyrand once described: "It is worse than a crime, it is a blunder."

OBAMA AND XI, PLUS TRUMP

Two books, both about politics and both written by young political figures, are instructive for our next comparison. One is *Audacity of Hope*, authored by Barack Obama in 2006. He was 45. The other is *Up and Out of Poverty* by Xi Jinping, published in 1992 when he was 40.

At the time, Xi was serving as party secretary in the county of Ningde, a relatively underdeveloped area in Fujian province—the lowest level of local executive jurisdiction. His book included page after page of reflections on the development policies he was trying out. Xi wrote about rearranging the county's agricultural economy by making each village specialize in just one type of produce in order to create economies of scale.[30] He wrote that the county should not copy more developed coastal areas that were building railways and ports; instead, it should be focused on building roads and expanding electricity capacity.[31] Most interestingly, Xi wrote that poverty alleviation should not come through welfare handouts: it should be part and parcel of actual economic development. He set a target of allocating 90% of the county government's poverty alleviation budget toward economic development, so it would generate productive returns.[32] His book also included a detailed discussion of how to reassign management of the county's forests—the list goes on.[33]

The *Audacity of Hope*, on the other hand, was a manifesto of slogans. Obama wrote many words vociferously lamenting America's political dysfunction, which only grew worse during his tenure as president and beyond. He spent many pages on campaigns and fund-raising, and complained about the influence of money in U.S. politics (He later went on to raise more money—and attend more fund-raising events—than any presidential candidate in history).[34] Finally, he wrote large passages on hope. At the time of the book's writing, Obama, then a senator, had already occupied one of the highest political offices in America. But before that, he had zero experience governing. Merely two years following *Audacity of Hope's* publication, with only six years in the Senate, a legislative record with scant results, and a soaring speech in front of the 2004 Democratic National Convention, Obama was elected president of the United States.[35]

After publishing *Up and Out of Poverty*, it took Xi, another 20-year slog through the ranks before he finally became general secretary of the party and president of China.

In 2018, Xi, wrapped up the first five-year term at the top. During that time, he executed a major anti-corruption drive unprecedented in its scale and intensity. He led a major structural shift in the economy, reducing investment as a share of GDP and dramatically lifting consumption and services. The economy expanded to $13.1 trillion, added 66 million new urban jobs, and lifted 68 million people out of poverty, putting the country within striking distance of eradicating poverty, as defined by current standards. As if those accomplishments were not enough, Xi engineered the most significant military reorganization in the history of the People's Republic. Even on the most intractable problem—environmental degradation—Xi, made incredible progress. Over a three-year-period, the government implemented policies that reduced the volume of fine particles in the air in China by 32%.[36] It took London and LA decades to clean up their air and that was after a major deindustrialization; China under Xi, by contrast, remains the fastest-growing industrial economy in the world.

What did Obama do in eight years as president? Perhaps the scholar Vali Nasr summarized it best. The United States began its post-Cold War cycle under Clinton with the self-aggrandizing label of "indispensable nation," Obama ended the cycle by turning America into a dispensable nation.[37] He was a relatively popular president judging from polling data, but his actual accomplishments in office were meager. Domestically, his healthcare reform legislation was much-needed but implemented in a way that totally polarized American society. Healthcare costs have continued to rise.[38] Financial market reforms pursued in the wake of the 2008 financial crisis are also coming undone. Other reform initiatives, such as gun control, fell apart due to a lack of legislative blocking and tackling.

Internationally, Obama's foreign policy was characterized by hesitation and the continuation of a long and costly war in Afghanistan. When Obama left office in 2017, the United States was a deeply divided and pessimistic nation that had turned to identity politics and populism.

Another best-selling book was published around the same time as Xi's *Up and Out of Poverty*. Its author was a young American, who also was around 40, and a successful businessman. The book was *The Art of the Deal*. And, whereas his predecessors had scant political experience, Donald Trump had absolutely none.

Comparing these two sets of leaders from the same period of time show in glaring detail the contrast between the kinds of politicians each political system generates. Of the four American presidents, two were born into extraordinary privilege. A third one, Obama, was raised in relative comfort. Only Clinton can claim to have had hardscrabble beginnings. All four presidents had familiarity with only a narrow sliver of American society, and all had limited government experience before becoming president.

The Chinese leaders, on the other hand, all climbed the ladder from the bottom to the top. By the time they made it to the top as general secretary (or premier, in the case of Zhu) they had gone through many layers of government over several decades. The process gave them intimate knowledge of the intricacies of all levels of Chinese governance. All of them excelled under tough and complex conditions, which had conflicting policy goals and required overcoming vast bureaucratic and societal resistance.

Of the four Chinese leaders, three came from ordinary backgrounds. Only Xi is a princeling. However, he was a princeling born at the wrong time, and his background became a source of severe adversity while he was coming-of-age.[1] Before occupying the highest office in the land, they had each managed combined GDPs bigger than those of most countries. More importantly, they had each governed populations of tens of millions of people, and in Xi's case, over a hundred million.

In the Chinese bureaucratic lexicon, the word *li lian* is key. It means long periods of training, trial, and testing. *Li lian* is one of the most important criteria when the party evaluates its officials for promotion. And *li lian* is what seems to be thoroughly missing in American politicians.

Meritocratic Governance: It's the Org Department![39]

The differences between American and Chinese leaders are not by chance. They are a direct result of each country's political processes.

On the Avenue of Eternal Peace just west of the Forbidden City, a seven-story building—stately but otherwise nondescript—houses one of the most important organs of the Chinese party-state: the Organizational Department of the Central Committee of the Chinese Communist Party, or the Central Organizational Department (COD) for short.

The COD was established in 1924, less than three years after the party was itself founded. Its first minister was none other than Mao Zedong. Since then, some of the People's Republic's most important figures have headed the COD, including Zhou Enlai, China's founding premier, Liu Shaoqi, later a state president, and Chen Yun, eventually Second Chairman of the Central Advisory Commission. Even Deng Xiaoping served as head of the COD in the 1950s. Indeed, since 1949, of the

---

[1] Just as Xi was starting his career, his father, a senior party leader, was purged and imprisoned. This derailed Xi's own career at the very start.

56 people that have made it to the very top—the standing committee of the Politburo—13 have either risen to that level after serving as head of the COD or have served in both roles concurrently.[40]

As important as it has been to the party-state, the COD was essentially shut down for ten years during the Cultural Revolution. After that period, Deng began to rebuild the party-state. The COD's first head in the new era was Hu Yaobang, who later became general secretary of the party. Under Deng's direction, Hu used the COD to begin a large-scale process of reinstating thousands of officials who had been banished during the Cultural Revolution. Since then, the COD has become the mighty engine that powers modern Chinese governance.

Namely, the department carries out an elaborate process of bureaucratic selection, evaluation, and promotion that would be the envy of even the most successful corporations. Patronage continues to be a problem for the system, but by and large, merit remains the main driving force.

Every year, the government and its affiliated organizations recruit university graduates into entry-level positions in one of the three state-controlled systems: the civil service, state-owned enterprises, and government-affiliated social organizations, such as universities or community programs. Most new recruits enter at the lowest level, or *ke yuan*. Depending on the candidates' performance at that level, the Organization Department ranks all three pools and then promotes individuals through four managerial ranks: *fu-ke*, *ke*, *fu-chu*, and *chu*. The range of positions at these levels is wide, covering anything from running the healthcare system in a poor village to attracting commercial investment in a city district.

As young officials move up through the four grades, they are further evaluated and then promoted, stalled, or retired. The department reviews quantitative performance records; carries out interviews with superiors, peers, and subordinates; vets personal conduct; and confirms abilities through public polling data. Such public opinion surveys are extensive and frequent and are conducted at all levels of government. Questions might include general satisfaction with the country's direction and more mundane and specific local issues. Once the department gathers a complete dossier on all the candidates, committees discuss the data and promote winners. Exceptional workers are put on fast track.

The promotion tracks are diverse, and individuals can be rotated through and out of all three systems. An official can start with a job making economic policy and move on to a posting where he or she will deal with political or social policy. The official can go from a traditional government position to a managerial role in a state-owned enterprise or a university. The most successful of the candidates make it to the *fu-ju* and *ju* levels, during which many would typically manage districts with populations in the millions or companies with hundreds of millions of dollars in revenue. To get a sense of how rigorous the selection process is, this year, there are 900,000 officials at the *fu-ke* and *ke* levels, 600,000 at the *fu-chu* and *chu* levels, and 40,000 at the *fu-ju* and *ju* levels. Those numbers might seem large but *fu-ke* and *ke* officials make up only 0.06% of the population, *fu-ju* and *ju* make up 0.0028%.[41]

After the *ju* level, a very talented few move up several more ranks and eventually make it to the party's Central Committee, which consists of about 300 members. The entire process could take two to three decades and most of those who get there will have had managerial experience in just about every aspect of Chinese society. From there, the chosen few will be promoted into important roles within the Politburo after one or two terms as Central Committee members. Of the 25 Politburo members elected at the 19th party congress, 17 had managed provinces larger than most countries in the world and budgets larger than the average nation's. And in the Politburo's seven-member standing committee, all but one have such experience. In fact, one of the most important criteria for joining the Politburo or its standing committee is that the individual has what is called "overall governance" experience of a region (*di fang zhu zheng*). *Zhu Zheng* means that the person has had all-encompassing responsibility, including economic performance, social welfare, healthcare, housing, stability and security, and the environment.

Xi's career path is illustrative. In the 30 years during which he moved from a *fu-ke* level deputy county chief in a poor village to party secretary of Shanghai and member of the Politburo, he managed areas with total populations of over 150 million and combined GDPs of more than $1.5 trillion. His career demonstrates how meritocratic forces drive Chinese politics.[42]

A person with Obama's pre-presidential professional experience would never have become a small county manager in China's system, let alone come anywhere near the Politburo. Indeed, if we survey the entire field of post-Cold War American presidential candidates, none of them would. This is not to say that they were not capable leaders—many of them were. But they had nothing like *zhu zheng* experience. Little wonder that Clinton and Romney, having reached the very top of American politics, could be caught uttering words like "basket of deplorables" and "…47%

of the (American) people…are dependent upon government…my job is not to worry about those people."[43]

In fact, there are only two areas in which these American leaders beat their Chinese counterparts hands down: oratory skills and fund-raising abilities.

Good Emperor, Bad Emperor

In *The Origins of Political Order*, the political scientist Francis Fukuyama discussed the "bad emperor problem." A political system without regularly held elections, he argued, won't be able to get rid of a bad leader. That sounds right at the abstract level, and China might seem vulnerable to the problem. After all, on March 11, 2018, the Chinese National People's Congress approved constitutional changes that included lifting the two-term presidential limit. And in October 2022, Xi was elected to a third term as general secretary of the party and state president in the following year.

Western media and the Chinese chatterati were in uproar. "China's Xi allowed to remain 'president for life' as term limits removed," proclaimed the BBC. CNN similarly declared "China clears way for Xi Jinping to rule for life." Fukuyama, writing in the *Washington Post*, asserted that China might be succumbing to a new bad emperor.[44] But such pronouncements completely misinterpret the nature of the Congress' action and gloss over what are some truly consequential political reforms.

In my article for *The Washington Post*, I explained that leaving aside debates about whether Xi is a good emperor or a bad one—or a good one who might turn bad—the presidential term limit had no bearing on how long a top Chinese leader could stay in power, and lifting it by no means creates lifetime rule for anyone. After all, the real position of power, the general secretary of the Chinese Communist Party Central Committee, has never had term limits.[45]

As to the issue of lifetime rule, the party does have institutional mechanisms—both mandatory and customary—that govern the retirement of its officials. In fact, the party constitution specifically states that no position has lifetime tenure. This system has developed over decades and reaches wide and deep, from the Politburo to ministerial to provincial positions. The exact age limit has varied over time and by position, but it has mostly ranged from 65 to 70. The custom for most senior leaders has been to retire at 68, which is usually extended so that the official can complete his or her term. Exceptions have been made for the position of general secretary (one served, successfully, through his late 70s), but time is always finite. In other words, it is possible that Xi will lead the country for longer than his recent predecessors, but he will not rule for life.[46]

This is not to say that the recent reforms were inconsequential. Quite the contrary: they have the potential to fully fuse the party and the state, which is good for China simply because the party has developed into the most competent political institution in the country and in the world.[47]

Since the founding of the People's Republic in 1949, the leadership of the party has always been central to China's political DNA. In my article for Foreign Affairs analyzing the impact of the third plenum of the party's 18th Congress, I summarized the evolution of the relationship between party and state.[48] The system has gone through significant growing pains. In its early days, China adopted the Soviet system that separated, in institutional form, the party and government. The top organs—the party central committee, the National People's Congress, and the state council—were parallel. But in substance, the party led everything. This produced significant conflicts that may have been partially responsible for the disastrous Cultural Revolution.

When Deng began his reforms 40 years ago, he pushed a policy of administrative separation between party and government. But that was due to the particular circumstances of post-Cultural Revolution China. At the time, many senior leaders whom Mao had purged were rehabilitated and returned to their previous positions, but those officials all came from the centrally planned economy. Deng believed that China needed market economics and wanted to unleash younger and more forward-looking officials to execute his reform agenda. Even more importantly, he wanted to rebuild the party institution. In the following four decades, the party has developed into one of the most elaborate and effective governing institutions in the world, and in history. It is responsible for achieving the greatest improvement in the standard of living for the largest number of people in the shortest time.

The party is now front and center of Chinese governance, something the recent constitutional reform enshrined by formally unifying the role of President and General Secretary of the Chinese Communist Party Central Committee. It also moved the wording about party leadership from the preamble to the body of the constitution.[49] At the governing level, the reform created a super agency, the National Supervisory Commission, to combat corruption. This body is an extension of the party's Central Disciplinary and Inspection Commission, and it will further institutionalize the party commission's tremendous anti-corruption drive.

It is in this context that the removal of the presidential term limit is a significant move. Although the party's leadership has always remained politically paramount, the administrative separation of party and government had continued to produce institutional contradictions and confusion. This reform went quite far in correcting this problem at the institutional level.

With China's rise as a major power, the office of the president has assumed greater importance, especially in China's interactions with the rest of the world. Formally merging it with the office of the party general secretary will create a more efficient and coherent governing structure within, and more transparency and predictability in China's dealings with the world. It signals the maturing of the Chinese political system which is now ready to show the world with clarity how decisions are made and who is in charge.

The current Chinese system is a good combination of principle and flexibility. The principle of no lifetime tenure, combined with a retirement mechanism, prevents rule for life. Yet, a degree of flexibility allows a good leader to govern longer. Xi will of course retire someday. But as long as he continues to lead successfully, it may be a long way off in the future.[50]

Until then, the case cannot be stronger that Xi is a "good emperor." As Zhang Weiwei, a professor at Fudan University, has written, modern Western political philosophy places great emphasis on preventing "bad emperors" from retaining power—he uses the term *xia xia ce* (the least bad option)—while China's system aims for finding the right person for the job in the first place—called *shang shang ce* (the best of the best options). In this case, the system's aim is to reach for and preserve a "good emperor" advantage while checking the "bad emperor problem."[51]

In any case, the American system has failed in its main mission. It has not kept unsuitable figures from coming to power. It has actually helped put them in place.

Xi is now beginning his third term. No one knows for sure how long he will serve. But with his track record, it is understandable that there is a genuine desire for him to stay in power (According to an opinion survey by Harvard's Kennedy School, Xi consistently receives the highest domestic approval ratings of any leader in the world, by far.[52]). If the

United States got a leader like him, Americans might want to keep him or her forever, too (Just kidding). But, sadly, liberal democracy in its current state seems incapable of producing someone half as good.[53]

NOTES

1. Plato. *The Republic*. Trans. Desmond Lee. Penguin Classics, 2007.
2. Mill, John Stuart. "Thoughts on parliamentary reform." *Collected Works of John Stuart Mill vol. XIX*. University of Toronto Press, 1977, pp. 322–331.
3. Watson, Burton. *The Analects of Confucius*. Columbia University Press, 2007, p. 116; Marx, Karl, and Engels, Friedrich. *Manifesto of the Communist Party*. New York: International Publishers, 1948, p. 30.
4. Lynn-Jones, Sean M. "Why the United States Should Spread Democracy." Discussion Paper, 98–07, Belfer Center for Science and International Affairs, Harvard Kennedy School, March 1998.
5. Blake, Aaron. "Is Bill Clinton One of the Best Presidents in History?" *The Washington Post*. 6 Sept. 2012.
6. Ritter, Gary W. "Education Reform in Arkansas: Past and Present." *Reforming Education in Arkansas: Recommendations from the Koret Task Force*, 2015, pp. 27–42; Maraniss, David. First in His Class: A Biography of Bill Clinton. Simon and Schuster, 2008.
7. "On this Day (November 4) in 1992: Clinton Beats Bush to the White House." BBC News. 4 Nov. 1992. Retrieved in 2018 from: http://news.bbc.co.uk/onthisday/hi/dates/stories/november/4/newsid_3659000/3659498.stm; Troy, Gil. "What Hillary Can Learn From Bill for the Democratic Debate." *Times*. 12 Oct. 2015.
8. Johnson, Haynes, and David S. Broder. The System: The American Way of Politics at the Breaking Point. Back Bay Books, 2009.
9. Chollet, Derek, and James Goldgeier. *America Between the Wars: From 11/9 to 9/11*. PublicAffairs, 2009.
10. Friedman, Thomas L. "Why Putin Doesn't Respect Us." *The New York Times*. 4 Mar. 2014; Friedman, Thomas L. "We Have Never Been Here Before." *The New York Times*. 25 Feb. 2022.
11. The "three pillars" are civil service, state-owned enterprises, and social organizations. Public employees can be rotated through and out of all three tracks. See: Li, Eric X. "The Life of the Party: The

Post-Democratic Future Begins in China." *Foreign Affairs*, vol. 92, no. 1, January/February 2013, pp. 34–46.
12. Naughton, Barry. *The Chinese Economy: Transitions and Growth*. MIT press, 2007, pp. 116–118.
13. Robert, Kuhn L. "The Man Who Changed China: The Life and Legacy of Jiang Zemin", 2005, pp. 74–77.
14. Ibid., pp. 77–78.
15. Ibid., pp. 91.
16. Wang, Orange. "China's Guangdong GDP for 2021 Set to Top that of South Korea and Most Other Countries." *South China Morning Post*. 24 Jan. 2022.
17. Shanghai Statistics Bureau. *Shanghai Statistical Yearbook [上海统计年鉴]*. 1986, 1992; Yu, Lulu. "New Wave of Hope Driving Shanghai." *South China Morning Post*. 27 Jun. 1988.
18. World Bank. "World Development Indicators." Data retrieved in 2018, from World Development Indicators Online (WDI) database; World Bank. "World Integrated Trade Solution." Data retrieved in 2018, from World Integrated Trade Solution (WITS).
19. Huang, Mengfu. *China Private Economy Development Report No. 1 [中国民营经济发展报告No. 1]*. Social Sciences Academic Press [China], 2003, pp. 8–9.
20. Brahm, Laurence J. *Zhu Rongji and the Transformation of Modern China*. Wiley, 2002, pp. xxv-xxxiv.
21. Ibid., pp. 19–28.
22. Ibid., pp. 161–183.
23. Ibid., pp. 256–258.
24. Zhu, Rongji. "Government Working Report [政府工作报告]." 2003. Retrieved from: http://www.gov.cn/gongbao/content/2003/content_62011.htm
25. Brahm, Laurence J. *Zhu Rongji and the Transformation of Modern China*. Wiley, 2002, pp. 261–280.
26. Guizhou Statistics Bureau. *Guizhou Statistical Yearbook [贵州统计年鉴]* 1987, pp. 2–9.
27. Yang, Bo and Wu, Feiran. "A Tale of Hu Jintao Establishing Anshun Private Economy Reform Experimental Zone [胡錦濤創立安順民營經濟改革試驗區的故事]." *China Economic Herald* [Hong Kong, China], 11 Mar, 2013.
28. Smith, Jean Edward. *Bush*. Simon and Schuster, 2017, pp. 11.

29. Bush, George W. "Remarks on the National Economy, Sterling, Virginia," *PPPUS-GWB Vol. 1*, 19 Jan. 2006.
30. Xi, Jinping. *Up and Out of Poverty*. Foreign Language Press, 2016, pp. 1–10.
31. Ibid., pp. 74–80.
32. Ibid., pp. 98–108.
33. Ibid., pp. 117–121.
34. Roberts, Dan, and Powell, Kenton. "Revealed: Obama's Record-Breaking Effort to Tap Wealthy Donors for Cash." *The Guardian*. 12 Nov. 2013.
35. Obama, Barack. *The Audacity of Hope: Thoughts on Reclaiming the American Dream*. Canongate Books, 2007.
36. Greenstone, Michael. "Four Years After Declaring War on Pollution, China Is Winning." *The New York Times*, 12 Mar. 2018.
37. Nasr, Seyyed V. *The Dispensable Nation: American Foreign Policy in Retreat*. Anchor, 2014.
38. Parsons, Christi, and Mascaro, Lisa. "Obama, Who Sought to Ease Partisanship, Saw It Worsen Instead." *Los Angeles Times*. 14 Jan. 2017.

    Abutaleb, Yasmeen. "U.S. Healthcare Spending to Climb 5.3 percent in 2018: Agency." *Reuters*. 15 Feb. 2018.
39. This section is partly adapted from the author's article in *Foreign Affairs* and his 2013 TED Talk. See: Li, Eric X. "The Life of the Party: The post-democratic future begins in China." *Foreign Affairs*, vol. 92, no. 1, January/February 2013, pp. 34–46; Li, Eric X. "A tale of two political systems." *TED Global 2013*.
40. They were: Mao Zedong, Ren Bishi, Zhou Enlai, Chen Yun, Deng Xiaoping, Kang Sheng, Hu Yaobang, Qiao Shi, Wei Jianxing, Song Ping, Zeng Qinghong, He Guoqiang, and Zhao Leji.
41. Li, Eric X. "The Life of the Party: The Post-democratic Future Begins in China." *Foreign Affairs*, vol. 92, no. 1, January/February 2013, pp. 34–46.
42. Ibid.
43. Reilly, Katie. "Read Hillary Clinton's 'Basket of Deplorables' Remarks About Donald Trump." *Times*. 10 Sept. 2016; Moorhead, Molly. "Mitt Romney Says 47 percent of Americans Pay No Income Tax." *PolitiFact*. 18 Sept. 2012.
44. Fukuyama, Francis. "China's 'Bad Emperor' Returns." *The Washington Post*. 6 Mar. 2018.

45. Li, Eric X. "Why Xi's Lifting of Term Limits Is a Good Thing." *The Washington Post*. 2 Apr. 2018.
46. Ibid.
47. Li, Eric X. "Party of the Century: How China is Reorganizing for the Future." *Foreign Affairs*, 10 Jan. 2014.
48. Ibid.
49. On March 11, 2018, Chinese National People's Congress (NPC) amended the constitution to include an article, number 36, that explicitly defined socialism with Chinese characteristics as under the leadership of the Communist Party of China. This, in effect, strengthens and clarifies the legal legitimacy of party leadership within the Chinese constitution compared with previous inference from the constitution's preamble—as jurists around the world have yet to reach a consensus on the legal force for constitutional preambles; See: Zhang, Laney. "Global Legal Monitor." *China: 2018 Constitutional Amendment Adopted*, The Law Library of Congress, 18 May 2018, www.loc.gov/law/foreign-news/article/china-2018-constitutional-amendment-adopted/; and Orgad, Liav. "The Preamble in Constitutional Interpretation." *International Journal of Constitutional Law*. 2010, pp. 714–738.
50. Li, Eric X. "Why Xi's Lifting of Term Limits Is a Good Thing." *The Washington Post*. 2 Apr. 2018.
51. Zhang, Weiwei. "Meritocracy Versus Democracy." *The New York Times*. 9 Nov. 2012.
52. Pazzanese, Christina. "Grading 10 Top World Leaders." *The Harvard Gazette*. 17, Dec. 2014.
53. Li, Eric X. "Why Xi's Lifting of Term Limits Is a Good Thing." *The Washington Post*. 2 Apr. 2018.

CHAPTER 7

How to Rule

Ever since the Industrial Revolution ushered in a period of unprecedented prosperity and power for the United States and Europe, intellectuals the world over have come up with numerous explanations for how the West did it. Adam Smith's *The Wealth of Nations* attributed it to market capitalism and free trade.[1] Max Weber's *The Protestant Ethic and the Spirit of Capitalism* placed the modern West's success within religious and cultural contexts.[2] Friedrich Hayek's *The Road to Serfdom* zeroed in on individual freedom.[3]

In the second half of the twentieth century, Soviet socialism rose to challenge Western ideas. But its ultimate demise only took the fervor for Western thought to new heights. In recent years, contemporary scholars have gone still further. They've broken Western governance down into modules to be exported everywhere. The historian Niall Ferguson, for instance, summed it up as six killer apps.[4]

But as I wrote in previous chapters, failures abound and successes have been rare in the mad rush to copy the West. Meanwhile, the Chinese model stands alone as one of the biggest successes of our time. Yet there is scant work, either scholarly or in the popular press, to systematically explain it. It is beyond the scope of this book to offer a new theory of political governance, of course, much less some kind of roadmap for other countries to follow. But a few observations are useful. To borrow Ferguson's phrase, Chinese political governance has its own killer apps: meritocratic governance (as described in the previous chapter), experimental governance, entrepreneurial governance, and strategic governance.

Experimental Governance: You Are Special, Try It!

It is not possible to do a precise count, but I would wager that the words "special"—*te*—and "experimental"—*shi*—appear more frequently in Chinese official policy documents than nearly any other technical word.

The most regularly cited examples may be the special economic zones set up during Deng Xiaoping's reform era. In these zones, officials conducted policy experiments on everything from foreign trade to investment and taxation. The most famous among them was the Shenzhen Special Economic Zone, which turned a sleepy fishing village north of Hong Kong into a major metropolis, home to some of China's most innovative companies, including Tencent and Huawei.

But experimental governance was part of the Chinese party-state DNA going back much further. In fact, rather than an import from the Soviet Union, it began well before the founding of the People's Republic in 1949. During the land reform movement that began in 1928, for example, Mao Zedong advocated for officials to conduct trials in small areas to learn what worked and what didn't. They would then gradually expand their policies to larger areas, constantly adjusting to local circumstances. Mao and the Communists' success contributed to their ability to eventually take national power and lay the foundation for the party's long-term political dominance. The process, as German political scientist Sebastian Heilmann termed it, was "experimentation under hierarchy."[5]

In short, when Deng launched his economic reform in 1978, he was not pulling his methods from thin air. He was borrowing from an earlier tradition—and one with which his contemporaries were familiar. Indeed, it was Deng's contemporary, Chen Yun, who coined the motto of the reform era: "crossing the river by touching the stones beneath."

Te Qu, from Special to Normal

The term *te qu*, or special zone, is one of the most common policy phrases in China. Deng used the term to name the first significant such initiative, the Shenzhen Special Economic Zone (known as Shenzhen *te qu*). But the phrase had much deeper historic roots. It was borrowed from the

Shan Gan Ning *te qu*, the name of the revolutionary base Mao established with the Red Army on the borders of Shanxi, Gansu, and Ningxia Provinces in 1937.

Beyond the *te qu* in Shenzhen, in 1979, the Central Committee and the State Council also launched such zones in Zhuhai, Shantou (in Guangdong Province), and Xiamen (in Fujian Province). Three considerations went into the selection of cities. First, they were all close to Hong Kong and Taiwan, which were much more developed than the mainland. Officials hoped that the prosperity would spill over, in terms of both market and talent. Second, China's centrally planned economy was the strongest in the northeast and the Chinese hinterlands. The coastal regions of the southeast were both less controlled and more conducive to opening up. And last, unlike many inland regions that had an abundance of natural resources such as coal, the coastal regions lacked natural resources and were, therefore, more motivated to try out market-oriented development.

In those *te qu*s, the government simplified the approval process for private (especially foreign) investments, cut business taxes, and prioritized public spending on infrastructure. In the following two decades, the *te qu* economies spearheaded China's economic growth and attracted enormous amounts of foreign direct investment (FDI).

The experiments worked so well that by 1985, Beijing wanted to make it easier to try them on an ad hoc basis. That year, the National People's Congress authorized the central government to begin making the rules for economic reform initiatives. Legal scholar Peter Corne calls the resulting rules "quasi-laws."[6] Research by Sebastian Heilmann shows that, in the first 20 years of Deng's reforms, regulations of this kind—those that include the terms "experimental" or "temporary" in their names—made up over 30% of all economic laws and regulations nationwide (Fig. 7.1).

Experiments in Healthcare

The practice of experimental governance played an important role during the Mao era. The political scientist Wang Shaoguang studied the organization of China's healthcare sector since the founding of the People's Republic. His studies found that policies for financing healthcare were in a continuous process of experimentation, learning, and adaptation for more than 60 years.

Experimental Regulation in China, 1979–2006

- - - Share of regulations with experimental status in total of national regulations
——— Share of regulations with experimental status in total of national economic regulations

Fig. 7.1 Experimental regulation in China, 1979–2006[7]

Before 1949, according to Wang, the only way to get healthcare in rural China was to pay for it oneself. And few did. Conditions were miserable. For example, the infant mortality rate hovered at 25%. In 1955, multiple counties began experimenting with cooperative medical systems (CMS), which became a catalyst for nationwide reform.[8] As part of the CMS, China organized collective village-wide financing systems that pooled together public welfare funds from agricultural cooperatives and doctors' proceeds to pay for farmers' healthcare fees. The accounts helped spread risk and provided free preventive care. They resulted in significant reductions in medical fees paid by farmers.

These experiments were then expanded into province-wide policy initiatives. Eventually, the Ministry of Health and the State Council approved nationwide implementation. By 1957, China had more than 10,000 such cooperative medical organizations.[9] But the party central committee—with Mao's direct support—wanted more. Between 1958 and 1962, coverage exploded from 10 to 46%.[10]

The CMS movement also experienced its downturns, especially after 1962 when the government changed policy directions. But after 1969, things were back on track. By 1976, 92.8% of agricultural collectives (85% of the rural population) had adopted the CMS).[11]

Throughout the two-decade-long adoption process, there were many lessons to learn and adjustments to make. Rules that caused waste and inefficiency were corrected over time. But the policy experiments drove a dramatic improvement in public health, in infant mortality, immunization, and life expectancy during the first 30 years of the People's Republic—at a time when the country's per capita GDP remained one of the lowest in the world. At the end of the Cultural Revolution and before Deng's reform era, China's health services were internationally recognized for their fairness and accessibility and became a model for the World Health Organization as it sought to advance healthcare around the world.[12]

As this example shows, experiments are not always led from the top-down (In fact, between 1992 and 2003, Professor Mei Ciqi of Tsinghua University has found, experiments were equally likely to be initiated by the central government, by the provincial governments, or by the local government.[13]). During the Deng era, there were several economic and social policy experiments that were initiated at the county level and later, after they became successful, were expanded by higher levels of government. For example, Deng's so-called household responsibility system sought to essentially privatize agricultural production and, as a result, the rural collectives that undergirded the CMS financing system were weakened and eventually phased out.

This was a trying time for rural healthcare in China. In fact, the dismantling of the CMS) without an effective replacement is now seen as one of the biggest failures of the Deng era. Attempts to resuscitate CMS faltered because of internal government resistance, the collapse of the collective economy, and a lack of government funding.[14] A new trial, the "China Rural Health Insurance Experiment," which was based on a proposal by the World Bank with technical assistance from the RAND Corporation, failed.[15]

By the late 1990s and early 2000s, rural healthcare had become a nationwide crisis. Ninety percent of rural residents lacked any health coverage at all. Although farmers' incomes had risen dramatically because of the Deng's economic reforms, one big illness could push a family right back into poverty. This was an amazing regression from what China had achieved by the end of the 1970s.[16]

In late 2002 and early 2003, the dire conditions of China's rural healthcare could no longer be ignored. Blanket media coverage of the crisis led to sustained public outcry.[17] The central government finally swung into action. It initiated a series of new experiments to redesign the CMS to make it suitable for the country's new economic and social conditions. This set of policy trials was called New Community Medical System (NCMS). The NCMS initiative went through the typical process of trials, collecting data, adjustments, and expansions.[18]

By 2008, the NCMS covered nearly all administrative villages in the country.[19] It boasted new features such as direct government funding, a focus on catastrophic illnesses, and larger risk pooling. A decade later, China has achieved near-universal coverage—albeit at a fairly basic level. After a disastrous and unnecessary regression, China's rural healthcare was finally back on its feet. This should go down in history as a significant example of self-correction by experimental governance.

The Test of Taxes, *Ying Gai Zeng*

One of the most significant recent policy experiments to have gone nationwide was a corporate tax reform known as *ying gai zeng*—let's call it the YGZ reform, for short, which implemented a value-added tax. The experiment started in 2012 and completed its nationwide roll-out in 2016. For an economy as large and as complex as that of China, this was no doubt an enormous undertaking.

Before the YGZ reform, a large portion of China's corporate tax receipts came from a revenue tax levied as a percentage of sales. For local governments, the revenue tax was their largest source of income, making up approximately 30% of all local tax receipts.[20] The system had worked well enough during the period of rapid economic growth; it provided strong incentives for local governments to implement business-friendly policies to attract companies and help them grow their top lines.

But by the time China emerged from the 2008 global financial crisis, there was a need for change. Investment-led growth was no longer the only driver. The Chinese economy needed to increase demand-driven growth. And that demand would have to come in high-value sectors, especially in the service industries.

But the revenue tax, which resulted in double taxation in many cases, stemmed such growth. For example, a manufacturing company that used third-party design services paid a straight revenue tax on its sales. The cost it paid to the service provider could not be deducted for tax purposes. Meanwhile, the service provider also had to pay a revenue tax on the money it received from the manufacturer. In such a situation, the incentive would be for the manufacturing company to bring all services in-house, resulting in unnecessary and inefficient vertical integration. The tax system essentially discouraged specialization, which was key for building up higher-value services.

The replacement of the revenue tax with a value-added tax was meant to correct the structural misalignment. Businesses would be incentivized to outsource any parts of their operation that were not related to their core competency, mostly services, to third-party providers. The costs businesses paid to those providers would be deducted when the businesses paid the VAT, eliminating the double taxation. In time, the system would help China develop high-value-added service businesses.

In 2012, China was already the second-largest economy in the world, with a gigantic industrial base and complex tax structures. The YGZ reform was a huge shift that would affect millions of businesses and many layers of government. Regional and local governments, which were a formidable interest group, could stand to lose big. Revenue taxes, with few exceptions, had gone entirely to local governments, but the VAT receipts were to be divided between central and local governments on a 75/25 split. The reform, in other words, could have spurred a major redistribution of the nation's tax revenues.

Faced with an important policy imperative but daunting implementation challenges, the Chinese government resorted to a tried and true method: experiment! And an experiment Beijing did, in a carefully staged process. Step one, roll the new system out in chosen sectors in a select geography; step two, expand it to multiple geographies; step three, expand it to more sectors in multiple geographies; step four, spread it to all sectors in multiple geographies; step five, cover all sectors nationwide (Table 7.1).

In January 2012, Shanghai was chosen as the first site for YGZ. That made sense. Shanghai was one of the wealthiest metropolitan areas in the country and had a broad range of business sectors. In fact, it already had a burgeoning service sector and would, therefore, see significant potential benefits from the reform. Still, the experiment began on a small scale. Only the transportation logistics sector and a limited number of service sectors, such as information technology, cultural products, and consulting, were affected at first.

After several months of trials in Shanghai, a major problem surfaced. Consulting companies saw their taxes go up significantly. Consulting

Table 7.1 China's policy experiment during YGZ reform

Date	Region in experiment	Industry in experiment
JAN 1, 2012	Shanghai	"1 + 6" Transportation Industry (exclude railway) and Six Modern Service Industries (Technical Service and R&D, Information and Communication Technology, Cultural and Creative Services, Logistics Supporting Service, Tangible Movable Property Leasing, Consultation and Assurance Service)
SEPT 1, 2012	Shanghai, Beijing	
OCT 1, 2012	Shanghai, Beijing, Jiangsu Province, Anhui Province	
NOV 1, 2012	Shanghai, Beijing, Jiangsu Province, Anhui Province, Fujian Province, Guangdong Province	
DEC 1, 2012	Shanghai, Beijing, Jiangsu Province, Anhui Province, Fujian Province, Guangdong Province, Tianjin, Zhejiang Province, Hubei Province	
AUG 1, 2013	Nationwide	Expanded to include Broadcasting, Film, and Television Services
JAN 1, 2014	Nationwide	Expanded to include Railway Industry and Postal Service Industry
JUN 1, 2014	Nationwide	Expanded to include Telecommunication Industry
MAY 1, 2016	Nationwide	Expanded to include Construction Industry, Real Estate Industry, Financial Industry, Consumer Service Industry, Estate Transfer Industry

Sources Shanghai Municipal Tax Service, State Administration of Taxation

firms' costs were mainly personnel—and consultants were highly paid professionals. Those costs were not deductible in the trial system. The reform would, in the short run, hurt one of the very business sectors that it was intended to help. The Shanghai government, which was empowered to make quick adjustments, responded immediately with a stopgap measure, temporarily changing the rule to cap the tax payments for consulting firms at the pre-reform rate.

Over a longer period, the impact of the higher tax rate was neutralized and the new system significantly expanded business opportunities for the consulting industry. Because clients were able to deduct consulting fees from their tax obligations, consulting firms were able to raise their prices to get part of that benefit. Overall, the new regime encouraged businesses to use more consulting services and thereby helped expand the sector as a whole.

The YGZ reform, which has now been put in place nationwide, has been a significant driver in China's economic transition toward a more service-oriented model. It has also resulted in a substantial reduction in the taxes that businesses pay. Companies that were included in the policy trials saw their taxes reduced by nearly $20 billion in total. Over a five-year period, that figure was expected to reach more than $258 billion.[21]

The World's Largest Governance Lab

At any given moment, there are thousands—if not tens of thousands—of policy experiments like the New Community Medical System and the YGZ reform being conducted around China. It would thus be no exaggeration to say that contemporary China is the largest governance laboratory in the world. It has its political system to thank for that.

Experimental governance would be very difficult in a liberal democracy in which most policies are made by legislation. As an example, consider the Trump administration's 2017 tax cut. Myriad interest groups actively sought to influence the legislative decision. Economists and sociologists made various predictions about the impact of the tax cut on the American economy and society—all in the abstract. It would clearly have been useful to be able to subject such a large policy change to a process of trial and error before enacting it. Because that is impossible in the U.S. context, the burden on legislation is so high that it is hard to get new laws on the books in the first place.

Two other features of liberal democracy make policy experimentation difficult as well. One is the multi-party system at different levels of government. If a policy proves effective in Illinois, it would be impossible for its governor, or even the president of the United States, to order Texas to try it too. The latter may be run by a different political party. The other is elections. Duration is key to effective experiments, which rely on learning through practice. But in a liberal democracy, power changes hands frequently making cumulative institutional learning very difficult if not impossible.

ENTREPRENEURIAL GOVERNANCE: MAYORS AS CEOS

Chinese governance is not just experimental. It is also entrepreneurial. Go back to 1992. On an early autumn holiday—October 1, China's national day—Zhang Xinsheng, the young mayor of Suzhou, went to work.[22] He had an important guest who had arranged to visit at the last minute. The visitor was Lee Kuan Yew, the legendary founding prime minister of Singapore. Lee was on a tour of Jiangsu Province, where he was evaluating potential opportunities for economic development cooperation between China and Singapore.

The idea for such cooperation had come up earlier, when Deng visited Singapore soon after he became China's top leader. Among the Asian tigers, Chinese officials especially admired the city-state. In merely one generation, under Lee's leadership, Singapore had gone from a small fishing village to a modern global center for trade and finance. At the time, attracting foreign investments was the top priority for just about every Chinese local official. Potential investments from Singapore were naturally the most coveted.

Lee's delegation went to Wuxi, which was then one of the most industrialized cities in the province. After that visit, he asked whether it was possible to pay a visit to Suzhou, Wuxi's polar opposite, as well.

There was no real road between the two cities—just a narrow unpaved country path. It took Lee's convoy two hours to travel the 60 kilometers to reach Suzhou. He was meant to spend less than half a day there, so the local officials had to rush in their efforts to persuade Lee to bet on their city. As the Singaporeans began to leave for the train station to go to Shanghai, Zhang saw his chance and grabbed it! He jumped into Lee's Mercedes Benz limo for the 20-minute ride to the train station.

Like a salesman giving an elevator pitch, Zhang began his rapid fire. He had studied Singapore's investment strategy for its large foreign currency reserve, he said. Given Singapore's own small size, he continued, diversification was vital. China would be the future, the only place with the scale to absorb major investments and generate returns. China was also ready to learn from Singapore, giving the latter a unique opportunity to bring knowledge alongside its capital. Why not build a Singapore-like industrial city within Suzhou? "I will guarantee you special policy treatments, ensure the success of your investment," he proclaimed.

Lee was rather surprised by the mayor's aggressiveness. "A capable mayor like you would be promoted soon. Then what?" he challenged Zhang. "Yes, my successor may give you some trouble in the beginning," replied Zhang, "but soon after, he will have to follow the path I set. The people of Suzhou want the Singapore they see on TV, with jobs, housing, and a garden city."

The convoy arrived at the train station and Lee hopped aboard the train. A few minutes later, the prime minister got back off and asked the mayor, "Does Suzhou have an airport?" The answer: "No, not yet."

Eighteen months later, in early 1994, the Suzhou Industrial Park was launched with an initial investment of $32.5 million from the government of Singapore, which got a 65% equity stake in the endeavor. By 2017, the Suzhou Industrial Park had attracted foreign direct investments of $28.2 billion. Its GDP had reached $36 billion, making its GDP per capita approximately $45,000—equivalent to Hong Kong's. Its Human Development Index, meanwhile, was neck-and-neck with Singapore's.[23]

Zhang, as Lee predicted, didn't stay mayor forever. Instead, he went to Harvard and got a master's degree in urban development. He returned to China in 2000 and was promoted to the central government. He served as Vice Minister of Education until his retirement.

A Market Place of Governance

The young mayor's endeavor was a success story of the reform era, but what he did was by no means an exception. In fact, a hallmark of modern Chinese governance is that mayors and county party secretaries often become entrepreneurs. The cities and counties they run are akin to companies in competitive marketplaces. Rather than creating value for their shareholders, however, local officials compete on behalf of the public in order to move up the career ladder. Professor Zhou Li-An of Peking University has called the process a "political tournament."[24] Competition is fierce, driving China's economic development and policy innovation.

Modern entrepreneurial governance began in the 1980s as the so-called Su Nan model, which the sociologist Fei Xiaotong has credited for jumpstarting economic development in Jiangsu Province.[25] In the early days of market reform, there was no capital, no entrepreneurs, and no rules governing private enterprise. So local governments took the initiative to form collectives called town and village enterprises (TVE), mostly in the light manufacturing sectors. Local governments nominally owned the companies, and local officials served as their managers. Profits were shared by the community. The TVEs became very successful and drove the first wave of industrialization and urbanization in rural communities along the east coast.

In the 1990s, as China's markets matured, the government directed a new round of reforms that turned TVEs into actual stock-holding corporations. Now private investment—both domestic and foreign—flooded into the enterprises. Soon, China was the manufacturing powerhouse that it is today.

By the mid-1990s and 2000s, attracting investment to start new businesses was a top priority for virtually every local government. Some went to extreme lengths. Kunshan in Jiangsu Province was one example. The city set the goal of attracting manufacturing businesses from Taiwan, which at the time was a leading hub in Asia. Not only did the Kunshan government put in place incentives for Taiwanese businesses like tax exemptions, it also deployed teams to help the Taiwanese executives navigate their everyday lives, including arranging healthcare and schooling for their children. At onetime, the Kunshan mayor and vice mayors even made public their cell phone numbers and announced that Taiwanese executives could call them at any time, day or night, for any business or personal issues. In a few years, Kunshan had won the moniker "little Taipei" with a huge number of Taiwan-invested companies mostly in the electronics industry. The city of two million people—relatively small by Chinese standards—saw its GDP skyrocket above those of cities many times its size.[26]

Entrepreneurial governance has also spurred China's domestic private sector. Of late, of course, the term "state capitalism" has come into fashion to describe China's economic system. But private companies have been a real engine for growth. In 1979, when Deng's reform began, private companies made up a mere 1% of the economy.[27] As of this writing, the private sector accounts for more than 60% of the economy and over 80% of total employment.[28]

Many of the leading private companies exist thanks to entrepreneurial governance. Sunny Optics[1] is a typical example. It started in 1984 as a TVE in the small town of Yuyao in Zhejiang Province. The company began by producing low-end lenses for cameras at a rather low gross margin. Local government officials used their connections with neighboring governments to help the company expand nationwide. In the mid-1990s, as part of the TVE reforms, the local government transformed it into a modern stock-based business. In order to help the

---

[1] Chengwei Capital was an early investor of this company.

company and others like it move beyond low-end, low-margin products, the local government began campaigns to recruit technical talents from larger cities. At one point, the local government offered direct subsidies of RMB130,000 ($20,000) to any professional with a master's degree who moved to Yuyao and worked for five years. Those with doctorates could get RMB200,000 ($33,000). Today, Sunny Optics is a leading global player in optical components with a market capitalization of $20 billion.

Such examples, large and small, are numerous. By contrast, those developing countries that pursued privatization above all else have faced failure after failure. "The success of local governments as entrepreneurs," Professor Jean Oi of Stanford University, has written, "suggests that privatization is not the only way to stimulate economic growth. By the late 1980s a strong public–private cooperation was developing, resulting in what some have called a symbiotic relationship between private enterprises and local officials."[29]

Strategic Governance: Planning Makes Perfect

China's final killer app is strategic governance, exemplified best by the development of its national rail system.

In 1978, Deng, freshly installed in office, visited Japan. The rapprochement between the two former mortal enemies signaled a fundamental pivot. China was poor and agrarian; Japan was among the most advanced industrial powers in the world. Amid the pomp and circumstance that accompanied the historic event, one image captured the imagination of the Chinese public. On national television and in newspapers, they saw Deng riding Japan's bullet train, the Shinkansen, and marveling at this miracle of modern industry and technology. At the speed of 200 kilometers an hour, the Shinkansen had two lines covering 1,175 kilometers. It was the largest, fastest, and most advanced high-speed rail in the world. In China, it all seemed like a very distant dream.

But in 1990, Beijing began to seriously consider building its own high-speed rail. The Ministry of Railway formerly suggested adding it to the country's eighth Five-Year Plan, to begin in 1991. The initial project would be a modest one-line link between Beijing and Shanghai. The suggestion spurred an intense internal debate about China's development priorities, and eventually, the government decided to put off high-speed rail in favor of roads and civil aviation.

It wasn't until 1999 that the leadership came back to the idea of a national high-speed rail. Over the following few years, policymakers put together a long-term vision. China would have not just one-line linking two cities. It would boast a nationwide network of 16,000 kilometers[30] of track that would link all provincial capitals and cities with populations over 500,000. The service would cover 90% of China's 1.3 billion people. The completion date was set for 2020.

The plan, rather simply entitled "The Medium to Long Term Rail Network Plan," shocked everyone. It would require China to build more high-speed rails than ever laid by the rest of the world combined!

And so it did. The project started with financing. By announcing the Rail Plan, the central government stimulated a major competition among local governments to be included in the development of the network and opened up a broad array of financing options. The eventual model Beijing settled on was to get 50% of the capital—about RMB1.6 trillion (approximately $280 billion)—from the Railway Ministry and 50% from local governments.

The Railway Ministry was also able to attract large multinationals with the most advanced technologies, which China lacked at that time, to participate. The competition among those companies gave China leverage in negotiating favorable terms. The initial contract went to a consortium led by the French company Alstom. Alstom's technology was immature at the time compared to its competitor, Siemens. But China's game plan was to eventually develop its own capabilities. By choosing less mature technologies, it was able to essentially co-develop what it needed.

Trial-and-error was key to the rail project. The Railway Ministry, for example, experimented with a German technology called Maglev, or magnetic levitation, in Shanghai. Tourists there still marvel at the amazing 430 kilometer per hour train that carries them from Pudong Airport to the city's subway system in eight minutes. But that was to be the first and only such line in the world. It proved too expensive, and the German company that supplied the rail owned all the technology without giving China a chance to develop its own know-how. After other experiences like that, China's high-speed rail network eventually achieved a remarkable 70% indigenous technology deployment.[31]

By 2017, China had already built 25,000 kilometers of the world's fastest (350 km per hour) and most advanced high-speed rail network, far exceeding the original goal for 2020. In the same year, the network carried 1.2 billion passengers. By 2022, the operating mileage of China's high-speed railway network had exceeded 42,000 km.[32]

For countries with large territories, the impact of good transportation infrastructure is enormous. Large-scale railway development in the United States in the nineteenth century played a major role in advancing American industrialization. The building of the interstate highway system in the middle of the twentieth century significantly expanded interstate commerce and facilitated America's post-war economic growth.

Perhaps that is why the United States has, for decades, dreamed of building its own high-speed rail network. It has yet to lay a single mile of track. And there is still no beginning in sight. The United States seems to have lost its ability to make long-term strategic plans and implement them. China, meanwhile, has a proven method: a centralized political authority in the form of the party-state that governs for a long duration so that it can plan for the long term; an elaborate system to develop capable and experienced government executives who can deliver; and continuous experimentation to make sure that policies are right for the country. A major element in all that—indeed, the most important tool of strategic governance—is the Five-Year Plan.

The Visible Hand of the Five-Year Plan

When the Soviet Union collapsed, one thing just about everyone in the world was sure of was that the so-called centrally planned economy had been swept into the dustbin of history.

Ever since the early 1980s, the obviously underperforming communist economies had turned central planning into a laughing stock. In 1987, President Ronald Reagan joked to the *New York Times*:

> [A Soviet man] goes to the official agency, puts down his money and is told that he can take delivery of his automobile in exactly 10 years. 'Morning or afternoon?' the purchaser asks. 'Ten years from now, what difference does it make?' replies the clerk. 'Well,' says the car-buyer, 'the plumber's coming in the morning.'[33]

Just about every country in the world eventually ran away from the centrally planned economy as fast as it could—Cuba and North Korea being the exceptions. Even China made market economic reform the centerpiece of its governance. As it did, though, a small but important fact escaped the world's notice. The Five-Year Plan, the most important tool of the centrally planned economy, survived. Not only has it survived, in fact, it has assumed ever-greater strategic importance over the past 40-plus years. How could that be? Simply put, rather than ditching the Five-Year Plan, China adapted it.

Originally, the Five-Year Plan was a Soviet import, primarily a system for top-down centrally planned and executed economic management with no thought about the market. The system heavily favored the development of heavy industry. Even sectors that were highly fragmented by nature, such as agriculture, were managed at the national level. The approach did help China grow—as it did the Soviet Union—by marshaling the resources needed to craft a basic industrial infrastructure. But it led to gross misallocation of resources, lower productivity in many sectors, and complete disregard for consumer demand.

After a time, of course, China needed a new model that both kept the good aspects of the old economy and updated what no longer worked. And so, Beijing retreated from the management of all aspects of the nation's economy and instead focused on active involvement in larger projects of long-term strategic importance. The vast agriculture and consumer products industries, for example, were left to the market. At the same time, Beijing expanded the scope of the Five-Year Plan to many areas beyond the economy, such as education, the environment, and welfare. According to research by Tsinghua University's Yan Yilong, the percentage of the plan that dealt with the economy dropped from over 60% in the Sixth Five-Year Plan (1981–1985) to 12.5% in the Twelfth Five-Year Plan (2011–2015).[34] In essence, in the past 40 years, the Five-Year Plan has been transformed from a tool primarily used for economic management into something for all of governance (Table 7.2).

Hu Angang of Tsinghua University[36] has identified four models of the Five-Year Plan: the internal collective model, the one-man show model, the consultative model, and the society-wide collective model.[37]

The first and second Five-Year Plans (1953–1962) and the fifth and sixth (1976–1985) were made using the internal collective model. Ministerial officials drew up the drafts and national leaders collectively finalized them. The process was not open to the public. The late second, third, and fourth Five-Year Plans (1966–1975) were a one-man show. Mao had virtually all the decision-making power then.

The seventh through the tenth plans (1986–2005) were developed using the consultative model. It was during this period that the

Table 7.2 Proportion of quantified indicators of different types in each five-year plan (6th five-year plan period to 13th five-year plan period)[35]

	6th Five-Year Plan	7th Five-Year Plan	8th Five-Year Plan	9th Five-Year Plan	10th Five-Year Plan	11th Five-Year Plan	12th Five-Year Plan	13th Five-Year Plan
Economic growth	15.2%	21.4%	26.9%	23.5%	10%	9.1%	4.2%	8%
Economic structure	45.5%	35.7%	30.8%	23.5%	23.3%	13.6%	8.3%	8%
Total proportion of economic indicators	60.7%	57.1%	57.7%	47%	33.3%	22.7%	12.5%	16%
Education and technology	15.2%	7.1%		3.8%	11.8%	23.3%	9.1%	16.7%	16%
Resources and environment	3%		3.6%	7.7%	11.8%	20%	27.2%	33.3%	40%
People's livelihood	21.2%	32.1%	30.8%	29.4%	23.3%	41%	37.5	28%
Total proportion of social indicators	39.3%	42.9%	42.3%	53%	67.7%	77.3%	87.5%	84%

process adapted most comprehensively to the complexities of the market economy. Decision-making was still centered around the party's collective leadership, but it was expanded into wider circles of professional experts and business communities.

Finally, the society-wide collective model began with the 11th Five-Year Plan (2006–2010) through the present one. Their development was much more open, with participation from the wider public. For example, the 13th Five-Year Plan took three years to complete. The process began in 2013, during the third year of the 12th Five-Year Plan. Beijing made an interim evaluation of that plan, and based on its assessment, drew up a new analytical framework. In 2015, the party central committee developed an interim document called the *Suggestions*, which was formalized at the fifth plenum later the same year. The *Suggestions* was then further developed and became the 13th Five-Year Plan in March 2016 at the National People's Congress.[38]

Four types of activities, Professor Wang Shaoguang and Yan Yilong have written, were part of the development of the current Five-Year Plan. First is *diaoyan*, or investigation and research. It has long been a hallmark of party governance. "Without *diaoyan*," Mao famously said, "no one has the right to speak." Over the decades, the party has gotten the process down to an art. It involves extensive on-the-ground investigations conducted by multiple levels of officials and researchers. Detailed information is collected from virtually all sectors of Chinese society. It is summarized, analyzed, and reported to the top.

The second type of activity is broad consultation. Throughout all stages of the development of the Five-Year Plan, from the initial brainstorming to the writing of *the Suggestions* and the final document, ideas, plans, and targets are sent to a wide range of reviewers, including government agencies, think tanks, businesses, and community organizations for comments and suggestions.

The third activity—at least with the most recent plans—is public participation. It is different from what happens in Western democracies, where interest groups actively seek to influence public policymaking. In China, officials go directly to the people to solicit public views on policy priorities. Forums, seminars, and discussions are conducted at multiple levels during the drafting of a Five-Year Plan.

The last type of activity is what the party calls "democratic centralization." Although that might sound contradictory, it actually means that although broad participation and collection of data and opinions are required for the process, final decisions are made by the party leadership.[39]

The system, when it works, can effectively broaden public participation in policymaking without the pitfalls of interest groups potentially capturing the political process. In effect, the party can maintain its political autonomy to make decisions based on long-term collective interests while being responsive to the widest public demands possible.

In the West, various coalitions[40] have captured the political system for their own benefit, resulting in what the political theorist Frank Fukuyama has called a vetocracy.[41] The system has robbed liberal democracies of their ability to plan and govern with the long term in mind. Any political system, liberal or otherwise, should seek to produce capable leaders, execute policies competently, deliver results, and make decisions based on long-term collective interests. China's party-state system—albeit far from perfect—is demonstrating a surprising ability to realize these goals even as liberal democracy fails.

Perhaps the West and other developing countries have something to learn from the Chinese model: Meritocratic, experimental, entrepreneurial, and strategic governance seem to work.

Notes

1. Smith, Adam. *The Wealth of Nations*. pp. 16–83.
2. Weber, Max. The Protestant Ethic and the Spirit of Capitalism. Routledge, 2001, pp. 122–123.
3. Hayek, Friedrich August. *The Road to Serfdom: Text and Documents: The Definitive Edition*. Routledge, 2007, pp. 69-73.
4. Ferguson, Niall. *Civilization: the Six Killer Apps of Western Power*. Penguin UK, 2012, pp. 12–13.
5. Heilmann, Sebastian. "Policy Experimentation in China's Economic Rise." *Studies in Comparative International Development*, vol. 43, no. 1, 2008, pp. 1–26.
6. Corne, Peter Howard. "Creation and Application of Law in the PRC." *The American Journal of Comparative Law*, vol. 50, no. 2, 2002, pp. 369–443.
7. Heilmann, Sebastian. "Policy Experimentation in China's Economic Rise." *Studies in Comparative International Development*, vol. 43, no. 1, 2008, pp. 1–26.
8. Wang, Shaoguang. "Adapting by Learning: The Evolution of China's Rural Health Care Financing." *Modern China*, vol. 35, no. 4, 2009, pp. 370–404.
9. Xu, Jie. "A Historical Review of the Rural CMS [对我国卫生经济政策的历史回顾和思考]." *China Health Economics*, no. 10, 1997.
10. Cretin, Shan, Albert P. Williams, and Jeffrey Sine. "China Rural Health Insurance Experiment," 2007; Wang, Shaoguang. "Adapting by Learning: The Evolution of China's Rural Health Care Financing." *Modern China*, vol. 35, no. 4, 2009, pp. 370–404.
11. Wang, Shaoguang. "Adapting by Learning: The Evolution of China's Rural Health Care Financing." *Modern China*, vol. 35, no. 4, 2009, pp. 370–404.

12. Between 1949 and 1980, China's average life expectancy surged from 35 years to 68 in 1980, infant mortality rate fell from 250 per 1,000 births to less than 50 per 1,000 births. Cited in Wang, Shaoguang. "Adapting by Learning: The Evolution of China's Rural Health Care Financing.".
13. Mei Ciqi et al. "The Characters of Policy Experiment: Evidence From People's Daily During 1992–2003." *Public Policy Review*, vol. 3, 2005, pp. 8–24.
14. Zhu, Aorong. "A Study of China's Cooperative Medical System [中国农村合作医疗保障制度的研究]." *China Rural Health Management*, vol. 1, 1988, pp. 51–54.
15. Wang, Shaoguang. "Adapting by Learning: The Evolution of China's Rural Health Care Financing." *Modern China*, vol. 35, no. 4, 2009, pp. 370–404.
16. Feng, Xueshan et al. "The Impacts of Economic System Reform on Rural Health Services." *Health Economics Studies*, vol. 5, 1994.
17. World Bank. "Rural Health Insurance–Rising to the Challenge." Rural Health in China: Briefing Notes Series (2005).
18. Wang, Shaoguang. "Adapting by Learning: The Evolution of China's Rural Health Care Financing." *Modern* China, vol. 35, no. 4, 2009, pp. 370–404.
19. Wang, Xiaojing. "NCMS Achieves Full Coverage in Advance [新农合提前实现全覆盖]." *Farmer's Daily*. 11 Jul. 2008.
20. Ministry of Finance, People's Republic of China. *Finance Yearbook of China*. 2016.
21. "China cut 1.7 Trillion RMB of Tax in Last 5 Years Thanks to Reform." *People's Daily Online*. 12 Oct. 2017.
22. Minli, Han. "The China-Singapore Suzhou Industrial Park: Can the Singapore Model of Development be Exported?" PhD diss., 2008.
23. Lee, Kwan Yew. "From Third to First World: The Singapore Story, 1965–2000," 2000, pp. 649–654; Xu, Weiwei. "*Lee Kuan Yew Memories in China: Suzhou Industrial Park [李光耀中国往事: 苏州工业园区"青出于蓝"]*." 21st *Century Business Herald*. 24 Mar. 2015. Retrieved from: http://news.sipac.gov.cn/sipnews/yqzt/yqzt2015/lgy/mtjj/201503/t20150324_346763.htm; China-Singapore Suzhou Industrial Park. Data retrieved in 2018 from: http://www.sipac.gov.cn/zjyq/yqgk/201801/t20180120_677084.htm.

24. Zhou, Li-an. "Governing China's Local Officials: An Analysis of Promotion Tournament Model [J]." *Economic Research Journal*, vol. 7, 2007, pp. 36–50.
25. Fei, Xiaotong. "Small Town, Big Issue [小城镇, 大问题]". *Love My Hometown [爱我家乡]*. Beijing: Qunyan Press. 1996. pp.51–98.
26. Chien, Shiuh-shen. *Kunshan as "Little Taiwan": China's Most Industrial County-level City*. East Asian Institute, National University of Singapore, 2007.
27. "From 1 to 65%, the 27 Years of Private Economy." *CCTV.com*. 21 Dec. 2006.
28. "China's Private Sector Contributes Greatly to Economic Growth: Federation Leader." *Xinhua*. 6 Mar. 2018.
29. Oi, Jean C. "The Role of the Local State in China's Transitional Economy." *The China Quarterly*, vol. 144, 1995, pp. 1132–1149.
30. The initial plan drafted in 2004 called for 13,000 km, this was expanded to 16,000 km in 2008.
31. Gaotie Jianwen [高铁见闻]. *Great Power Speed: The Rise of China's High-speed Rail [大国速度: 中国高铁崛起之路]*. 2017.
32. "More than 3,000 km of New Railway Lines to Operate in 2023, Including 2,500 km High-Speed Lines." *Global Times*. 3 Jan. 2023.
33. Roberts, Steven V. "Washington Talk; Reagan and the Russians: The Joke's on Them." *The New York Times*. 21 Aug. 1987.
34. Yan, Yilong. *Goal-Based Governance: The Visible Hand of Five-Year Plan [目标治理: 看得见的五年规划之手]*. 2013, p. 160.
35. Hu, Angang. "The Distinctive Transition of China's Five-Year Plans." *Modern China*, vol. 39, no. 6, 2013, pp. 629–639.
36. Ibid.
37. Wang, Shaoguang and Yan, Yilong. A Democratic Way of Decision-Making: Five-Year Plan Process in China. 2015, pp. 62–89.
38. Wang, Shaoguang and Yan, Yilong. "Reveal: How Was The 13th Five Year Plan Made [独家揭秘"十三五"规划如何出炉]" *Xiakedao*. 28 Oct. 2015.
39. Wang, Shaoguang and Yan, Yilong. *Great Wisdoms that Vitalize A Nation: How China Makes Its Five-Year Plan [大智兴邦: 中国如何制定五年规划]*. 2015.
40. Olson, Mancur. *The Rise and Decline of Nations: Economic Growth, Stagflation, and Social Rigidities*. Yale University Press, 2008, pp. 60–94.

41. Fukuyama, Francis. "American Political Decay or Renewal." *Foreign Affairs*, vol. 95, no. 4, 2016, p. 63.

CHAPTER 8

China Today—Myths and Realities

We now hear many in the West complain that they got China wrong. Judging from the current problems between the West and China, it is apparently the case indeed. I venture to suggest that the culprit was Western media and politicians who, due to their biases and need for political expediency, for decades misrepresented China to their publics. To be fair, China is not the only country they misled their own publics about. They do this with so many. How else could they have manipulated their public opinions and led their countries into so many debacles overseas, such as Iraq and Afghanistan. But China is the most consequential one. Without correction, such misrepresentation and misunderstanding could lead to irreversible damage to the world.

In this chapter, I again use the case study method to demonstrate a few examples where the perceived and oversimplified China is far from realities.

In the fall of 2017, the CCP held its 19th Party Congress. At the gathering, which cemented Xi Jinping's leadership, the Chinese president unveiled to the nation a development blueprint for the next few decades. His over 30,000-word report—delivered without breaks in a three-and-a-half-hour address—sent analysts scrambling to decipher the direction the world's largest nation had decided to take.

Theirs was a laborious task, especially considering the report's opaque official jargon and extensive policy details. But, as I wrote in the Washington Post, they might have saved themselves the time and read *The*

Economist's editorial on the congress instead. Had they done so, they would have known exactly what not to think.[1]

I explained as follows. In October 1992, while the party held its 14th Party Congress, *The Economist* editorialized that the party had "stepped backwards." The magazine called the fusion of socialism and capitalism that the CCP espoused at the congress an "oxymoron."[2] Five years later, in 1997, it characterized the 15th Party Congress as full of "hollow promise(s)"—from privatization to unemployment goals—that would soon be broken. Dashing raised expectations, the editors opined, was a "recipe for civil strife."[3]

The list goes on. The 16th Party Congress in 2002 saw a party in "crisis" and facing "unrest."[4] By the time the 17th Party Congress swung around in 2017, "politically, little ha[d] changed."[5] And by the advent of the 18th Party Congress, China had become "unstable at the grassroots, dejected at the middle strata and out of control at the top," as an anonymous source was quoted saying.[6] Finally, in *The Economist's* 2017 cover story on the 19th Party Congress, readers were warned the world not to "expect Mr. Xi to change China, or the world, for the better."[7]

The Economist may have believed that China was stepping backwards in 1992, but it was that year Deng Xiaoping launched a new wave of reforms with his famous Southern Tour, which set China on the path of economic greatness. The "muddling through" years between 2002 and 2012 saw China's GDP quadruple and its economy become the world's largest, by purchasing power.

The Economist is not alone, of course. A regular subscriber of the *New York Times*, or other mainstream Western media, would be left with the impression that China was little more than corrupt, polluted, heavily censored, grossly unequal nation quick to abuse human rights. Although Western media cannot deny that China is an economic juggernaut, reports are still full of warnings about some economic catastrophe just over the horizon, whether driven by over-leveraging, real estate bubbles, trade wars, or any number of other crises.

As a recent critic suggested, Western media outlets should prioritize reporting on the thoughts of the general Chinese population, rather than elevating the voices of minority groups to the mainstream. The lack of coverage on the views of ordinary Chinese people has resulted in distorted perceptions of the country by foreign audiences as well as governments.[8] Similarly, in a short study for Oxford University's Reuters Institute for the Study of Journalism, the broadcast journalist Daniel Griffiths found that coverage of China in leading Western outlets—the *New York Times*, the BBC, and *The Economist*—had "a narrow news agenda."[9] Of the more than 100 news stories on China over a given period of time, 53% covered politics and the economy, and another 15% included topics on human rights and the environment. Of the political coverage, about half focused on official corruption. Even without actual data, one needs only imagine the near total negativity in stories that report on human rights and the environment.

Corruption, of course, has been a big problem. Even Chinese media has not lacked for coverage of it. But to spend half of an outlet's political coverage on corruption seems excessive—especially when the Chinese political system lifted 800 million people out of poverty and has kept producing some of the most capable political leaders in the world. Indeed, although there is no doubt that many of the issues raised by Western media and academics are real, China is much more complex than its portrayed caricature.

Corruption—Saints or Thieves[10]

For years, Western media and academics have identified corruption as the Achilles' heel of China's political system. Mainstream Western media have published major exposés of it; the *New York Times* won a Pulitzer Prize for one.[11] Most of the stories predicted that corruption will prove the ultimate downfall of the party-state. The irony is that no one seems to agree with that assessment more strongly than the party's general secretary himself.

Since Xi rose to China's top leadership position in 2012, he has led an anti-corruption drive the intensity and duration of which caught most China observers, domestic and international, by surprise. (The Chinese historian Eryuehe has called it the harshest anti-corruption movement in 2000 years![12]) From 2012 to 2018, Xi, with the help of his fellow standing committee member and anti-corruption tsar Wang Qishan, swept up some 2 million officials, including 254 "tigers" (those who rank at or above deputy provincial or deputy ministerial level).[13] Critics have accused Xi of using corruption as a way to attack political rivals. No doubt, some political competitors were among those convicted; but so many others were as well that the intention of the campaign should be clear.

There is no doubt that the party is much more worried about corruption than even the *Times*. But the two have differing definitions of what corruption is—and to understand why, it is worth examining the concept of corruption within a larger historic and intellectual context.

Corruption, in its contemporary form, has become a subject of global attention and scholarship only in the past 30-plus years. Before that, the Cold War shielded rampant graft behind ideology. The Philippines' Ferdinand Marcos and Indonesia's Suharto were accused of corruption. But they were protected by their Western allies. The same happened on the other side.

In the very early days after the Cold War, a new global consensus on corruption was formed—and without much empirical data to back it. The argument went as follows: Corruption happens because of incomplete economic liberalization, a lack of political competition, a curtailed judiciary and press, and a weak civil society. Proponents of this vision developed standardized measurement systems to produce single-dimension indexes to chart corruption. According to such indexes, corruption— which is basically equated with bribery—is qualitatively the same across all countries and varies only in quantity.[14] Among such indices, Transparency International's Corruption Perception Index (CPI) is the most authoritative.

Since such measures imply that the root causes of corruption are the same everywhere and that the severity of the problem can be accurately measured, it was only natural to conclude that a standardized prescription could treat the problem as well. Namely, economic liberalization (i.e., privatization), political opening (i.e., multi-party elections), and protections for an independent judiciary, press freedom, and a strong civil society. Political scholar Michael Johnston summarizes this kind of development in his book *Syndromes of Corruption*.[15] And a myriad of respected institutions issued "how-to" manuals to put the ideas into practice, including USAID's *Handbook for Fighting Corruption*, World Bank's *Helping Countries Combat Corruption*, and UNDP's *Corruption and Good Governance*. But like their commercial cousins, there is a problem with these self-help books: they don't quite work.

Take the example of Indonesia. After 40 years of severe corruption during the Sukarno-Suharto eras, the country began to implement all the "right" prescriptions in 1998. More than 60 political parties were formed to compete in elections, the press was set free, judges became independent, and companies were privatized. Yet just about every study has shown that corruption has only gotten worse. In the words of Monash Professor Andrew MacIntyre, Indonesia went from "one Suharto to hundreds of little Suhartos."[16] Examples like this abound, particularly in the developing world.

In due course, scholars have started to re-examine the dominant consensus. The academic world has learned that corruption is a complex, multi-dimensional, and multi-faceted phenomenon. Furthermore, corruption and its effects vary qualitatively across different places and are nearly impossible to measure.[17]

Today, the most commonly accepted definition of corruption is the abuse of public trust for private benefits. However, the distinction between public and private varies considerably between stable and transitioning economies. In the developed West, the boundaries between the two have been clear for decades. In a rapidly transitioning economy like China, the line is constantly shifting. What is public today could become private tomorrow. Moreover, in a stable economy, even a small quantity of corruption can be very damaging, whereas in a transitioning economy the effects are much less certain.

Corruption also takes many forms. One example is what Johnston refers to as "influence market corruption," which is particularly rampant in developed liberal democracies.[18] It is corruption that has been legalized in the forms of political contributions, special interest lobbying, and revolving doors between government and pressure groups.

The United States, for example, fares very well in TI's Corruption Perception Index. But the American people seem to disagree. 77% of them say elected officials are influenced by financial contributors; 59% of Americans say elections are for sale[19]; 70% of Americans say the political system is controlled by special interests and not responsive to the country's real needs; and 93% of Americans say politicians do special favors for campaign contributors.[20] Such numbers would seem to represent rather widespread corruption. Yet they are never counted in any of the ranking systems because they do not capture anything illegal.

Now let's consider the case of China. Corruption is not new. Every dynasty suffered from it. But the root causes of Chinese corruption are rather unique. One of them is embedded in the DNA of the Confucian Mandarin class—*shi da fu*—the centuries-old non-hereditary and meritocratic ruling bureaucracy. The *shi da fu* class is defined by its moral claim that Mandarins should be selflessly devoted to the people. As Fan Zhongyan, the eleventh-century philosopher and statesman described the

Mandarin elite, they should be "the first to worry of the world's troubles, and last to enjoy its pleasures."[21] Over many centuries, Chinese people used this cultural expectation to form a moral standard for their paternalistic rulers.

Yet in contrast to this claim, Confucius articulated the term *xiaokang* to describe an orderly and comfortable society. Here private desires and personal interests, including those of bureaucrats, can be accommodated. And, of course, the party proclaims to be building for China exactly that— a *xiaokang* society. These two conflicting concepts have guided Chinese officialdom for centuries and represent the root cause of corruption there.

Recall the story of Hai Rui, the corruption-fighting minister who lived during the Ming dynasty, a period in Chinese history when officials' salaries were the lowest, anti-corruption campaigns were the fiercest, and levels of corruption were stubbornly high. Hai Rui, whose government salary was so meager that he could barely support his family, was said to eat meat only once a year on his mother's birthday. His two wives both committed suicides.

The gap between selflessness and the good society has gotten more severe over time. During the first 30 years of the People's Republic, the level of corruption was low because nearly everything was public. Market reforms brought about private property, which exacerbated the growing disparity between public service and private wealth. Today, a rich Chinese citizen's dinner could cost more than the entire monthly salary of Wang Qishan, the party's legendary Politburo standing committee member and anti-corruption tsar from 2012 to 2017 (who later became Vice President of China). This is one of the roots of Chinese official corruption.

It is clear that a ready-made solution wouldn't suit China: If the country were to adopt the checks and balances by dividing political power into three branches, as advocated by some experts, the result could very well lead to the current quantity of corruption times three. In fact, the solution may well be to strengthen the party as the most viable vehicle to contain corruption, instead of scrapping existing institutions and replacing them with imported ones.

That is what Xi seems to be accomplishing with his ferocious anti-corruption drive. Officials live in fear of being caught on camera hosting a fancy banquet or wearing an expensive wristwatch. Some critics have argued that the campaign is unsustainable because it attacks the symptoms but does not cure the disease. That may be true. But at the very least its harsh discipline will most likely reduce corruption significantly in the foreseeable future. The problem may inevitably flare up again, but even a pause is surely better than an untenable solution that would flop in reality.

In the long term, the inherent *shi da fu* conflict will likely never be resolved, but it will have to be managed. Here, it is worth discussing something economists have long mused about: "good corruption,"[22] or practices that allow the expedited implementation of worthy economic activities by skirting outdated and inefficient rules. Because such practices involve the breaking of rules, which carries personal risks to officials who allow rules to be broken, bribes become a necessary risk premium—especially when a country is going through significant changes, when old rules no longer work and new rules are not yet developed. China underwent just such a period in the past 30–40 years. "Good corruption" was tolerated as the country experienced drastic growth. But over time, bad corruption has far exceeded good corruption, to the extent that it is even threatening the legitimacy of the party-state itself.

Still, the concept of "good corruption" may explain why China has soared while corruption has hurt economic rivals like India. In his book, *Cracking the China Conundrum*,[23] Yukon Huang proffered a fresh perspective. In India, Huang ventured, corruption is also severe and has indeed impeded economic development. The difference in economic outcomes, therefore, is likely because of differences in the two country's fundamental political constructs.

In the Chinese party-state, the party is the institution that governs the state as the ultimate autonomous political authority. Party officials, therefore, behave as stakeholders of state assets. They may collect bribes from private entrepreneurs, who want favorable access to land or other state resources. But because the officials behave like stakeholders, they also have an interest in the success of the commercial enterprises. The more successful the private companies, the more productive (and valuable) the state resources the officials hold become. Even corrupt Chinese officials, then, have reason to go out of their way to help the businesses that bribe them succeed.

In India, on the contrary, government officials do not behave as stakeholders of the country. Instead, the bribes corrupt Indian officials collect are like tolls. They have no interest in the success or failure of those who bribe them. Actually, the more difficult they make the lives of the businesses under their jurisdiction, the more bribes they can collect. Perhaps that is why India's corruption has had a vast economic cost, whereas

China's has far less of one. In China, corruption's damage has been mostly political and social.

Xi's campaign may have significantly reduced corruption and restored public trust.[24] But its success has come at a cost. Entrepreneurial governance, one of the hallmarks of the party's success in the reform era, may have taken a hit. Quantitative evidence is hard to find, but there are plenty of stories of local officials losing incentive to try new things. Fear of making mistakes or breaking rules—even without the intention of corruption—has paralyzed decision-making at many different levels.

There is evidence that the party leadership knows as much. On numerous occasions, the Politburo, and Xi himself, has called for the rejuvenation of entrepreneurial spirit—*dan dang*, or the daring to take the responsibility and act—in governance. But in the pressure cooker of China today, *dan dang* is difficult. The party seems to have judged that, at the moment, the urgency to stem corruption outweighs whatever negative impact doing so has on entrepreneurial governance. It may very well be right. But managing the balance will continue to be a challenge. Officials' ability to get it right determine how long the party can govern China successfully.

Censorship and Free Speech

The Age of "Cyber Utopianism"[25]

At the turn of the century, as the Internet revolution kicked off, liberal techno-optimists abounded.

The Internet, they believed, would open a brave new world liberated from top down control.[26] Societies with liberal politics would actually flourish as more openness and transparency would strengthen their values and institutions. For example, a 2000 article in Wired captured the spirit of the time:

> We are, as a nation, better educated, more tolerant, and more connected because of – not in spite of – the convergence of the Internet and public life. Partisanship, religion, geography, race, gender, and other traditional political divisions are giving way to a new standard – wiredness – as an organizing principle for political and social attitudes.[27]

It was this confidence that led the United States to abandon virtually all government regulations on telecommunications and to largely prohibit future regulations on the Internet with the Telecommunications Act of 1996.[28]

Meanwhile, the liberal optimists believed, authoritarians would have to watch out. Popular discontent would eventually spread and unseat them. Media mogul Rupert Murdoch famously proclaimed that advances in communications technology posed an "unambiguous threat to totalitarian regimes everywhere."[29] Naturally, Western observers included China among them. Efforts to place controls on the Internet were met with rebuke and scorn. Free speech and free press advocacy groups such as Reporters without Borders routinely censured the country for its Internet restrictions.[30] By their and *The Economist*'s telling, China's heavy censorship of the Internet kept its people in the dark behind a Great Firewall—like a "giant cage."[31] Bill Clinton went so far as to predict that system couldn't last long, because it was as if "trying to nail jello to the wall."[32]

The Reckoning

Well, it has. And the West isn't so optimistic any more. Contrary to their predictions, social media has actually subverted liberal political institutions and social norms in America and Europe. The term "fake news" is a daily theme. America is polarized to an astounding degree, largely abetted and amplified by an unfettered Internet. Identity politics, driven by social media, have become so pervasive that universities, supposedly the paragons of free speech, have barred politically incorrect scholars and commentators from speaking on campuses.[33] U.S. authorities have even blamed social media, manipulated by Russia, for altering the results of the 2016 election.

In his book, *Identity*, the political scientist Francis Fukuyama reflected on his own understanding of politics and the Internet. He recalled believing at the onset of the Internet revolution that it would be "an important force for promoting democratic values." But now he sees social media as "accelerating the fragmentation of liberal societies."[34] It turns out that, contrary to the predictions made in *Wired* magazine, "partisanship, religion, geography, race, gender, and other traditional political divisions" have all be dramatically exacerbated by increasing "wiredness."[35]

A similar set of issues—revolving around nationalism and immigration, also propelled by the Internet—is dividing European societies.

In Germany and Italy, social media routinely galvanizes public protests against the liberal establishment. After the murder of a young German by a migrant in Chemnitz in August 2018, social media helped mobilize large protests. The liberal media, including the *New York Times* and CNN, called them "mobs."[36] They certainly didn't use such terminology when the Internet was being used instead to incite protests against political systems they did not like, as in Ukraine and during the Arab Spring and during the Hong Kong protests in 2019.

Yet now that liberal societies are convinced that the Internet is a danger—whether because of "fake news" or because of the spread of right-wing ideas; calls for censorship abound. Some countries, including Germany and Australia,[37] have enacted new laws. Internet giants are under tremendous political and social pressure to self-censor their content. Many, such as Facebook and YouTube, have begun to do so.[38] The most telling example, of course, was the decisions by Twitter and Facebook to ban Donald Trump's accounts.

When the West was confident of its power, the narrative was that the more open the merrier. U.S. President Barack Obama, on his state visit to China in November 2009, held a town hall meeting and argued, to the dismay of his hosts, that "the more freely information flows, the stronger societies become."[39] To the liberal West, speech with zero restriction was the path to truth—until now.

The Chinese Riposte

China, on the other hand, defied predictions. When Google was effectively forced to exit China in 2010 due to censorship, a grim chorus resounded in the Western media that China's economy and its Internet industry would suffer. China was forsaking economic development for political control, they said. *The New York Times* maintained that Google's exit would "weaken [China's] links to the global economy."[40] *Time* Magazine's Beijing bureau chief argued that censorship was "the Chinese government's interference with the Internet actually saps people's interest in using it," and that further censorship would "hamper its own Internet companies" and "impede its economic progress."[41] *The Atlantic* claimed that the Great Firewall would curb innovations and hurt Chinese Internet companies.[42]

Yet more than a decade later, China's Internet has been growing at an unstoppable rate. It has become the world's largest and most vibrant economic and social cyberspace with over one billlion users and growing.[43] The Internet has penetrated every aspect of Chinese life, and much deeper than in the West. Hundreds of millions of people communicate, transact, entertain, and travel thanks to the Chinese cyberspace. While the *New York Times* and other sites are blocked, *CNN*, *Financial Times*, *USA Today*, *Fox News*, and many other news outlets are freely accessible to all. Entrepreneurial internet companies have created billions of dollars in economic value over just a few years. In 2018, before the crackdown on the big-techs—more on this later, of the top 20 Internet companies in the world, nine were Chinese![44] Contrary to dire predictions, China's Internet exploded and its companies soared—and even with censorship. And, of course, the Chinese economy, and its interconnectedness with the world, has continued to grow—so much so that the United States started a trade war and then a technology war to try to stop it.[45]

At the same time, Beijing has insisted on exercising strong political control over online speech, continuing its ban on Facebook and Twitter. Its Great Firewall—a massive government-directed monitoring system combined with self-regulation by hosting companies—makes China's cyberspace one of the most controlled in the world. When social crises occur, key-word barriers are erected to prevent amplification that would threaten stability.

The fact that China has been able to achieve both vibrancy and control has confounded critics. But it is possible because the nature of the Internet should never have been defined by the dichotomy between free expression and censorship. China's response to the Internet may explain why, as a freewheeling web seems to be tearing apart many liberal societies, China's society remains relatively cohesive. At the same time, China has not sacrificed the social and economic benefits of the new economy.

In 2012, the Singaporean politician George Yeo and I wrote that China's Internet control was much more complex and nuanced than most in the West understood.[46] We referenced the work of a pioneer in understanding the information revolution, Norbert Weiner. In his book *Cybernetics*, published in the 1960s, Weiner separated human responses to new challenges into two types: ontogenetic and phylogenetic.[47] Ontogenetic activities are organized and carried out through centrally designed institutions to shape the development of society. Phylogenetic responses, on the other hand, are evolutionary—analogous to the way bacteria behave in mutual interaction without organizational oversight.

166   E. LI

The development of human civilization has been characterized by the constant struggle between two opposites: the ontogenetic attempts to control the phylogenetic, and the latter's undermining of the former. The relationship is both adversarial and symbiotic, much like *yin* and *yang*. In today's context, political authority is ontogenetic whereas cyberspace is phylogenetic. The health of human society depends on a balance between the two.

As it turns out, liberal societies fit Weiner's analysis well. Cyber-utopianism blinded the liberal West into allowing the phylogenetic forces of the Internet to undermine and subvert the ontogenetic structures of liberal democracy's political institutions. Indeed, the easy scalability of the Internet makes it perhaps the most powerful phylogenetic invasion of the body politic in recent times.[48] The Internet is not an unmitigated force for good. It can also do harm, something liberal societies overlooked.

The approach of the Chinese government was akin to traditional Chinese medicine, with an emphasis on the Internet being an organic part of the body politic. Too much intervention is as bad as too little. Constant monitoring is necessary so that one knows when and how much to intervene. The word in Chinese is *tiao*, which means continuous tuning of a complex system.

In some ways, the Internet is just another way to monitor the body. Social media in particular has helped the Chinese government overcome an age-old problem of poor feedback. Social media brings problems to the immediate attention of China's leaders, who can react with immediate policy reforms. At the same time, however, the government exercises control to prevent such discontent from spreading too widely—leading to mass movements that could endanger social stability.

A regular observer of China's Internet would find that some discontent is usually allowed to spread and discussion tolerated. And then, generally after a few days, it is shut down. Beijing does not always get the balance perfect. Sometimes things are allowed to spread too fast and too wide, leading to outrage disproportionate to the problem at hand. Sometimes they are suppressed too quickly and harshly, depriving the political leaders of useful feedback and the public of a necessary relief valve. But over a long span of time, the party has exercised *tiao* rather effectively.

To see how, two incidents are worth studying.

The Accident That Could Have Stopped China

In 2011, a terrible train collision in Zhejiang province killed 40 people. A national uproar followed. Soon, fake news had completely taken over Weibo (China's Twitter). In the first three days following the accident, 9.6 million Weibo messages (at the time a huge number) flooded the Internet. Many of them were manufactured rumors: the rescue was a debacle with live people falling out of the lifting equipment; a cover-up was underway to hide a much higher casualty number; the captain at the wheel of the train had only ten days of training because of pressure to quickly expand rail service.

All of these rumors were eventually proven false. But at the time, fake news generated tremendous public anger, which led to more fake news. The vicious cycle overwhelmed any fact-checking or rational discourse. China's liberal media, led by Caixin's *New Century Weekly*, took the opportunity to reject China's entire development model and the political system itself: "China, go slower, wait for your people" became a rallying cry.[49] Its immediate target was the nation's high-speed rail project, which ignored the fact that the locomotives involved in the accident were not part of the project.[50]

Mainstream Western media chimed in to call the high-speed rail project a failure. The West saw the voices on Weibo as evidence of mass dissatisfaction with China's development path.[51] *The Wall Street Journal* called it a "Weibo watershed" moment.[52] The BBC opined that the high-speed rail project encapsulated all of the characteristics that made the Chinese development model bad—and that the accident "ripped apart" both the "grand packaging of high speed rail and the pompous robe of the China model."[53]

It was a real possibility that those predictions would prove correct. We have seen this movie over and over again in the past 20-plus years in so many countries: societal changes breed conflicts, a trigger incident ignites dissatisfaction, fake news fans a revolution, and all hell breaks loose—Ukraine, Libya, the Arab Spring, and now Europe and America.

But China did not let that happen. After two weeks of hesitation, the government moved in to contain the rumors by censoring certain content. A month later, the government ordered Weibo to institute a mechanism to control the dissemination of false information and harmful rumors.

Looking back, it is obvious that there was a significant disconnect between cyberspace and the real world. At the time of the accident, the Beijing-Shanghai high-speed rail line was just finishing its first month of operation and had already carried five and a quarter million passengers—not too shabby by any measure. For the rest of the rail system, trains continued to operate at full capacity as usual. The rescue was conducted quickly and competently. By all measures, the Chinese rail system, even with the accident, was and is one of the safest in the world. In a bit of irony, after an Amtrak accident in Philadelphia four years later, the *New York Times* decried the poor state of U.S. rails and used China's system as a counterpoint, since the latter has one of the lowest accident rates in the world. The paper used a picture of "Harmony"—China's first high-speed rail line—to illustrate its point.[54]

Today, by virtually every public opinion poll, the Chinese people are satisfied with the party-state and direction of their country. They have seen their lives improve dramatically. One accident could not have changed that.

Shortly after the accident, I wrote in *The Christian Science Monitor* that a pseudo-political opposition within China, mostly made up of media and intellectual elites, had taken the expressions of anger in the digital public square and created an Orwellian 1984 of Chinese public opinion.[55]

In the decade between 2005 and 2015, rapid growth of the Internet created a digital public square, and its ferocity became a unique phenomenon. While the vast majority of China's 800 million netizens used the Internet for entertainment and commerce, a smaller group used it to vent dissatisfaction about life, society, and the world. They expressed their most intense feelings about what they were most dissatisfied with in the loudest voices possible. The nature of the Internet was such that these sentiments were amplified and assumed a semblance of dominance. Its manifestation was by definition partial and parochial, extreme and unrepresentative. Little wonder that any casual visitor to the Chinese digital public square during that period would find a China filled with the most extreme expressions of populism and nationalism. Those who understood the nature of this medium would know that these expressions while legitimate were far from reflecting the general views of average netizens, much less the population at large. When put into an objective analytical framework, it is, at best, but one of the barometers of public opinion, and certainly not the most significant. At worst it was what Foreign Policy magazine termed the "People's Republic of Rumors".[56]

In his recent book *Identity*, Francis Fukuyama theorized that what he called "thymos," or "the craving for dignity" within individuals makes it difficult for citizens to behave rationally in the real world. Citizens, as Fukuyama shows, are not rational animals and can act against their interests. When coupled with anti-intellectualism, that excessive yearning for political rights tended to manifest corrosive effects on Western contemporary societies. Likewise, Chinese netizens under the same influence have behaved similarly.[57]

It's not hard to imagine "thymos" derailing China's development. If Beijing were unable to contain the spread of online falsehoods, and if Chinese society were as polarized as America's, a cyber storm of this magnitude could have assumed a life of its own and crept into the real world. The government could have buckled under pressure and, at the very least, halted the development of the high-speed rail. Soon, the outcry could have threatened political and social stability. And that scenario would have been tragic for the Chinese people.

Revolution (Almost) in the Air—Wumai and Celebrity

At some point between 2010 and 2011, a new word entered into the Chinese popular lexicon: *wumai*. It refers to dense pollution that contains harmful fine particles called PM2.5—the type that, in those years, had started to blanket many parts of the country, especially during the winter months. In Beijing, residents could go for days, even weeks, without seeing any blue sky. On the worst days, visibility was only 100 meters, the air smelled like chemicals, and the city's air quality index exceeded 500—at least 20 times greater than levels the World Health Organization deems safe. According to the Ministry of Environmental Protection, by 2013, China's air pollution was at its worst in some 52 years, with 13 provinces hitting record-high levels of air pollution.[58]

Public awareness and discontent spread quickly on Weibo and other Internet platforms. Soon, it dominated the national discourse. In the month of January 2011, the word PM2.5 was mentioned on Weibo only about 200 times. In January 2013, it was mentioned more than three million times.[59] As public rancor about *wumai* spread, the government did not jump in to restrict the conversation. Sometimes, it even encouraged the discussion. Every time *wumai* entombed a city for days on end, pictures and angry protests dominated virtually all Chinese Internet channels. Official media echoed public discontent and reported on the seriousness of the situation, possible sources of the pollution, and potential solutions. In 2014, Premier Li Keqiang even declared a "war on pollution,"[60] and the government began in earnest to implement policies to combat *wumai*.

Then, in February 2015, a celebrity broke the Chinese Internet. Chai Jing, a popular television host and investigative reporter, produced and starred in a TED Talk styled documentary called "Under the Dome"[61] that aired on the official Renmin website—the online version of China's highest-level official newspaper, the *People's Daily*. The 104-minute video began with a very personal story—Chai's daughter had been diagnosed with a prenatal tumor—then it dived into the pollution crisis. The implication, that pollution had caused the tumor, was clear. (Most later reports showed no such causality.) In interviews with government officials, business executives, and ordinary people, Chai placed the blame squarely at the feet of the country's entire political and economic system: rapid development that used too much dirty coal, state-owned enterprises' monopoly power on energy supply, and the environmental agencies' abdication of responsibility.

The timing was just right for a cyber storm. The *wumai* problem was reaching the height of its seriousness during the winter months. The government's "war on pollution" had not had enough time to deliver discernible results. The annual National People's Congress session was just days away, and people's attention was on politics. Chai's emotional appeal reached an astonishing 200 million views in 48 hours; it felt like the revolution was in the air.

Yes, pollution was a serious problem, but a total overhaul of the country's political governance and economic system was not the way to fix it. After a few days of this massive online movement, the government acted decisively, issuing orders to delete the documentary from major Chinese video websites, and it was shut down.

Fast forward to 2018 and 2019, and China has made impressive progress on its war against pollution. Pollution was still a problem, but improvements had been dramatic. The quantity of fine particles in the air had been reduced by 32%, and the number of *wumai* days were cut even more significantly. In the winter of 2018–2019, Beijing saw blue skies on most days.

The progress was thanks to a combination of policy initiatives, widely known as the "10 Measures," that were sustained over half a decade.[62] Coal burning was reduced, factories were shut down or moved, and auto emission standards were more strictly enforced. No doubt, China's fight against pollution is nowhere near victory. And there will be more ups and downs given the country's enormous industrial production and consumer base. But what ultimate success requires are sustained policy efforts, not revolution (Table 8.1).

The case highlights the benefits of China's management of Internet speech. The Internet channeled public dissatisfaction with air pollution, feedback that spurred the government into action and resulted in significant improvements. The "Under the Dome" documentary, which amplified popular discontent beyond proportion and risked societal breakdown, was quickly contained with direct intervention.

In that sense, the health of China's cyber universe is good. Economically and socially, the Internet is flourishing. Politically it has become a tool for managing rapid change. Regulations have not kept up with the new realities, causing frequent problems of public safety. Social and economic divisions have widened considerably. Yet, even so, China has avoided the kind of populist movements that have swept other societies. Thanks to steady governance and social stability, China has been able to solve many of the problems that came with rapid change without

Table 8.1 Air pollution prevention and control action plan ("Ten Measures")[63]

1	Reduce pollutant emissions through renovation of key industries and clean transformation
2	Strictly control high energy consumption of high-pollution industries' production capacity
3	Improve public transport and clean energy production
4	Develop natural gas, coal methane, and other clean energy supplies
5	Strengthen energy saving and environmental indicator constraints on construction, land, power and water supply
6	Implement incentives and constraints on new energy saving mechanisms
7	Enforce laws and standards for industrial restructuring and upgrading
8	Densely populated urban areas around the Bohai Sea, including Beijing, Tianjin, the Yangtze River Delta, Pearl River Delta, and other regions, must establish joint prevention and control mechanisms on atmospheric environmental targets and assessment systems
9	Establish local government emergency management in response to heavily polluted weather, and limit emissions from polluting enterprises and vehicles
10	Develop a code of conduct that can be applied to the whole society, with local government taking overall responsibility on local air quality

social unrest. It seems that China's effective management of the Internet deserves some credit.

Perhaps it's time for people to set aside their ideological impulses and realize that the Internet does not fit a dichotomy of free expression versus censorship. It is much more complex than that, as China's experience shows.

Some countries are already taking note: India has demanded that Facebook and Google remove derogatory materials. Some European countries have done the same. It is rather obvious that countries differ widely as to what kind of speech can be polarizing and destructive, so perhaps we should not apply a universal standard for managing the Internet. Countries should be allowed to mediate it based on their own social conditions. Eventually, as in the real world, cyberspace will not be flat but will have interconnected mountains and valleys.

On the Rule of Law[64]

If one concept of political governance has universal appeal, it would have to be the rule of law. In fact, virtually all governments claim to want it. In 1992, the World Bank even made it a prerequisite of successful economic development, linking it to "efficient use of resources and productive investment."[65]

China is no exception. The PRC's 1982 Constitution stated that "no organization or individual may enjoy the privilege of being above the Constitution and the law."[66] In 1997, the party declared at its 15th Party Congress that, at the most fundamental level, China's strategy was "governing the country according to law and making it a socialist country of rule of law."[67] And most recently, President Xi has made the rule of law a centerpiece of his "new era."[68]

But what is the rule of law? Does the United States model it? Can a country like China realize it? A little digging reveals that the concept is greatly misinterpreted in the general media and political discourse. A more in-depth survey of the history, theories, and practices of the rule of law would demonstrate that it is not an exclusive creation of liberal societies. Further, it is in the West that rule of law is most imperiled. Ironically, non-liberal societies—especially China—may hold more promise in realizing the benefits of the rule of law.

The Liberal Myth of Rule of Law

Asked to define rule of law, elites around the world would say something like the following: A country with a strong rule of law is governed by a constitution that guarantees individual rights and sets out the rules for democratic elections. Its political institutions are defined by a separation of power that provides for an independent judiciary that adjudicates disputes impartially and has the power to review legislation to ensure its compliance with a constitution. All are equal before the law.[69]

They may elaborate further with the obvious merits of the rule of law. When rules are set in advance and in general terms, and they are applied equally by an independent judiciary, businesses and individuals can operate with security and predictability. Rights and property cannot be taken away arbitrarily—a necessary condition for economic development and even human dignity and well-being.

Under this tautological narrative, liberal societies are rule-of-law countries and non-liberal societies are not. In China, the argument goes, the party holds arbitrary power over the law and even the constitution. The judiciary, which is under the party's supervision, is not independent and cannot therefore be impartial—let alone serve as a check on the party's political authority. In such a system, any individual rights stipulated in the constitution are meaningless, and businesses and individuals cannot operate because they don't enjoy the basic security of property and liberty.

By about every abstract measure of the rule of law, then, China would seem to fail. Some have labeled its system instead as rule by law. Rule by law, in their interpretation, is simply using laws as a means to efficiently exercise the rule of the party.

But this narrative is built on shaky ground.

The first problem is that common discussions of the rule of law have little basis in fact. Let's start with the United States, which considers itself an exemplar of rule-of-law governance. Ronald Dworkin, a prominent thinker on the issue, even calls the country the "Law's Empire."[70]

But there are some puzzling facts. If general rules are set in advance and applied with consistency and predictability, why are there so many lawsuits in America? The United States is the most litigious society in the world. Few enter into a lawsuit knowing for sure that they will win or lose—a truth that is hard to explain if the rule of law delivers perfect predictability.

A further problem is that a Supreme Court ruling of 5–4 decides so many consequential constitutional judgments with broad and far-reaching effects on American life. And votes swing, sometimes as a result of one justice's health, age, or personal experience. That is hardly a demonstration of predictability. For example, some traced the Supreme Court ruling that made same-sex marriage constitutional at least in part to the personal acquaintances and life experience of one justice, Anthony Kennedy.[71] Overnight, same-sex marriage became constitutionally sanctioned. Yet, not a word changed in the U.S. Constitution.

Even a determination no less important than who should occupy the U.S.' highest office was decided by a 5–4 vote in the Supreme Court in 2000.[72] And if Americans didn't understand that rule of law means rule by one vote in so many cases, the recent Supreme Court confirmation of Justice Brett Kavanaugh would never have become so intense and so partisan a struggle.[73]

It turns out that the rule of law has never been as neat as its advocates portray. In fact, four major misconceptions about the rule of law in general and the implications in the Chinese political context are worth reviewing.

1. The Rule of Law is Liberal

It is a historical fact that the rule of law predated liberalism by more than a millennium. When Aristotle first conceptualized the rule of law, it perfectly supported the Athenian slave society. Equality simply meant that the law was applied equally according to its own terms.[74] According to the political theorist Judith Shklar, Aristotelian rule of law was perfectly compatible with a state in which part of the population is declared subhuman, such as the governments of the United States through the civil rights movement, Nazi Germany, and apartheid South Africa in more recent times.[75] John Locke's proclamation, "where-ever law ends, tyranny begins," thus seems weak in this analysis.[76]

Even the Magna Carta, long credited in the popular imagination with cultivating liberal society based on the rule of law in England and the wider world, was but a myth. As the eminent scholar Edward Jenks has pointed out, it was a contract between the barons and earls and the king, who signed it under duress. If anything, it further consecrated feudal privileges instead of advancing progressive liberties.[77] No wonder, then, that legal scholar Brian Tamanaha has pointed out that the idea that only liberal democracies can have rule of law is "unjustifiable" and "smacks of stuffing the meaning of the rule of law with contestable normative presuppositions."[78]

2. The Rule of Law Solves the Problem of Unlimited Governmental Power

One of the most common criticisms of China and other non-liberal countries is that given weak rule of law, a ruler (or party) can govern unchecked, trampling human rights as it goes.

But this view is theoretically mistaken. The rule of law has never, not even at the conceptual level, resolved the issue of how to check sovereign power. How can laws restrict the lawgiver, be it king, party, or parliament? "He that is bound to himself only," Hobbes said, "is not bound."[79]

The conservative German jurist Carl Schmitt further consolidated this view in the twentieth century. Though his ideas later became associated with the Third Reich, his early theories have stood the test of time.[80] In his writings, Schmitt argued that the origin and effectiveness of law required an authority beyond the law itself. He asserted that a society's political will—not an abstract, just norm—defined the unity's fundamental political existence. Political decision-making always preceded law.[81] One implication is that Constitutions are formed by political will, and are not legitimized by previous law. Ordinary legislation too are objects of political decision-making. In *Political Theology*, Schmitt further argued that to decide the gap between general laws and particular applications a sovereign authority was required to make judicial interpretations central to justice.[82]

Even within England's liberal tradition, the idea of a fundamental political arrangement influencing the law rings true. First, the legitimacy of the Magna Carta as a legal document originates from a promise extracted by the nobles from the English sovereign. While for a time the Common Law tradition it fostered provided for a basic legal framework and principles above the powers of legislators, it wasn't long until Jeremy Bentham and other legal reformers in the nineteenth century repudiated that logic in favor of parliamentary sovereignty (supremacy over the law).[83] Judicial review of legislation was rejected—for no justification could be found for judges to override the people's will. In the United States, that most significant document of liberal legal principles—the Constitution, carries specific provisions on how everything within it can be changed by the proclaimed sovereign will of the people as long as certain procedures are followed.

Recognizing the theoretical predicament that law-makers can't be bound by the laws they make, Tamanaha posited that there are only three ways in which the rule of law *can* limit sovereign power in practice: political necessity leads the ruler to voluntarily or involuntarily pledge to be bound by the laws; customs develop over long periods of time and create a cultural environment in which all believe themselves to be bound by laws; and governments require officials to strictly follow the rules when conducting routine and mundane tasks.[84] All three, however, are products of cultural and political development, not natural consequences of the rule of law itself.

Xi recognized as much at the Fourth Plenary Session of the 18th Party Congress in October 2014. He made the development of the rule of law a centerpiece of his political agenda and said that "the party leads the people in establishing the constitution, the party leads the people in executing the constitution, and the party must be bound by the constitution."[85] Such pronouncements may seem contrary to the rule of law, but such contradictions have always been inherent to the theory. Party-led rule of law is no more an oxymoron than parliamentary-led or court-led rule of law.

3. The Rule of Law Overcomes the Follies of the Rule of Man

Among all the misconceptions about the rule of law, the idea that the rule of law stands counter to the rule of man is perhaps the most pernicious. As the saying goes, the rule of law is impartial and just while the rule of man is arbitrary and unjust. But again, Aristotle points to much more ambiguity. He placed reason at the center of the rule of law, arguing that "the law is reason unaffected by desire."[86] In this telling, because man was necessarily influenced by human passion and biases, the rule of man would make for an unstable or even unjust society. It would therefore be preferable for a society to be governed by general rules set in advance and strictly applied.[87]

At the same time, though, Aristotle also emphasized that the outcome of the rule of law depends on the quality of judges and, in complex cases, it would be better for laws to be less rigid so that judges can have more discretion.[88] This Aristotelian conflict has never really been resolved. The French judge and political philosopher Montesquieu argued against the role of judges for fear that "the life and liberty of the subject" would be "exposed to arbitrary control."[89] Yet, he, more than any other political thinker, was responsible for creating the intellectual foundation for the independence of the judiciary, which assigns tremendous power to judges.[90] There is no getting away from the cruel reality that the law does not act or speak by or for itself; all laws must be interpreted and acted upon by human beings.

In fact, in many Western countries, rule of law now means rule of judges. So much so that experts have begun to condemn their power. In his recent book, the American journalist David Kaplan called the U.S. Supreme Court "the most dangerous branch" of government, one that is mounting an "assault on the Constitution."[91] In this case, the line between the rule of law and the rule of man is surely blurred.

But do such conspicuous instances of the rule of man subvert the rule of law? Not necessarily. In fact, a strong case can be made that a strict view of formal legality, which stipulates the rigid application of the letter of the law without human discretion, is contrary to the ideals that underpin the rule of law.[92] Rule of law should not be morally or substantively neutral; procedural justice is not substantive justice and could very much produce the opposite. Human beings must intervene to ensure the law actually generates just outcomes—and such interventions are necessarily political.

China has had just as much difficulty as any other nation grappling with the relationship between the rule of law and the rule of man. After the Cultural Revolution, the party-state sought to fix the system that had allowed Mao's absolute personal rule by building more impersonal versions of the rule of law.

A public speech by Xiao Yang, the Chief Justice of the Supreme People's Court of China, in 2003 captured the mood of that era:

> Today's world is one of the rule of law. The prosperity of a nation, the integrity of its politics, the stability of its society, the development of its economy, the solidarity of its ethnic groups, the flowering of its culture, and the contentment and well-being of its people, all hinge upon the maintenance of law and order and the soundness of the legal system. China is no exception. The national strategy of a country determines its future and destiny. At the end of the twentieth century, China… publicly proclaimed

to the world that we would adopt the rule of law as our governance strategy.[93]

Adopt the strategy it did. China went so far as to implement computer sentencing so as to take personal discretion completely out of certain legal decisions.[94] Whether such methods are consistent with the fundamental intent and conception of the rule of law is very much debatable. In the end, computer sentencing, which flourished in certain provincial courts in the early 2000s, did not take off on a large scale. Although such software is still being used in Chinese courts, it is primarily for aiding investigative work such as evidence analysis rather than for making binding legal decisions.[95]

4. The Rule of Law Underwrites Social Justice in Modern Democratic Societies

In recent decades, the rule of law has been invoked as the ideological and institutional framework that can deliver social justice in liberal democratic societies. But this view ignores the theory's intrinsic contradictions.

From Aristotle through the medieval period, rule of law hardly represented any form of universal social justice, since slavery and feudal privilege were both institutionally enshrined and strengthened by the rule of law. Even in the liberal tradition of the modern era, the rule of law was not about social justice—at least not as we understand it today. John Locke, one of the most significant thinkers of the liberal rule of law, placed property at the center of it all. For Locke, a "state is a society of property owners,"[96] and the raison d'etre of the rule of law was the "protection of the propertied members of society against the demands of the indigent."[97]

Even centuries later, when social welfare became central to the political agenda of Western liberal societies, many political and legal thinkers thought that such politics were anathema to, and spelled the destruction of, the rule of law. Prominent among them were the constitutional theorist A. V. Dicey[98] and the economist Friedrich Hayek. For Hayek, the welfare state's pursuit of substantive equality by redistribution of wealth was against the very tenets of the rule of law.[99]

In China, this debate is perhaps just beginning. Forty years of untrammeled, market-driven growth has produced serious side effects, most notably environmental degradation and an expanding gulf between rich and poor. Since 2000, China's Gini coefficient has surged over 0.4, the recognized warning level for dangerous levels of inequality. In 2017, rural residents, which account for 42% of the population, had an annual per capita disposable income of RMB 12,363. That was about one third of the average per capita disposable income of urban residents, which stood at RMB 33,616.[100]

At the 19th Party Congress held in 2017, Xi stated that China's development paradigm had shifted from rapid growth to high-quality development.[101] In short, he recognized that the redistribution of economic gains would be the central political task of his era. Still, since 2004, the protection of private property has been enshrined in China's Constitution.[102] Some liberal opinion leaders, such as Zhang Weiying, Wu Jinglian, and Mao Yushi, have used the concept of liberty and the law's protection of private property (in other words, procedural justice) to oppose active government policies to achieve substantive equality through taxation and other political means,[103] just as Hayek did in the West decades ago.

Herein lies the extraordinary irony: China, a socialist country, is the only major economy in the world that still has neither a property tax nor an inheritance tax. As the political leadership seeks to build Xi's new era by bringing general prosperity to all, there will surely be stiff resistance from the country's political elites and among its commercial powers. We can expect that the concept and interpretation of the rule of law will be a central theme in the great debates to come.

Chinese Rule of Law

The theory and practice of rule of law contains so many self-contradictions that it is an "essentially contested concept"[104] as the term was defined by the social theorist W. B. Gallie.[105] That is, disagreements about what it truly means are inherent in the concept itself. Understanding as much is necessary to see how the concept applies in China—or anywhere else, for that matter.

1. Confucius and the Law

The great political debate, indeed, the essential struggle that has defined Chinese civilization for generation after generation, occurred more than two thousand years ago. It was the struggle between legalism and Confucianism (*fajia vs. rujia*). Very simply, Legalism was the procedural justice version of the rule of law. During the Warring States period (475–221 BC), when China was divided into separate kingdoms battling endlessly for dominance, the kingdom of Qin came from behind to surpass all others in economic and military power. It eventually unified China in 221 BC through the implementation of strict legal codes by Shang Yang, the reformer prime minister.[106]

The legalism the Qin practiced was brutally impersonal and soon led to rebellions. The Qin dynasty collapsed after only 14 years.[107] The Han dynasty took over, and the ensuing debates over political philosophy lasted nearly a century. Many schools of thought emerged, even flourished. But the central rivalry was between Legalism and Confucianism.

If Legalism was essentially the value-neutral application of generalized rules, Confucianism was centered on the concept of the "mandate of heaven." Moral legitimacy was the basis of just rule. The ruler held a divine right to rule, but only as long as he looked after the welfare of the people. If he failed in his duty, he would risk overthrow. Being a good ruler thus entailed not only giving orders but also engaging in moral conduct. In short, Confucianism was mostly about substantive justice.

The Confucian "Mandate of Heaven" contrasted sharply with the European doctrine of the divine right of kings, which asserted that a monarch received power directly from God and was subject neither to earthly authority nor to the will of the people.[108] In a sense, as long as the procedure (royal succession) was followed correctly, the rule was legitimate. In the modern era, this could be interpreted to mean that, as long as election procedures are correctly carried out, a leader in a liberal democracy is legitimate no matter how bad he or she is. The Chinese tradition is decidedly not that.

A simplified version of history would say that, in the great struggle between Legalism and Confucianism in the early years of the Han dynasty, the latter emerged victorious and served as the political foundation of China for two millennia.[109] But it's more complex than that. In fact, most historians name this defining period in Chinese political history as the Qin-Han Era. They group the Qin dynasty (Legalism) and the Han dynasty (Confucianism) together. As the Chicago University professor Zhao Dingxin explains in his book, *The Confucian-Legalist*

State, although the Han dynasty instituted Confucianism as the official state ideology, Legalism always remained an integral part of China's political constitution.[110]

Indeed, procedural justice has served as the practical method of governance throughout all Chinese dynasties. The public generality expects prescriptiveness and equality in the carrying out of rules. However, Confucianism served a higher purpose. Three aspects—constraint on the ruler, substantive justice, and communitarian values—are particularly important.

The Confucian doctrine both conceptually and institutionally sought to supply a needed check on sovereign rule. The ruler answered to a moral responsibility that was higher than a mere legal procedure. The ruler, by declaring his obligation to a higher moral law effectively bound himself, and his legitimacy rested upon honoring his vows. Even the Chinese philosopher Mencius suggested that a ruler who violated the moral code could be abandoned.[111] And that "right of resistance"[112] was taken seriously, as attested by the violent overthrows of dynasties every two or three hundred years—new dynasties with renewed mandates of heaven would emerge, honoring that code.

At the institutional level, Confucianism developed the highly elaborate Mandarin governance system through which a large cadre of powerful scholar-officials effectively administered the country. These *shidafu*s were the embodiment of Confucian morals and served as an institutional check on the absolute power of the emperor. They also had the right to disagree with or even criticize the emperor.[113]

The Confucian check on sovereign power also served as the political and legal structure for the delivery of substantive justice when procedures could not meet the task. In China's dynastic history, there were many examples of procedural outcomes that were contrary to the moral values of society; and, in the good cases, morality prevailed.

Observers might consider all this to be against the spirit of the rule of law, as understood in the West. Very much the opposite is true.[114] Dworkin, for example, put forth the idea that morality forms the background and is an integral aspect of positive law. It is the responsibility of judges to make decisions that are consistent with the moral and political consensus of the community. This imperative is above and beyond the rules in the book.[115]

To be sure, Confucian morality is distinct. But even here, there is a meaningful overlap between Confucian rule of law and liberal rule of law. In the West, theorists, mostly left-leaning, have argued that liberal rule of law "is irredeemably flawed" as Tamanaha has written, because it presumes that people come together to form a society for the common good.[116] This criticism has only intensified and broadened since the financial crisis of 2008, now from both the left and the right.[117] Liberal rule of law's overt emphasis on procedural justice based on the fundamental value of individualism has contributed to the decline of substantive justice. Communitarianism, in this context, unites the left and the right in its call for substantive justice, be it income equality or social cohesion. In the face of the dominance of the abstract supranational legalism of Brussels and Washington, communitarianism is in all likelihood going to grow even more robust in the first half of this century.

And this is precisely the role Confucianism played for centuries in its subordination of Legalism. The values and purposes of the community have served as the overarching vault that houses Chinese rule of law. Rules are to be applied strictly but only in accordance with the Confucian spirit. Communitarian faith lies in the foundation of Confucian politics—*tian xia wei gong ... shi wei da tong* (heaven and earth for all, such is the great common).[118]

Just like Aristotle and his intellectual heirs who have struggled with the idea of the rule of law in the West, the Chinese recognized long ago that the law cannot be soulless. The rules have to be harmonized with values—no easy task.

2. The Party and the Law—Present and Future

One question that has driven prolonged political debate is: the party or the law, in China, which is bigger? Which should be bigger? (*dang da hai shi fa da?*) Conservatives say the party is and should be; liberals say the party is, but the law should be. Both miss the point.

The structure of Chinese rule of law is the combination of legal procedures and party oversight to ensure the protection of the spirit of the law. Over the past 40 years, the country has developed a truly elaborate and advanced system of laws. But the common criticism is that enforcement is lacking,[119] although but most experts agree that China has gotten better in that respect.[120]

The contentious issue is the role of the party. The Central Committee Politics and Law Commission remains the nation's highest power on legal matters. And the party disciplinary commission structure holds all party members accountable to the party's internal rules, which are different and stricter than the public codes.[121]

But even this is well within the conceptual framework of the rule of law in the Western tradition. The party represents political sovereignty. In theory, the law cannot bind the sovereign. But the party declares itself to be bound, and the people expect such constraint as a basis of the party's political legitimacy. In this very practical way, the party is indeed bound by the laws, at least no less than any other sovereign power.

More importantly, the party, through its Central Committee Politics and Law Commission, serves as the ultimate recourse on substantive justice, just as the Confucian politico-moral structure did for centuries and liberal values and institutions do now in the West. Of course, the values that undergird substantive justice in both cases are quite different. The party upholds China's Confucian-Socialist ideology just as the West's institutions uphold the moral codes of liberalism.

When procedural justice produces an outcome that the general society does not believe is substantively just—and such disagreement is strong—the party has the authority to step in and tip the balance. In contemporary China, such cases have been rare, but they have happened.[122]

The party's political power over legal procedures also serves as the ultimate guarantor that procedural justice will not supersede the polity's fundamental values, just as Dworkin, argues that liberal society's consensus on moral imperatives forms the foundation of laws and their applications.[123] In China, the party plays this role instead of an "independent" judiciary. Therefore, like so many other questions, wondering whether the party or the law is bigger is a fool's errand.

To be sure, conceptual clarity does not prevent real-world messiness. In China, the development of the rule of law has been and continues to be plenty tangled. Party committees at different levels often interfere arbitrarily with legal proceedings. There is a thin line between ensuring substantive justice and wanton political interference on behalf of special interests, or worse, straight corruption.

On the other end of the spectrum, excessive legalism plagues Chinese rule of law, too. In an understandable attempt to move away from the rule of man after the Cultural Revolution, the legislature and the legal system have codified increasingly larger portions of civil and commercial activities. In many areas, such as environmental protections and domestic disputes, the legal codes are elaborate and are meant to be applied in a unified fashion nationwide. Yet many of these codes, if upheld strictly without consideration for actual circumstances and differentiation across regions and social groups, would prove rather unsuitable and contrary to the purposes of social justice.[124]

Overcoming the myriad conflicts that are both inherent in the rule of law and particular to China's circumstances will be a long and arduous process. But there are reasons for optimism. Both the party and the general public want a society in which rules are made in advance and are applied equally. At the same time, Chinese society's general consensus on values and moral imperatives—socialism and national renaissance—is the strongest now than in perhaps a century and a half. The former is the two-thousand-year Confucian patrimony of an egalitarian and just society for the "common good" expressed in modern form. The latter was the culmination of the struggles to survive that unified an entire people in the modern era. Chinese rule of law, whichever direction it may evolve, has a soul. The party, if it guards against corruption and elitism, will continue to embody that soul and will thus be accepted by the people.

Perhaps it is time we free the rule of law from the unwarranted ideological bondage of liberalism. As UCLA's Randall Peerenboom points out in his book, *China's Long March Towards the Rule of Law*,[125] China does not need liberalism to have the rule of law. In fact, there are many ways to fulfill the promises of the rule of law in a pluralistic world.

The irony is that, in liberal societies, the state of the rule of law is concerning. Across the West, the moral consensus has been shattered. Communities are decaying and the people are polarized over basic values such as identity, marriage, race, and equality. Liberalism has fallen victim to the worst impulses of the post-modern world—relativism and nihilism. Perhaps as a result, procedural justice has become a pure political and adversarial game. Soulless laws cannot sustain legitimacy for long. Western elites would be well advised to look inward rather than embarking on rule of law roadshows around the world.

On the Covid Pandemic

As the Covid pandemic is coming close to ending after three years of wreaking havoc around the world, Western media is already hard at work to rewrite history on China's record. Many Western media outlets are reporting the following story: The virus emerged in Wuhan, China in early 2020. The Chinese government responded ineptly. As the virus spread around the world, China implemented draconian controls and made its people live in misery for three years and caused huge damage to its economy and global supply chains.[126]

It would take only moderate effort to find news reporting that is less than three years old to remember what actually happened. In January 2020, the Chinese government decisively locked down the city of Wuhan. In only two to three months, it actually stopped the spread of the virus in the country. By just about every measure, the Chinese efforts were both heroic and highly effective; government competency, societal cohesion, and trust in public institutions were shown at their highest levels in recent history.[127] At the same time, the United States and Europe were in complete disarray. Their economies stopped, their societies polarized, and their deaths skyrocketed.

For the rest of 2020 and almost the entire year of 2021, the Chinese people, compared with the rest of the world, lived nearly normal lives. Other than restrictions on international travels, nearly everything functioned as before. There were very few lockdowns; people traveled around the country; schools were open. Even mask-wearing was uncommon during those two years. The infection and death numbers remained extremely low.[128] China's economies were also among the least affected.[129]

Then Omicron emerged in late 2021 and it changed the picture. The variant was more contagious but less deadly. The U.S. and Europe kept opening up, as they were unable to contain the virus to begin with and were already co-existing with the virus. China had a choice, to open or keep the Covid zero policies that had kept its people safe and economy running for nearly two years. It decided to be cautious. This is understandable in the spring of 2022 as Omicron data still had a short history. The fact that the 20th party congress was planned for autumn 2022 with an important leadership transition might have also made the government highly risk-averse. This decision resulted in larger-scale lockdowns, most notably the two-month lockdown of Shanghai. The government kept the Covid zero policies for another six months into the fall of 2022. When it became clear that the contagiousness of Omicron made these policies unsustainable and the lower deathrate made it less dangerous, the government made a U-turn in December and opened up.

Infections and death numbers climbed as China reopened. And, yes, some might argue that China waited too long to re-open. Maybe six months too long; maybe nine months too long. And yes, the initial opening saw quite a bit of chaos as hospitals scrambled to accommodate patients and pharmacies ran out of cold medicines. But remember, this is a country of 1.4 billion people!

When Covid is finally over and we look back and examine it in totality, I believe China's record would be among the best in the world, i.e., the lowest deathrate and the least damage to its economy.

Notes

1. Li, Eric X. "Western Media Is Still Wrong. China Will Continue to Rise." *The Washington Post*. 24 Oct. 2017.
2. "China's Sort of Freedom." *The Economist*. 17 Oct. 1992.
3. "Out of the Shadow of Deng." *The Economist*. 18 Sept. 1997.
4. "China's Future: Troubles Ahead for the New Leaders." *The Economist*. 14 Nov. 2002.
5. "The Mysterious Mr Hu." *The Economist*. 18 Oct. 2007.
6. "Xi Jinping: The Man Who Must Change China." *The Economist*. 27 Oct. 2012.
7. "Xi Jinping Has More Clout Than Donald Trump. The World Should Be Wary." *The Economist*. 14 Oct. 2017.
8. Mu, Chunshan. "Foreign Media Face a Trust Crisis in China." *The Diplomat*. 16 Jul. 2021.
9. Daniel, Griffiths. "The International Media Coverage of China: Too Narrow an Agenda?" *Reuters Institute Fellow's Paper*, 2013.
10. This is an adaptation from the column in South China Morning Post. See: Li, Eric X. "No 'How-To' Book from the West Can Curb Corruption in China." *South China Morning Post*. 13 Aug. 2013.
11. Barboza, David. "Billions in Hidden Riches for Family of Chinese Leader." *The New York Times*. 25 Oct. 2012.
12. Eryuehe. *Eryuehe Talks About Anti-Corruption [二月河说反腐]*. People's Publishing House, 2015, pp. 13–14.
13. "Visualizing China's Anti-Corruption Campaign." *ChinaFile*. Retrieved in 2018 from: http://www.chinafile.com/infographics/visualizing-chinas-anti-corruption-campaign.
14. Johnston, Michael. *Syndromes of Corruption: Wealth, Power, and Democracy*. Cambridge UP, 2005, pp. 17–23.
15. Ibid.

16. MacIntyre, Andrew. "Institutions and the Political Economy of Corruption in Developing Countries." In *Workshop on Corruption, Stanford University*, vol. 31. 2003.
17. Williams, James W., and Beare, Margaret E. "The Business of Bribery: Globalization, Economic Liberalization, and the 'Problem' of Corruption." *Crime, Law and Social Change*, vol. 32, no. 2, 1999, pp. 115–146; Rose-Ackerman, Susan. *Corruption and Government*. Cambridge University Press, p. 4.
18. Johnston, Michael. *Syndromes of Corruption: Wealth, Power, and Democracy*. Cambridge UP, 2005, pp. 42–43.
19. Saad, Lydia. Americans Not Holding Their Breath on Campaign Finance Reform. *Gallup News*. 11 Oct. 1997.
20. Johnston, Michael. *Syndromes of Corruption: Wealth, Power, and Democracy*. Cambridge UP, 2005, p. 67.
21. Fan articulates the expectation that intellectuals take moral responsibility to serve in his famous literary work "Memorial to Yueyang Tower" (先天下之忧而忧, 后天下之乐而乐). See: Fan, Zhongyan. *Memorial to Yueyang Tower [岳阳楼记]*. Beijing: Shijie tushu chuban gongsi, 2012.
22. MacDougald, Park. "The Surprising Relationship Between Corruption and Economic Growth." *Foreign Policy*. 16 Jul. 2013.
23. Huang, Yukon. *Cracking the China Conundrum: Why Conventional Economic Wisdom Is Wrong*. Oxford UP, 2017, pp. 106–108; Huang, Yukon. "The Truth About Chinese Corruption." *Carnegie Endowment for International Peace*. 29 May 2015.
24. In *2018 Edelman Trust Barometer*, China achieved the most significant increase in people's trust and rose to the top to the Trust Index. Edelman pointed out, the anti-corruption campaign following the 18th National People's Congress has improved the efficiency and transparency of government agencies. See: "Edelman Trust Barometer Executive Summary." 2018.
25. The term "cyber utopianism" first appeared in *Information Arts: Intersection of Art, Science, and Technology*, by Stephen Wilson, MIT Press, 2002, p. 477. It was further defined and popularized by Morzov. See: Morozov, Evgeny. *The Net Delusion: The Dark Side of Internet Freedom*, 2011.
26. Li, Eric X., and Yeo, George. "Globalization 2.0: China's Parallel Internet." *Huffington Post*. 20 Jan. 2012.

27. Breslau, Karen. "One Nation, Interconnected." *Wired*. 1 May 2000.
28. Lepore, Jill. "The Hacking of America." *The New York Times*. 14 Sept. 2018.
29. Kotkin, Stephen. "How Murdoch Got Lost in China." *The New York Times*. 4 May 2008.
30. Reporters without Borders. "Chinese Regime's True Face—One of the Worst Free Speech Predators." 9 Jan. 2018.
31. "China's Internet: A Giant Cage." *The Economist*. 6 Apr. 2013.
32. Clinton, Bill. "Speech on China Trade Bill." Paul H. Nitze School of Advanced International Studies, Johns Hopkins University, Washington, D.C., Speech, 8 Mar. 2000.
33. Bruni, Frank. "The Dangerous Safety of College." *The New York Times*. 11 Mar. 2017; Dwoskin, Elizabeth. "Ann Coulter Speech at UC Berkeley Canceled, Again, Amid Fears for Safety." *The Washington Post*. 26 Apr. 2017; "A War of Words on College Campuses." *CBS News*. 21 Jan. 2018.
34. Fukuyama, Francis. *Identity: The Demand for Dignity and the Politics of Resentment*. Farrar, Straus and Giroux, 2018, pp. 179–180.
35. Breslau, *Wired*, 2000.
36. Bennhold Katrin. "Mob Protests in Germany Show Vigor of Far Right." *The New York Times*. 31 Aug. 2018.
37. "Social Media: How Can Governments Regulate It?" *BBC*. 8 Apr. 2019.
38. Roose, Kevin. "Facebook and YouTube Give Alex Jones a Wrist Slap." *The New York Times*. 27 Jul. 2018.
39. Branigan, Tania. "Barack Obama Criticises Internet Censorship at Meeting in China." *The Guardian*. 16 Nov. 2009.
40. Wines, Michael. "Stance by China to Limit Google Is Risk by Beijing." *The New York Times*. 23 Mar. 2010.
41. Schuman, Michael. "Can China's Economy Thrive with a Censored Internet?" *Time*. 26 Oct. 2011.
42. Bao, Beibei. "How Internet Censorship Is Curbing Innovation in China." *The Atlantic*. 22 Apr. 2013.
43. Below is adapted from China's Parallel Universe, co-authored by Eric X. Li and George Yeo, originally published in SCMP in 2012.

44. Meeker, Mary. "Internet Trends 2018." *Kleiner Perkins*. 30 May 2018; Meeker, Mary. "KPCB Internet Trends (2011)." 18 Oct. 2011.
45. China's trade with the rest of the world grew about 40% between 2010 and 2018, although trade as a percentage of China's GDP has been significantly reduced. Data retrieved from: https://wits.worldbank.org.
46. Li, Eric X., and Yeo, George. "Globalization 2.0: China's Parallel Internet." *Huffington Post*. 20 Jan. 2012.
47. Wiener, Norbert. *Cybernetics or Control and Communication in the Animal and the Machine*. MIT Press, 1965, pp. 169–170.
48. Bill Davidow talked about how the Internet's "hyper-connection" can spread "contagions" like pandemics in his book. See: Davidow, William H. *Overconnected: The Promise and Threat of the Internet*. Open Road Media, 2011.
49. Ye, Tan. "The Train Collision Reflects Institutional Drawbacks [动车事故折射体制弊端]." *FT Chinese*. 26 Jul. 2011.
50. According to *Code for Design of High Speed Railway (TB10621-2009)*, high speed rail is defined as any railway whose operation speed exceeds 250 km/h. The railway in this accident did not meet that standard.
51. Moore, Malcolm. "Anger in China as Bodies 'Fall from Carriages' During Train Crash Clean-Up." *The Telegraph*. 25 Jul. 2011.
52. Chin, Josh. "Weibo Watershed? Train Collision Anger Explodes Online." *The Wall Street Journal*. 26 Jul. 2011.
53. He, Qinglian. "High-Speed Rail Accident Questioned the China Model [高铁事故拷问中国模式]." *BBC*. 29 Jul. 2011.
54. Clark, Nicola. "Low U.S. Rail Spending Leads to Poor Safety, Experts Say." *The New York Times*. 20 May 2015.
55. Li, Eric X. "China's Critics Don't Represent the Voice of the Chinese People." *The Christian Science Monitor*. 9 Aug. 2011.
56. Larson, Christina. "The People's Republic of Rumors." *Foreign Policy*. 8 Jul. 2011.
57. Fukuyama, *Identity*, 2018, pp. 115–123, 163–183.
58. Wong, Edward. "On Scale of 0 to 500, Beijing's Air Quality Tops 'Crazy Bad' at 755." *The New York Times*. 12 Jan. 2013; Fung, J., and Hunt, J. "China Seeks to Curb Worst Air Pollution in 50 Years." *The Guardian*. 18 Dec. 2013.

59. Wong, Herman. "2013 Will Be Remembered as the Year That Deadly, Suffocating Smog Consumed China." *Quartz*. 19 Dec. 2013.
60. "China to 'Declare War' on Pollution, Premier Says." *Reuters*. 5 Mar. 2014.
61. For full documentary: https://youtu.be/T6X2uwlQGQM.
62. Ghauri, Clare S. "China Announces Ten 'Tough Measures' to Combat Atmospheric Pollution." *The Climate Group*. 25 Jun. 2013.
63. Ten Measures: The Action Plan Was Issued by the State Council in 2013. For full-text, see: http://www.gov.cn/zwgk/2013-09/12/content_2486773.htm.
64. This section is taken from article written by the author for American Affairs. See: Li, Eric. "China and the Rule of Law." *American Affairs*, vol. 3, no. 3, 2019.
65. Talvitie, Antti. *Governance-the World Bank's Experience*. The World Bank, 1994.
66. China, Constitution. Constitution of the People's Republic of China (Adopted on December 4, 1982 by the Fifth National People's Congress of the People's Republic of China at its Fifth Session). Foreign Languages Press, 1983, p. 14.
67. Jiang Zemin's Report at the 15th National Congress of the Communist Party of China. 12 Sept. 1997. Full text available at: http://www.bjreview.com.cn/document/txt/2011-03/25/content_363499.htm.
68. Fourth Plenary Session of the 18th CPC Central Committee in 2014 was the first time for a Party session to center on rule of law. The general target is to form a system serving "the socialist rule of law with Chinese characteristics" and build a country under "the socialist rule of law". See: *Communiqué of the Fourth Plenary Session of the 18th Central Committee of the Communist Party of China*. 23 Oct. 2014.
69. Tamanaha, Brian Z. *On the Rule of Law: History, Politics, Theory*. Cambridge University Press, 2004, p. 55.
70. Dworkin, Ronald. *Law's Empire*. Harvard University Press, 1986, pp. 407–410.
71. Stolberg, Sheryl Gay. "Justice Anthony Kennedy's Tolerance Is Seen in His Sacramento Roots." *The New York Times*. 21 Jun. 2015.

72. Chemerinsky, Erwin. "Bush v. Gore Was Not Justiciable." *Notre Dame Law Review*, vol. 76, 2000, pp. 1093.
73. Fisher, Marc. "Behind Kavanaugh Fight, a National Struggle Over Trust, Identity and Sex Roles." *The Washington Post*. 27 Sept. 2018.
74. Tamanaha. *On the Rule of Law*, 2004, p. 7.
75. Shklar, Judith N. "Political Theory and the Rule of Law." *The Rule of Law: Ideal or Ideology*, vol. 1, no. 1, 1987.
76. Locke, John. *Locke: Two Treatises of Government*. Cambridge University Press, 1988, pp. 400–401.
77. Jenks, Edward. *The Myth of Magna Carta*, vol. 4, no. 14. 1904.
78. Tamanaha, Brian Z. "The History and Elements of the Rule of Law." *Singapore Journal of Legal Studies*, 2012, pp. 232–247.
79. Hobbes, Thomas. *Thomas Hobbes: Leviathan* (Longman Library of Primary Sources in Philosophy). Routledge, 2016, p. 184.
80. *The Oxford Handbook of Carl Schmitt*. Ed. Jens Meierhenrich and Oliver Simons. Oxford UP, 2017.
81. Schmitt, Carl. *Constitutional Theory*. Trans. and Ed. Jeffrey Seitzer. Duke UP, 2008, p. 125.
82. Schmitt, Carl. *Political Theology: Four Chapters on the Concept of Sovereignty*. Trans. G. Schwab. University of Chicago Press, 2005, pp. 29–35.
83. Tamanaha. *On the Rule of Law*, 2004, pp. 25, 57.
84. Ibid., pp. 115–117.
85. "CPC Sets New Blueprint for Rule of Law." *China.org.cn*. 23 Oct. 2014.
86. Aristotle. *Politics*. Trans. Benjamin Jowett. Oxford UP, 1963, p. 140.
87. Aristotle. *On Rhetoric: A Theory of Civic Discourse*. Trans. A. K. George. Oxford UP, 2006, pp. 31–33.
88. Aristotle. *Nicomachean Ethics*. Ed. and Trans. Roger Crisp. Cambridge UP, 2012, pp. 113–114.
89. De Montesquieu, Charles. *Montesquieu: The Spirit of the Laws*. Eds. Anne M. Cohler, Basia Carolyn Miller, and Harold Samuel Stone. Cambridge UP, 1989, p. 157.
90. Bentham, Jeremy, and Hart, Herbert Lionel Adolphus. *Of Laws in General*, vol. 177. London: Athlone Press, 1970; Manning, John F. "Justice Scalia and the Idea of Judicial Restraint." *Michigan Law Review*, vol. 115, 2016.

91. Kaplan, David A. *The Most Dangerous Branch: Inside the Supreme Court's Assault on the Constitution*. Crown, 2018, p. 347.
92. Ibid., p. 96.
93. Xiao, Yang. "Singapore Academy of Law Annual Lecture 2003: Economic Development and Legal Evolution in China." *Singapore Academy of Law Journal*, vol. 16, no. 1, 2004, p. 1.
94. Ji, Weidong. "The Judicial Reform in China: The Status Quo and Future Directions." *Indiana Journal of Global Legal Studies*, vol. 20, no. 1, 2013.
95. "Meng Jianzhu: The Intelligent Judicial Assistance System Will Not Replace Judge's Independent Judgement [孟建柱: 智能辅助办案系统不替代司法人员独立判断]." *ChinaNews.com*. 11 Jul. 2017.
96. Laski, Harold J. *The Rise of European Liberalism*. Routledge, 2018, p. 153.
97. Strauss, Leo. *Natural Right and the History*. University of Chicago, 1953, p. 234.
98. Dicey, Albert Venn, and Wade, Emlyn Capel Stewart. *Introduction to the Study of the Law of the Constitution*, 1915.
99. Hayek, Friedrich A. *The Road to Serfdom: Text and Documents: The Definitive Edition*. Routledge, 2014, pp. 80–111; Hayek, Friedrich A. *Law, Legislation and Liberty: The Mirage of Social Justice*, 1978 ed., vol. 2. University of Chicago, 1976, pp. 62–100; Hayek, Friedrich A. *The Political Ideal of the Rule of Law*, 1955.
100. "Urban–Rural Gap of Annual Disposable Income Narrowed in 2016." *Xinhua News*. 20 Jan. 2017; Tobin, Damian. "Inequality in China: Rural Poverty Persists as Urban Wealth Balloons." *BBC News*. 29 Jun. 2011.
101. See Xi Jinping's report at 19th CPC National Congress. 18 Oct. 2017.
102. "China's Constitution Amendments to Have Far-Reaching Influence." *People.cn*. 28 Dec. 2003.
103. "Zhang Weiying: Restricting Government Taxation Is a Precondition of a Society Based on Rule of Law [张维迎: 法治社会前提条件是对政府征税的约束]." *Caijing*, 2011; Wu, Jinglian. "Finding Road to Prosperity from *Rise of Great Powers* [从《大国崛起》看各国富强之道]." *Tongzhou Gongjin*, vol. 4, 2007; Mao, Yushi. "Do

Not Have Blind Faith in SOEs [不要再迷信国企]." *FTChinese.* 29 Dec. 2018.
104. Waldron, Jeremy. "Is the Rule of Law an Essentially Contested Concept (in Florida)?" *The Rule of Law and the Separation of Powers.* Routledge, 2017, pp. 117–144.
105. Gallie, Walter Bryce. "Essentially Contested Concepts." *Proceedings of the Aristotelian Society.* Wiley, 1955, pp. 167–198.
106. Lewis, Mark Edward. *The Early Chinese Empires: Qin and Han*, vol. 1. Harvard UP, 2009, p. 30.
107. Ibid., p. 19.
108. Zhao, Dingxin. *The Confucian-Legalist State: A New Theory of Chinese History.* Oxford UP, 2015, pp. 52–55.
109. Ibid., p. 275.
110. Ibid., pp. 262–294.
111. For example, Mencius held that the murder of the tyrannical last king of the Shang was the punishment of the outcast rather than regicide. See: *Mencius*: Book I Part B.
112. Tamanaha. *On the Rule of Law*, 2004, p. 24.
113. For a detailed historic explanation of this Confucian-legalist tradition, see: Michael Loewe, *The Government of Qin and Han Empires: 221 BCE–220 CE*, 2006; Zhao Dingxin, *The Confucian-Legalist State: A New Theory of Chinese History*; and from a liberal perspective, Doh Chull Shin, *Confucianism and Democratization in East Asia*, 2011; Joseph R. Levenson, *Confucian China and Its Modern Fate.*
114. For examples, see: Wang, Jing. The Legalization of Morality in Ancient China (zhongguo gudai daode falvhua yanjiu). Diss. Hebei University, 2008.
115. Dworkin, Ronald. "Political Judges and the Rule of Law." *Arguing About Law.* Routledge, 2013, pp. 193–211.
116. Tamanaha. *On the Rule of Law*, 2004, p. 84.
117. See: Sandel, Michael J. *Liberalism and the Limits of Justice*; MacIntyre, Alastair. *After Virtue*; Piketty, Thomas. *Capital in the 21st Century*; Murry, Charles. *Coming Apart*; Putnam, Robert D. *Bowling Alone.*
118. Confucius. *The Book of Rites (li ji).* Intercultural Press, p. 100.
119. Cohen, Jerome A. "A Looming Crisis for China's Legal System." *Foreign Policy*, 22 Feb. 2016.

120. Wang, Jiangyu. "The Rule of Law in China: A Realistic View of the Jurisprudence, the Impact of the WTO, and the Prospects for Future Development." *Singapore Journal of Legal Studies*. Dec. 2004. Lau, Lawrence J. "From the Economy to Judicial Reform, China Is Settling into a 'New Normal'." *South China Morning Post*. 15 Mar. 2017.
121. Shigong, Jiang. "A Farewell to National Law Monism: The Confusion of Qiuju and Reconstruction of Legal Pluralism [告别国家法一元论——秋菊的困惑与大国法治道路]." *Dongfang Journal*, no. 2, 2018.
122. One example is the case of Yu Huan, who killed a loan shark who had sexually taunted his mother. His case made national headlines and ignited heated online debate. Finally, he had his life sentence cut to five years following a retrial. See: "China Slashes Murder Sentence in Loan-Shark Killing Case." *Reuters*. 23 Jun. 2017. Another example is the case of Lu Yong, a leukemia patient. He imported a generic version of Glivec, patented by Novartis, for himself and fellow patients. In 2003 he was arrested for illegally distributing the unapproved drug, but was acquitted in 2015 after an outpouring of public support. His story was made into the hit film Dying to Survive, raising public sympathy to cancer patients. See: Kuo, Lily. "Popular Cancer Drug Film Prompts China to Speed Up Price Cuts." *The Guardian*. 19 Jul. 2018.
123. Dworkin, Ronald. "Political Judges and the Rule of Law." *Arguing About Law*. Routledge, 2013, pp. 193–211.
124. For detailed analysis of this phenomenon, see: Zhu, Suli. *Rule of Law and Its Indigenous Resources [法治及其本土资源]*; Jiang Shigong, *A Farewell to National Law Monism: The Confusion of Qiuju and Reconstruction of Legal Pluralism [告别国家法一元论——秋菊的困惑与大国法治道路]*.
125. Peerenboom, Randall. *China's Long March Towards the Rule of Law*. Cambridge University Press, 2002, pp. 587–588.
126. See: Topaloff, Liubomir K. "Is COVID-19 China's 'Chernobyl Moment'?" *The Diplomat*. 4 Mar. 2020. Cheshire, Tom. "I Lived Through China's COVID Lockdowns for the Best Part of Three Years—It's a Miserable Existence." *Sky News*. 29 Nov. 2022. Toh, Michelle. "How China's Lockdowns Are Taking a Toll on Global Companies." *CNN*. 10 May 2022. Madhok, Diksha.

"From Apple to Disney, China's Covid Curbs Are Again Hurting Business." *CNN*. 4 Nov. 2022.
127. Li, Eric. "Xi Jinping Is a 'Good Emperor'." *Foreign Policy*. 14 May 2020.
128. As of December 28, China has a total of 101,683 confirmed cases of Covid-19 and 4636 cumulative deaths. Globally, the cumulative number of confirmed cases exceeded 280 million, and the number of deaths exceeded 5.4 million. Data retrieved from: http://www.gov.cn/xinwen/2021-12/31/content_5665 689.htm.
129. In 2020, China was the only major economy expanded, its GDP grew by 2.3%. In 2021, China's GDP grew by 8.1%, at its fastest in 10 years. See: "China GDP: Economy Ends Coronavirus-Ravaged Year with Strong Growth Surge." *South China Morning Post*. 18 Jan. 2021; "2021: China's GDP Growth Beats Expectations with 8.1%, Fastest in 10 years." *CGTN*. 17 Jan. 2022.

CHAPTER 9

China, the Liberal International Order, and the Future of Globalization

The world is evidently at a critical juncture in so many ways. China's oversized position in it will no doubt affect the future. What does China's development mean for the world and the order of the world? Here, we also encounter gross misrepresentations and misunderstandings. In this last chapter I present, only in broad strokes, how China, if properly understood and related to, could play a constructive role. And, unfortunately, the opposite would hold true as well.

It was a balmy evening in late August 2018. VIP guests, a who's who of the movie industry, uncomfortable in tuxedos and gowns, crowded into the theater for the opening film of the Venice Film Festival. It was the world premiere of "The First Man," the story of Neil Armstrong and the Apollo landing. Beset by jet lag, I slouched into my seat, planning to doze off unnoticed as soon as the theater went dark. I knew the story; I knew how it would end. It would be hard not to fall asleep.

But I was surprised. The film kept me on the edge of my seat for two hours and twenty minutes, my heart pumping fiercely at times. The acting was superb; the plot, although familiar, was filled with intense moments of suspense. But for me, the best part was seeing an America I never knew before.

It was an America that was secure in its own innate abilities and felt no need to shout its greatness to the world. The story showed an American ethos that championed community, strength, and self-reliance—not

© The Author(s), under exclusive license to Springer Nature 197
Singapore Pte Ltd. 2023
E. Li, *Party Life*, https://doi.org/10.1007/978-981-99-4522-1_9

rivals' weakness. The American people in the story—elite and ordinary—truly sacrificed for the collective. American politics enabled the country to lay out a national plan and rallied citizens around it in the face of external threats and despite internal divisions. This was in such contrast to today's American society wherein political and commercial powers enrich themselves while sending the sons and daughters of commoners to die in far-flung lands. The film's footage featured U.S. President John F. Kennedy's impassioned call-to-arms, "we choose to go to the moon in this decade and do the other things, not because they are easy, but because they are hard."[1]

My exposure to America began in the waning years of the Reagan era, when "government [was] not the solution ... government [was] the problem."[2] Since then, America has sped into overdrive propelling the individual to ever ascending heights—community and the collective be damned. Liberalism on steroids has also been sold around the world, wrapped in the package of liberal democracy and market capitalism—the universalization of these twin forces has dominated globalization.

Just over 30 years into this grand project, liberalism is combusting from within and is besieged from without. The same summer "The First Man" premiered, Rafael Reif, President of MIT, wrote an op-ed for the *New York Times* about the U.S.-China trade war. In it, he essentially called on Americans to stop whining. Yes, China might have taken some U.S. intellectual property. But most technological innovation in China, he argued, was indigenous. China was racing ahead on many fronts, such as 5G, mobile payments, quantum computing, artificial intelligence, and high-speed rail—all homegrown. What America needed to do, wrote Reif, was to get its act together and compete. His to-do list was long: invest in R&D and education, develop national science policies, attract more talent, build better infrastructure.[3]

I showed Reif's op-ed to one of the most senior American political figures. "Look, this is coming from the President of MIT," I said. "Maybe you should stop scapegoating China and focus on rebuilding your own strengths and compete."

"He is absolutely right!" he replied. "But you know, given our politics now, we are not going to be able to do any of these things."

Such loss of confidence in American political institutions is widespread. Trust in government is at an all-time low. Even the judiciary, which used to be immune to political polarization, is seeing its prestige spiral downward.[4] So much so that John Roberts, the Chief Justice of the U.S.

Supreme Court, publicly denounced U.S. President Donald Trump for saying that judges were political. "We do not have Obama judges or Trump judges, Bush judges or Clinton judges,"[5] Roberts said. But, of course, anyone who has watched the process of selecting justices for the high bench would know that Trump was right.

In the quarter century since globalization, both the United States and China have made tremendous economic gains. China, starting from a low base and with a population four times as large, gained more on relative terms. (Between China's accession to WTO in 2002[6] to 2017, it's GDP grew from $1.47 trillion to $12.24 trillion.) But the United States, already the world's wealthiest nation before globalization, also made enormous gains, not much less than China's on absolute terms. (Over the same time, its GDP grew from $10.98 trillion to $19.39 trillion.[7]) Measured by a per capita basis, Americans actually did better—their gains contained much more profit. That's because China's growth was mostly based on lower-end manufacturing, which received a much smaller share of value-added production. Perhaps the most illustrative example was found with the iPhone. When Apple first began to make iPhones in China in 2007, it generated an average revenue of $237.45 per phone for manufacturers. Only 3.6% ($8.46) of that revenue stayed in China.[8]

Yet there's another set of numbers that points to a mind-boggling reality: China's GDP grew eight times during this period of globalization, with its disposable income per capita growing nearly six times.[9] In America, the median household income had stagnated or even declined—and that was despite the slow but sustained decade of recovery since the 2008 financial crisis and near full-employment.[10] Meanwhile, American workers' job security and welfare declined markedly.[11] Where had all the money gone?

It went to the elite oligarchy of America liberalism: those very few who own and deploy capital and technology on global scales. They have come to control the U.S.' politics and economy and, by extension, much of the world's economy. Together, Wall Street and Silicon Valley might not even employ one million people—waiters and nannies included. But they reaped, and are keeping, most of the rewards of globalization and technological advancement.[12]

It isn't just stagnant incomes that have shattered the American middle class. Through globalization and technology, this oligarchy has ripped apart American communities in the unending pursuit to maximize their own economic gains. The loss of the post-World War II way of life has left American communities destitute and families broken.[13] Fifty thousand Americans kill themselves every year,[14] and another 33,000 die from the slow-motion suicide of opioid addiction.[15] Labor force participation has been declining steadily since the late 1990s. A federal count showed 7.2 million American men of prime working age had essentially dropped out of the workforce.[16]

This is unconscionable in the wealthiest country in the world. It is not an economic failure; it is a political one. Perhaps this is what people mean when they speak of making America great again. The American people want their country back from the financial and technology oligarchy.

Across the Atlantic, Europe's own oligarchy has been delivering exactly the same thing. In Britain, globalization transformed London into a cosmopolitan paradise. But since New Labor and its conservative successors entered government in 2010, the United Kingdom's public services have faced austerity, with spending cuts of up to 40 percent by 2020 in welfare, the National Health Services (NHS), and prisons. A further £12bn reduction in welfare spending was implemented by 2021, with more cuts for the NHS and prisons.[17] As a result, after a decade of austerity measures, spending on welfare benefits for the UK's poorest families shrank by nearly 25%, with a decrease of £37bn.[18] No wonder so many people rose up to take back political power—some in the form of Brexit and others—especially the young—in their public yearning for socialism.

On the Continent, elites in Berlin and Brussels impose their neoliberal economics and liberal ideology on the rest. Rebellions are bursting out everywhere. Poland and Hungary want control of their own borders. Italy wants control of its own economy. The French people periodically protest against their banker president—who was once heralded as the post-Trump world leader of liberalism, but is now revealed as out of touch with ordinary citizens. Even the compliant Germans have cut short the political life of Angela Merkel, one of the last stalwarts of the liberal *ancien regime.*

Liberalism is besieged on its own home turf, and both from the right and the left. Right-wing nationalist populism has become the dominant political force in the United States and several European countries, including Hungary, Poland, Austria, and even Germany. Socialist populism is rising from the left as well.

In their despair, and after intense introspection, these oligarchical elites and their coteries in the media finally had their epiphany: China did it to us!

On January 24, 2019, the grandee of global liberalism, the billionaire hedge fund mogul George Soros, showed up at Davos. His indictment of China reads like a Red Guard poster against capitalism during the Cultural Revolution. China is "undoubtedly the wealthiest, strongest and most developed in machine learning and artificial intelligence," he blustered. "This makes [President] Xi Jinping the most dangerous opponent of those who believe in the concept of open society." Invoking the specter of uncertainty on the question of global Internet governance, he proclaimed, "China wants to dictate rules and procedures that govern the digital economy by dominating the developing world with its new platforms and technologies," which "is a threat to the freedom of the Internet and, indirectly, open society itself."[19]

Meanwhile, David Brooks, the otherwise moderate *New York Times* columnist, named China as the enemy that could unify the left and the right.[20] His fellow columnist, Thomas Friedman, has regularly taken to the media to advocate confrontation with China. Perhaps he is so frustrated because China has refused to be flattened by his "flat world"?[21]

The United States has kept issuing national security assessments naming China, along with Russia, as major threats against American security.[22] It strains credulity that this is coming from a superpower with unmatched offensive nuclear capability with military bases dotting the globe—514 to be precise[23]—with a track record of invading more countries than all other nations combined in the past several decades. (To this day, the United States has never renounced the use of nuclear first strike.) China, on the other hand, remains a developing country with per capita income less than one-sixth of the United States.[24] and its military has not fired a single shot since 1985.[25]

In 2018, the Hoover Institution issued a report, "Chinese Influence and American Interests," co-chaired by Larry Diamond and Orville Schell. In the report, they warned of Chinese interference in various sectors of American government and society.[26] In their telling, Chinese students, academics, and businesspeople in America are all potential ideological threats. Even language schools like the Confucius Institutes are cause for concern. As Diamond put it in an op-ed for the *American Interest*, "this vast 'influence operations bureaucracy' is controlled by the highest levels of the party and state, with the aim of controlling the global narrative about China and preempting criticism of its domestic practices and international policies."[27]

Such arguments are actually laughable. If there is one area in which the Chinese party-state was utterly incompetent, it is the so-called "external propaganda"—*wai xuan*. For the longest time, every China commentator pointed to soft power as the one thing China lacked and least likely to acquire. And soft power was exactly what America and its liberal order had in abundance. As Joseph Nye, the originator of the idea, has written, American culture, ideals, and values have been extraordinarily important in helping Washington attract partners and supporters.[28]

Since when did the self-evidently superior liberal values of the West become so feeble as to be vulnerable to foreign students and language schools?

The Myth of Liberal Globalism

Today, it isn't Western liberal hubris that threatens world peace, but hubris turned paranoia. Just a few years ago, the warrior-priests of liberalism were so sure that they had found the "final form of human government"[29] that they took upon themselves to spread it by media, money, and military force. But now they claim that their invincible liberalism is besieged and that drastic measures—a Cold War or even a hot one—are needed to save it. How did that happen?

The answer is rather obvious. They managed to convince themselves that their final form of government was inherently and exclusively legitimate; liberal democracy and market capitalism were the only possible routes to prosperity and justice. Their efficacy was a foregone conclusion, whether they actually performed well or not.

If a CEO made such claims about his or her business model, we can be sure that the company would not be far from bankruptcy. But as the British political theorist John Dunn argued, the West, and the larger world for that matter, had fallen under "the spell" of liberal democracy.[30]

The unipolar moment after the Cold War deluded Western elites into thinking that liberal democracy and market capitalism were inevitably universal. But that moment was actually more like a bubble. And the bubble is bursting.

But fear need not replace hubris. American elites should be reminded that those who conceived of the republic—and those who struggled to maintain it over two centuries—were clear-headed about the enormous difficulties ahead of them. They understood liberal democracy's innate problems and precarious future. As Harvard's Graham Allison has pointed out, when Abraham Lincoln asked in his Gettysburg address whether liberal democracy could "long endure," it was not a rhetorical question. Americans would be well advised to listen to Allison's assessment of the current state of American political institutions:

> No one denies that in its current form, the U.S. government is failing. Long before Trump, the political class that brought unending, unsuccessful wars in Afghanistan, Iraq, and Libya, as well as the financial crisis and Great Recession, had discredited itself. These disasters have done more to diminish confidence in liberal self-government than Trump could do in his critics' wildest imaginings, short of a mistake that leads to a catastrophic war. The overriding challenge for American believers in democratic governance is thus nothing less than to reconstruct a working democracy at home.[31]

His assessment can be safely applied to the governments in Berlin, Brussels, London, and Paris.

Excessive insecurity on the part of the United States and its Western allies is not only damaging their domestic politics, but also poisoning international relations, particularly with China. Beginning with U.S. President Barack Obama's "pivot to Asia," the increasingly contentious relationship between the United States and China has been aggravated by Western revisionism, best summarized by Kurt Campbell, the National Security Council Coordinator for the Indo-Pacific in the Biden administration, in an article co-authored with Ely Ratner, in *Foreign Affairs*.[32]

Their story goes as follows: The United States made the "biggest and most optimistic bet" on China with Nixon's outreach in the early 1970s. This ambitious project continued for decades and accelerated with China's accession to the World Trade Organization in 2000. By bringing China into the so-called liberal rules-based international order, the West sought to induce China to gradually liberalize its politics and economy. In turn, China would move ever closer to the U.S.' political and economic vision.

But, argue Campbell and Ratner, China took advantage of its integration with the rest of the world in terms of trade, investment, and technology while steadfastly refusing to fulfill its promise of gradually becoming a full member of the order. Even worse than failing to uphold its end of the bargain, China used the order to become a major power intent on playing by its own rules. Although Beijing kept its intentions purposely ambiguous at first, since 2012 under Xi's leadership, China has declared outright its plan to pursue its own path. The West, in other words, was conned by China as it unwittingly helped incubate a formidable challenger to global liberalism.

Through this prism, everything China does is some form of ill-willed subversion that endangers world peace and prosperity. That's why China's 2016 establishment of the Asian Infrastructure Investment Bank (AIIB), to fill widely recognized deficiencies in existing international development lending met fierce resistance from the Obama administration. The Belt and Road Initiative (BRI), China's effort to build a modern silk road to spur integration and growth, is likewise seen as a major strategic threat because it offers alternative international arrangements.

I wrote in my response to the Campbell and Ratner essay that such assessments were based on false readings of history and a misunderstanding of the present and future of the world.

First, the idea that the opening between the West and China during and after the Cold War failed to change Chinese behavior is incorrect. U.S. President Richard Nixon's initiative to engage China did alter Chinese policies in the United States' favor by turning China into a de facto ally against the Soviet Union, which was arguably one of the most decisive factors in the outcome of the Cold War.[33]

Second, Beijing's participation in U.S.-led economic globalization has made China the world's largest contributor to global economic expansion. In turn, China has also played a significant stabilizing role in the global economy during times of distress. Chinese fiscal and monetary policies, for example, greatly contributed to the management of the global economy after both the Asian financial crisis in 1997 and the global financial crisis of 2008.[34] According to former U.S. Treasury Secretary Henry Paulson, the strong collaboration between U.S. and Chinese leaders was instrumental in persuading China not to sell U.S. securities during the 2008 financial crisis. This decision played a crucial role in preventing another Great Depression.[35]

Third, the post-war liberal, rules-based international order is a myth. The phrase is so long because it lumps together historic episodes and current realities. The post–World War II international order was centered on the United Nations, whose charter placed national sovereignty at the center of the international system. The Soviet Union, along with its allies, was a major enabler and participant of that order, which conferred no legitimacy to any ideology and specifically prohibited the use of military hegemony to enforce any particular international agenda. This was the kind of international order China signed on to after Nixon's outreach. And by most measures, China participated fully and constructively in the institutions it joined (as Campbell and Ratner even admitted).[36]

After the Cold War, however, the United States, followed by its Western allies, embarked on a grand project to rewrite the rules of the international system. As the writer Michael Lind recounted in an article in the *National Interest*,[37] it sought to transform its own position as the world's preeminent power into unchallenged hegemony that would allow it to unilaterally set and enforce rules for other sovereign states. And so, the United States, with its European allies, led a global campaign to universalize its liberal ideology. It even used economic and military means to induce and coerce other nations into ideological submission. In this, the United States and Europe became perhaps the most brazen and ambitious revisionist powers in recent history.

It is this revision of the post-WWII international order, with the misleading addition of the words "liberal" and "rules based," that China rejected. And its "no" was loud and clear from the get-go. In the decades since Deng Xiaoping launched his economic reforms, the Chinese have never missed a chance to strenuously and publicly reject liberal democracy and market capitalism. Ever since China decisively (and tragically) shut the door to Western universalism with the suppression of 1989's June 4th movement in Tiananmen Square, Western liberals have never stopped criticizing China for its refusal to accept their vision. It is disingenuous, then, for those same people to also accuse China of pretending that it did.

In his *Foreign Affairs* article, "The Myth of the Liberal Order," Allison sought to correct "an imagined past."[38] He pointed out that the "long peace" that followed World War II was not the result of some liberal order but the byproduct of the balance of power between the United States and the Soviets during the Cold War and the brief period of U.S. dominance after it. In fact, during the first four decades after the world war there was no global liberal order to speak of. On the contrary, the United States and its Western allies accommodated Soviet power, particularly in Eastern Europe. And that, not the liberal international order, was what kept the world at relative peace for many decades.

After the Cold War, the United States did enjoy a period of unmatched dominance, and it used that power, mostly in the form of economic inducements, to universalize liberalism. But, as Allison points out, the United States and its Western allies also used "military force to impose liberalism on countries whose governments could not strike back." As a result, after the Cold War, the world actually experienced more conflicts, mostly waged by the West, than during it.

Alas, the "End of History" pitch fooled not only the developing countries that adopted wholesale political and economic institutions that didn't work, but also, most ironically, the Westerners who sold it. The mirage of the "final form of human governance," as the political scientist Francis Fukuyama termed it, blinded Western societies from all of the liberal democracies' inherent problems; and worse, it convinced liberal democratic governments that they didn't need to win legitimacy through good performance since liberal democracy is inherently legitimate. As Western elites traveled around the world to tell everyone else that they needed reforms, they forgot that they could benefit from reforms too—and perhaps even more. Such internal neglect has led to today's dysfunction and decay.

Exacerbating the problem, the zeal to universalize liberal democracy has led to classic imperial overreach. Since the end of the Cold War, the United States has expended tremendous blood and treasure trying to force its political and economic vision onto others while its own industrial base was being hollowed out, its infrastructure fell into disrepair, its public education and health systems deteriorated, and its social fabric was torn apart. At the same time, its global misadventures have undermined the credibility of liberal democracy itself.

If Allison's accounting of the post-WWII long peace was correct, perhaps a balance of power that includes China would make the world environment more favorable to peace than a unipolar order. The strategic, political, and moral choices the American-led Western alliance and China make now will no double determine the fate of the twenty-first century. The choice is perhaps more in the hands of the West than China, simply because the former is the incumbent power. It has, essentially, two options: a new Cold War or "a world safe for diversity."[39]

COLD WAR II

Many in the United States are clamoring for a new Cold War with China. The urge is present both among the traditional political establishment, which consists of liberal interventionists and neo-conservatives, and the newly emergent nationalists represented by the Trump movement. The Biden administration claims that it is not seeking a new Cold War, but its actions certainly demonstrate plenty of Cold War approaches. These Americans should stop and think. Just because the United States won the last Cold War, does not mean it will win this one. In fact, as Lind wrote in the *National Interest*,[40] the odds are against the United States.

If I may draw an imperfect comparison just to provoke thoughts and stimulate debates, today's United States is, in many aspects, like the Soviet Union during the Cold War. Its social contract is in shambles, and its society has ossified. Its formerly large middle class is gradually sinking, and the political, economic, and social privileges that belong to the few are growing. Yet, its political institutions are grossly dysfunctional and incapable of making the reforms needed to meet these daunting challenges. Even its lauded market economy has stalled, and an old term—secular stagnation—has been trotted out to describe it.[41] Two years of Biden, with the Democratic Party controlling both the White House and the Congress, some necessary legislations were passed with huge fights and watered down with compromises. Now the United States is returning to divided government and more institutional dysfunctions are a virtual certainty.

Perhaps the most striking resemblance between the United States today and the Soviet Union during the Cold War is in the realm of ideology. Just like Soviet elites, American elites have been turning their country into a credo state. The new American creed rejects cultural integrity and problematic blood and soil nationalism. Instead, elites are defining America purely by the ideology of liberalism. The Soviet Union, too, was a classic credo state, albeit instead of liberalism, communism dominated national and cultural identities. But such systems are against human nature. Just like the Soviet creed could not suppress nationalism in the union's peripheral territories and even in Russia itself, the more American elites impose their ideology, the more the American people cling to their group identities (be they racial, religious, regional, gender, sexual orientation, or other).[42] In order to suppress identity politics, the elites prescribe more ideology. It becomes a vicious cycle that leads to more polarization and partisanship.

Another similarity with the Soviet Union is that, externally, as liberal democracy loses its luster around the world, the United States finds itself relying on its military might alone to project power. That, in turn, has led to its overuse. And military misadventures have begot a further weakening of American credibility, luring the superpower into yet more imperial overreach. The failure of U.S. military occupation of Afghanistan was the most recent example. Would the current ever deepening involvement in the Russia-Ukraine conflict be another?

Furthermore, the global environment in which America finds itself is totally different from that of the Cold War. During the Cold War, the line was clearly drawn between the Western and Soviet blocks. All of the United States' Western allies depended on it for their prosperity and even survival. The Soviet Union and its allies had virtually no economic links to the West. And there was no question that the U.S.-led Western bloc had a more vibrant economy than the Soviet one.

But the sides in today's new Cold War, if one does materialize, are enmeshed. And China, for its part, is in many ways even more integrated into the global economy than the United States. Being the largest trading nation in the world, and in history, China is the biggest trading partner of 124 countries—many of them U.S allies, compared with 76 for the United States.[43] China is seeking to deepen and expand its interconnectedness with the rest of the world through its BRI—a twenty-first-century Silk Road—by financing and building a web of roads, ports, and sea routes.[44]

When China launched the Asian Infrastructure Investment Bank (AIIB), to finance global infrastructure construction in 2016, it met determined resistance from the United States, which tried to scuttle the project. But it was America's closest ally, the United Kingdom that was the first major developed nation to break ranks with Washington and join the bank. Now many developing countries and a large majority of developed countries have joined,[45] while the United States has stayed out and kept up the pressure on other holdouts to stand firm. But recently, Italy and Switzerland have officially endorsed BRI.[46]

Even with the ever-increasing efforts by the United States to isolate China, European leaders, German chancellor Olaf Scholz being the first one to visit Beijing post 20th party congress and others might follow, are still continuing to engage.[47] What other options do they have? Their economies and social stability require them to continue to work with China.

This is even the case when conflicts turn into "hot war", as in Ukraine. The United States has been putting huge pressure on virtually all nations to join its sanctions on Russia. But amazingly, not just China and India refused, much of the global South also rejected the sanctions.[48]

That bodes ill for the United States if it insists on fighting a new Cold War against China. Most of the global South is not likely to pick America's side. And even some of its Western allies might sit on the fence. And unlike the USSR, China won't commit suicide. It might be the United States that does. Like the Soviet Union, the United States is consumed with intractable social, political, economic, and ethnic contradictions. And like the Soviet Union, it has decaying political and social institutions that are obviously incapable of solving these problems. Both attempted, perhaps as a sign of internal weakness, to aggressively impose their respective ideologies onto other countries worldwide; both find their military strength the most reliable in projecting power and have used it carelessly, courting disastrous defeats.

It is alarming to watch America, which only a short time ago faced the world with apparent total confidence, drawing down its own "iron curtain." After a nationwide scare over Russian election hacking, it now believes China is launching a "societal-wide" assault on its domestic affairs.[49] It is denying visas to Chinese scholars in international relations for fear that they might be spies or that their opinions could harm U.S. security.[50] It is forbidding its citizens to work for Chinese technology companies. A U.S. State Department official even took the American scholar Samuel Huntington's "clash of civilizations" thesis several steps further and publicly characterized the struggle with China a racial conflict. She referred to the conflict with the Soviet Union as "a fight within the Western family" and the rivalry with China as the first great power competition with a non-Caucasian power.[51] By this logic, as the columnist Fareed Zakaria wrote, we might also call the fight against the Nazis a mere family feud compared with a racial struggle with China.[52] These neo-Cold Warriors are inciting a clash of civilizations, and America, liberal democracy's final citadel, is fast losing all its cool.

One sure sign that the United States is losing confidence and submitting to fear is that its leaders, President Biden included, have resorted to rather emotional personal attacks on Xi Jinping himself.[53] This effort to demonize Xi is wholly unnecessary and counterproductive. Even in times of most heated disagreements, Chinese leaders have so far never made *ad hominem* attacks on U.S. leaders, not even on Trump. On the contrary, on a call, Xi Jinping calmly told Biden to cool down the feverish rhetoric about "democracy vs. authoritarianism" and work together to try to solve some real problems.[54]

China indeed is behaving more like America at the onset of the Cold War. It is focused on building its own national strength. Its political and social institutions, although not without significant problems, are by and large functional. Its people are relatively unified around the nation's goals, and it is not trying to sell, much less impose, its values or ideology onto others. Rather, it is merely trying to defend its own system against external ideological imposition by controlling its Internet and social institutions. This is akin to post-war America's focus on its own national wellbeing—on making liberal democracy safe and operable in America, not everywhere else,[55] and countering the ideological expansion of Soviet communism to that end.

It would be sad and unnecessary for America to choose, in this context, to launch a new Cold War that it will likely lose.

A World Safe for Diversity

At the height of the Cold War, a more confident America, facing an existential threat in the form of the Soviet Union, behaved very differently from today. Instead of paranoia, U.S. President John F. Kennedy called for "a world safe for diversity."[56] In that framework, Allison explains, the United States needed to adapt to the "reality that other countries have contrary views about governance and seek to establish their own international orders governed by their own rules."[57]

While accommodating diversity, Americans fundamentally believed in the effectiveness of their own political institutions, the efficacy of their social arrangements, and the attractiveness of their values. They could lead by example as a "shining city upon a hill," as U.S. President Ronald Reagan put it. It was perhaps this confidence, combined with the Soviet Union's loss of confidence in its institutions and values that contributed to America's victory in the Cold War.

Today's China is pointedly not engaged in any existential struggle with the United States (or the West in general, for that matter). As Professor Minxin Pei wrote, "China has neither the destructive capability nor the geopolitical motivation to destroy the U.S."[58] It would be better for everyone if the United States could restore confidence in its politics and society. After all, America retains formidable advantages for its development in the twenty-first century: its technological leadership, its entrepreneurial culture, its economic dynamism, and its ability to attract talents from around the world, to name just a few. If America would focus its energy on harnessing these assets and containing the ideological excesses of liberalism, it can surely compete effectively; and such competition would be constructive for the world. If the United States could fix its political dysfunction and restore social cohesion, it could really give China a run for its money; and that, I would argue, would be good even for China.

But if the United States chooses to expend precious resources on trying to stop China's development, spread its ideology around the world, maintain its costly and wholly unnecessary military-industrial complex, and periodically embark on ill-conceived military adventures, it would spell trouble for the world and court defeat for America itself. It would be better to focus on building one's own strength and allow different models of governance to flourish and compete on their own merits. In the process, if the world's nations are open-minded enough—not locked in ideological prisons—they might even be able to learn from each other.

It is rather unfortunate that in the present rivalry between the United States and China, Washington is making so many vehement demands for China to change its ways. In their trade negotiations, the Trump administration insisted that China curtail its support for its domestic industries. Washington claims that such practices give China unfair advantages. If Kennedy and Reagan were alive, they might wonder how America could have lost so much confidence in its free-market economics that it believes that it can only compete if its rival gives up its own, more effective model.

When China struggled its way out of the disastrous Cultural Revolution with its economic system in tatters, it did not demand that other countries give up market economics to level the playing field. Instead, it dramatically reformed its centrally planned economy and borrowed many Western best practices in the process. Wouldn't the United States be better off if it could find the courage to do the same? It need not even look to China. It can find in its own recent history examples of government-led collective endeavors that propelled the nation to greatness. The Apollo Moon landing, the building of the Interstate Highways, state underwriting of home ownership for virtually the entire middle class, to name just a few. All those were tremendous successes that took place before neoliberal ideology choked America's ability to adapt and reform.

When China began its reform era 40 years ago, Deng had confidence that the Chinese party-state could survive and even flourish by learning from others. He has been proven right. Does Biden, along with the rest of the American political and economic establishment, have confidence enough to loosen the ideological shackles of liberalism and learn from others and from their country's own past experiences?

We would all be better off if they did. If the word "diversity" is too charged, perhaps we can use a different one—pluralism—to remind us of what Kennedy meant. Can we abandon ideological rigidity and allow different countries to pursue their own development paths, to explore their own models of governance? Can we learn from each other? A world safe for pluralism would make the twenty-first century more peaceful and vibrant.

Globalism's Death and Globalization's Renewal

More than 30 years after the end of the Cold War, what seemed unstoppable has been stopped: globalization has run aground. Brexit and Trump's election as U.S. President effectively spelled the end of Anglo-Saxon-driven globalization. The United States and China are engaged in fierce trade and technology rivalries. What the historian Niall Ferguson termed Chimerica, the partnership between the United States and China that provided the comprehensive economic structure for globalization,[59] is no more. What was billed as a tremendous success of globalization—the European Union—is in trouble, with anti-globalization forces taking hold, or even taking power, in virtually all of its member states.

Perhaps it is time to reassess. Here, it is important to note the conceptual distinction between globalization and globalism. Globalization started as a rather practical concept in the 1970s, when the world was becoming increasingly connected through trade, investment, travel, and information.[60] But after the Cold War, globalization was injected with ideology, turning it into globalism. And now one can hardly distinguish between the two.[61]

Globalism is essentially the universalization of liberalism. It is rooted in the neoliberal doctrine of the Washington Consensus, which was carried out around the world by the Bill Clinton, George W. Bush, and Barack Obama administrations, along with some of their European counterparts.

The foot soldiers of globalism were the world's cosmopolitan commercial, media, and intellectual elites, whom Huntington termed "Davos Man."[62] Davos Men envisioned a world moving inextricably toward the adoption of a unified set of rules and standards in economics, politics, and international relations. National borders would gradually lose relevance and even disappear. Cultural distinctions would give way to universal values. Liberal democracy and market capitalism would spread the world over. Liberalism in all its facets would finally reign supreme.[63]

But it was not to be so. Globalism's ideological zeal led it astray. Despite all the economic wealth that has been created in the past quarter century, disillusionment is the norm almost everywhere. Countries that went through major political upheavals to conform to globalism, such as those of the so-called Arab Spring and various color revolutions, are mired in disorder and poverty. Even more notable is the intense backlash in the developed countries where globalism originated. Western countries have not only failed to share the economic gains from globalization equitably around the world, but also have produced vast inequality and social dislocation at home. As the American economist Jeffrey Sachs said, "I come from a country that not only doesn't care about the world's poor, it doesn't even care about its own poor!".[64]

And so, the United States seems to have a split personality. The liberal globalist elites who still control the media and many levers of government are behaving like revelers on a sinking Titanic, continuing their universalizing crusade. The State Department keeps printing its world human rights report as if it's a best seller. But Trump couldn't care less about any of that. Instead, he teared down liberal institutions, both domestically and internationally. In his administration's efforts to counter China's rise, for example, it began to close off America's so-called open society and gutted the WTO. The Biden administration pronounced that "America is back".[65] But its actions point to mere extensions of Trump's postures in substance. So many "America-First"-like provisions were in Biden's legislations that even the Europeans are complaining vehemently.[66] How are the liberals of the world going to universalize their values when their survival in their own countries is very much in doubt?

Globalism is dead, though few realize it because the corpse is so well dressed. The question is, can globalization find a way to continue? That's hard to say. But the normative answer is that it must. Going backwards would be costly and, perhaps, catastrophic. A violent stop to increasing interconnectedness would cause tremendous disruption; in some ways, recent attempts to reverse course already have. If iron curtains are drawn everywhere, conflicts would become the norm. It is up to us to avoid a repeat of the history of the first half of the last century.

A look back to the era of "Warring States" is helpful. That was a tumultuous time in ancient China before the Qin Emperor unified the country in 221 BC. It was a period when various kingdoms pursued their own interests with naked hard power. There were many violent wars, similar to European history before Westphalia and, of course, until after World War II.

To avoid descending into the same abyss, China has put forward a proposition, though not yet well articulated. But it deserves attention.

Globalization needs a new vision, a reincarnation. China, being the only major country in the world to have successfully engaged in globalization while resolutely rejecting globalism, is in a unique position to save the former. Davos Men cheered when Xi gave the keynote address at their annual gathering in January 2017 and advocated for the continuation of globalization in face of widespread reactionary pressures. But if they thought China would take up the banner of globalism, they were badly mistaken. In his entire address, he used the word "globalization" 24 times, but virtually never without the qualification "economic" before it. The Chinese position has always been clear, it was not globalization that caused many of the world's current problems. Rather, the problem was globalism carried to excess—by the very Davos Men in Xi's audience.[67]

So, how will China's idea save globalization? Here, I attempt to articulate a conceptual prototype:

> Globalization increases interconnectivity and interdependence among the nations and peoples of the world, improves economic productivity, and is therefore conducive to peace and prosperity for all. Globalism, which is globalization infused with the ideology of liberalism, has underdelivered and, in many cases, also caused harm, instability, and economic stagnation in both developed and developing countries. If globalization is to succeed and benefit more people, Western countries must separate it from their own norms and values. The primacy of culture and the sovereignty of nations must be the basis upon which globalization is carried out. Nations must be allowed the space to pursue their own development paths. On this basis, nations may compete on the merits of their own ways. And they may cooperate based on their own interests.

A Message to the Populist-Nationalists[68]

The populist-nationalist movements that are sweeping the world have brought globalization to this historic juncture. Anti-globalist and anti-liberal forces have gained large followings and even governing majorities in many major developed and developing countries: Austria, Brazil, Egypt, Hungary, India, Italy, the Philippines, Poland, Russia, Thailand, the United Kingdom, and the United States. They are surging even in France and Germany.

Some of them seem to target China as a potential enemy; former Trump ideologue Steve Bannon sounds most vehement. But he, and others like him, are misguided. China has succeeded in the globalization process precisely because it rejected the liberal doctrine that the populist-nationalist movements seek to overturn in their own countries. For many decades, long before Trump, China was the lone champion of national sovereignty in face of the globalists' liberalism. The fact that China successfully resisted globalist encroachments into its domestic affairs while achieving its development goals is the reason populist-nationalist movements don't exist there; there is no need.

The countries that are going through such upheavals are ones that have suffered the excesses of globalism and are seeking redress. In this context, leaders looking to restore national sovereignty will find China to be supportive of many of their goals. China would no doubt cheer other countries' efforts to regain control of their borders and determine their own immigration policies, for instance. Consider that it was the only major world power to provide moral and material support to Philippines' former President Rodrigo Duterte's anti-drug campaign.[69]

China also supports Hungarian Prime Minister Viktor Orban, another leading figure in the counter-globalist movement. On his visit to Beijing in 2017 to promote building railway links to increase trade between China and Central Europe, Viktor Orban had the following to say: "We need to see eye to eye without asking the other side to change themselves.... The West (should not believe that it) represents a superior ideal and expects other parts of the world to adopt international doctrines reflecting that .... China's political system is up to the Chinese, while Hungary's is up to Hungarians.... Nobody has the right to interfere as a self-appointed judge."[70]

In 2019, Italy's populist-nationalist coalition government made that country the first major developed economy to officially endorse BRI.[71]

It would be wise for American conservatives to see that the United States is much more at risk of being subsumed by their own Frankenstein liberal universal order than by China. The same applies to virtually all populist-nationalist political forces around the world. These movements must put forth a positive agenda. For now, they are mostly reacting to liberal excesses. If they remain so, they are at risk of taking the world backwards. And that would be a monumental betrayal of the people who put them in power.[72]

In his address to the United Nations General Assembly in 2017, Trump put forward a positive vision: "strong, sovereign nations let diverse countries with different values, different cultures, and different dreams not just coexist but work side by side on the basis of mutual respect."[73] This has been China's worldview all along. And it would be the strongest potential ally in ushering in a new international order that furthers a more constructive globalization. Would the next generation of American conservatives hold true to that vision?

A Message to the Liberal Globalists

The message to the liberal globalist establishment is a much simpler one: You have overdone it. It's time to reflect and reform.

The globalist establishment has been running the world for more than 30 years. Some of the globalists are well intentioned, and there is no doubt that the globalization they facilitated produced significant economic gains. However, their project has now collapsed under the weight of their own hubris, aggression, and greed.

The hubris came from the post-Cold War conviction in the infallibility of liberal democracy and market capitalism. Infallible ideas brook no dissent and instinctively reject the need for reform. This is why, even in the face of mounting evidence that the liberal program was failing in a vast number of countries that adopted it, globalists are still stuck to their dogma. Now they are being undermined or even overthrown by domestic forces using the very electoral system they designed and believed was perfect.

Extreme hubris leads to extreme behavior, including both military and economic aggression. Illegal invasions of sovereign nations were carried out at large scale. Destructive economic policies were imposed on countries that had no choice but to accept them. The IMF did it to many developing countries, and the EU did it to its own member states. In recent years, the United States has weaponized its control of the global financial system to punish nations, businesses, and even private individuals whom they believe are undermining their dominance.

Some liberals in the West have now, in their despair, taken to seek an alliance with their populist-nationalist nemesis to pin the blame for their system's failures on China. The notion that China rigged the game is misguided. China succeeded because it rejected globalism. In all likelihood, it would have failed if it followed the lead of post-Soviet Russia and many other developing countries in their headlong conversion to the Washington Consensus.

It is time for sensible liberal globalists to stop and reflect. Their movement's excesses have not only caused harm to developing countries around the world, they have now come back to destroy liberalism at home. Corporate greed has cut down the U.S. middle class, which was the bedrock of America's own liberal society. The French philosopher Bernard-Henri Levy, one of the world's most radical advocates of the universalization of Western values, led the intellectual drive to champion the European and American invasion of Libya—the collapse of which directly created the refugee crisis that might have irreversibly damaged liberalism in Europe. Such ironies still have not woken up many Western elites, certainly not Levy himself. He is now deep inside Ukraine, cheering on that war with his same old moral-crusade rhetoric.[74] It would be advisable for them to work on the three characteristics that drove them to the present predicament: hubris, aggression, and greed.

It is now abundantly clear that liberal democracy is not the final form of human government. Without significant reforms, it may not even be viable in the twenty-first century. And if liberal democracy perishes, the world will be worse off. Our century would be best served if there are multiple forms of political governance that are viable for their respective countries.

Liberalism, for all its faults and excesses, is a natural outgrowth of Western cultural development and can therefore be a suitable philosophy for the West, if it can be effectively reformed. But Western liberal elites need a change of mindset. They need to admit that liberal democracy, along with market capitalism, is not infallible and do not command inherent moral legitimacy. Only if they can do that, can meaningful reforms take place. At the same time, their efforts to universalize their political model and values must stop. They need to work hard to make liberal democracy work at home before trying to export it. Last but not least, they need to let go of some of the gains they reaped from globalization to share it more equitably within their own societies. That way, they will be able to rebuild their societies and public trust in institutions.

There are signs that reexaminations are beginning to take place among some Western intellectuals. Caroline Winterer, in her book, American Enlightenments, demonstrated an historic account that differed from the contemporary narrative of liberalism.[75] The story of a singular strand of modern universal ideas that began in Europe, flourished in the American revolution, and culminated in the twentieth-century American success was actually a myth concocted during the Cold War to serve the West's ideological needs. Winterer presented the modern era in her rendition of "Enlightenments"—plural—as an amalgamation of diverse and even conflicting ideas and experiences. At this moment, after the 2008 financial crisis and the Covid-19 debacle, after American troops left Afghanistan following 19 years of fruitless war, and as the United States and NATO are deepening their involvement in a dangerous military conflict with Russia in Ukraine, her suggestions might be more useful to the West than ever:

> The legacy of enlightenment for Americans is not so much of providing definitive answers and being sure about the rightness of our political ideals, as the narrative of a grand "American Enlightenment" proposes. Instead, the legacy of enlightenment in America is of asking important questions about our world—about nature, society, and government—and of being modest about our abilities to agree on what is true and good for Americans and for others. It seems to me that this is a more useful version of enlightenment for Americans today than a dusty mausoleum of self-evident truths.[76]

Meanwhile, there may be a thing or two Western liberals can learn from China's experience. They have been so steeped in the dogma of neoliberal politics that they might be blind to alternatives. China has demonstrated that state capacity can be deployed to solve big problems and over reliance on the market can be destructive. China has also shown that strengthening the political autonomy of executives can be conducive for effective reforms. Excessive focus on checks and balances—and branding any attempt at strong leadership as authoritarianism or autocracy—have led to decay in the West.

Stop preaching and invading, start reflecting, maybe even learning!

Globalization's Renewal

One of the globalists' better traits is their genuine desire to solve the world's problems. Challenges like climate change, mass migration, terrorism, and the spread of weapons of mass destruction cannot be addressed without nations—especially the United States and China—working together to develop collective responses. If we allow Cold War II to happen, the world will certainly face even more serious threats decades from now—or sooner. Western liberals must develop a modus vivendi with China for the sake of effective global governance.

After decades of staying in the background, following Deng's dictum of "hiding your strength and biding you time," China is now finally stepping into the limelight, if not by intention, then by necessity. The BRI, for instance, is China's effort to drive a new round of global economic growth in regions that were previously neglected or have yet to find suitable development models. The underlying idea is a simple one, derived from China's own development experience: If you want to get rich, build a road first. China seeks to use its capital and capacity to build infrastructure to more effectively and efficiently link up the economies through its western corridor to Europe and south through maritime routes to Southeast Asia. It is a long term and enormous undertaking with estimated $1 trillion in building expenditure that covers 60 countries and growing.[77] The BRI is perhaps the most ambitious project for global interconnectivity since the Marshall Plan—and it is probably much bigger than the latter.[78] It is the surest sign of China's determination to carry forward globalization against current widespread headwinds.

China's BRI will certainly encounter problems and missteps. But it would be to the world's benefit to embrace the idea and work together to realize its potential. In many ways, the project offers the best chance for a renewal of globalization precisely because of its clear differentiation from globalism. If done right, it would usher in a globalization that is more inclusive and more pluralistic. Globalism was fundamentally exclusionary in so many ways: ideologically and politically, it was structured to push for a single set of so-called universal values; militarily, its operation was backed by the U.S.-led military alliance which by definition excluded non-allies; economically, the system was controlled by rich developed nations and designed to keep developing countries as permanent peripherals and dependents. China's plan is fundamentally more inclusive. It imposes no ideological, political, or social values. China is militarily non-aligned and it seeks to champion the developing world because, although the largest economy in the world by purchasing power, it remains a developing country and will remain so for a long time.

Many fear that China may be following the footsteps of those hegemons that dominated the world in the past. But the lack of ideological imposition and military non-alliance makes China different. Its rhetorical toughness against Western impositions is not to be confused with any desire to dominate others. As China's foreign minister Qin Gang said recently, "China will never claim hegemony, but also will not bow to hegemony".[79]

The economic realities of the world are also different and may just make the practice of traditional hegemony obsolete. Jin Keyu argues that the power of economic networks will supersede traditional national hegemonic power and that China might be becoming a "global network leader".[80] BRI certainly fits that hypothesis—a world without a hegemon that operates through networks of networks. China, in this case, may be a new kind of world leader—a dominant player without dominating the world.

BRI is China's globalization proposition in its most concrete form. But it is only one aspect of a larger vision. Xi terms it a "human community of a shared destiny"—(*ren lei ming yun gong tong ti*).[81] It is still in its formative stage. And as with any overarching world view, it will necessarily involve conflicts and contradictions. But its basic tenets and broad contours have already emerged: continue to encourage economic interconnectivity, reject ideological imposition, respect national sovereignty, allow space for nations to walk their own paths, encourage competition of ideas and political modes without interference and coercion, develop mutual learning, and build interdependence. On this basis, perhaps nations can develop a new consensus on the rules of engagement to pursue a new version of globalization.

The Chinese proposition has the potential to offer the world a new philosophical framework to collectively address humanity's myriad challenges. If the West, as the incumbent leading power, could find the wisdom to participate in it—and shaping it, globalization may have a chance at renewal. In that case, the twenty-first century may well be a peaceful and prosperous one for all.

Notes

1. Kennedy, John F. "Moon Speech–Rice Stadium." *NASA Transcript*. Retrieved from: https://er.jsc.nasa.gov/seh/ricetalk.htm.
2. Reagan, Ronald. "Inaugural Address, January 20, 1981." *Ronald Reagan Presidential Foundation and Institute*. Retrieved from: https://www.reaganfoundation.org/ronald-reagan/reagan-quotes-speeches/inaugural-address-2/.
3. Reif, L. Rafael. "China's Challenge Is America's Opportunity." *The New York Times*. 9 Aug. 2018.
4. "Public Trust in Government: 1958–2019." *Pew Research Center*. 11 Apr. 2019. Retrieved from: https://www.people-press.org/2019/04/11/public-trust-in-government-1958-2019/; Jones, Jeffrey M. "Trust in U.S. Judicial Branch Sinks to New Low of 53%." *Gallup*. 18 Sept. 2015. Retrieved from: https://news.gallup.com/poll/185528/trust-judicial-branch-sinks-new-low.aspx.
5. Barnes, Robert. "Rebuking Trump's Criticism of 'Obama Judge,' Chief Justice Roberts Defends Judiciary as 'Independent'." *The Washington Post*. 21 Nov. 2018.
6. China formally ascended to the World Trade Organization (WTO) on 11 December 2001, but it only began to accrue the economic benefits of formally joining the world economy in 2002.
7. Data retrieved from: http://datatopics.worldbank.org/world-development-indicators/themes/economy.html.
8. Dedrick, Jason, Linden, Greg, and Kraemer, Kenneth L. "China Makes $8.46 from an iPhone. That's Why a U.S. Trade War Is Futile." *CBS News*. 9 Jul. 2018.
9. "China's Disposable Income Per Capita Was 4520 yuan ($565) in 2002 and 25,974 yuan ($3,820) in 2017, According to National Statistical Bureau." Data retrieved from: http://www.stats.gov.cn/.
10. Data retrieved from: https://www.bea.gov. For more discussions about Income inequality and middle class shrinkage, see: Irwin, Neil. "You Can't Feed a Family With G.D.P." *The New York Times*. 16 Sept. 2014; Piketty, Thomas, Saez, Emmanuel, and Zucman, Gabriel. "Economic Growth in the United States: A Tale of Two Countries." *Washington Center for Equitable Growth 6*. 2016.
11. Desmond, Matthew. "Americans Want to Believe Jobs Are the Solution to Poverty. They're Not." *The New York Times*. 11 Sept.

2018; "Americans' Job Satisfaction Falls to Record Low." The Associated Press. 17 Mar. 2010. Retrieved from: https://www.cnbc.com/id/34700568.
12. For detailed presentation of the plight of the American middle class, see: Hacker, Jacob S., and Pierson, Paul. *Winner-Take-All Politics: How Washington Made the Rich Richer—And Turned Its Back on the Middle Class.* Simon and Schuster, 2010.
13. Luce, Edward. *Time to Start Thinking: America and the Spectre of Decline.* Hachette UK, 2012; Putnam, Robert D. *Bowling Alone: The Collapse and Revival of American Community.* Simon and Schuster, 2001; Murray, Charles. "Coming Apart: The State of White America, 1960–2010." Crown Forum, 2012; Vance, J. D. *Hillbilly Elegy.* New York, NY: HarperCollins, 2016.
14. According to the National Survey on Drug Use and Health (NSDUH), Suicide was the tenth leading cause of death overall in the United States, claiming the lives of 47,173 people in 2017. Data retrieved form: https://webappa.cdc.gov/sasweb/ncipc/leadcause.html.
15. Brooks, David. "Let's Go for a Win on Opioids." *The New York Times.* 4 Apr, 2017.
16. Dokoupil, Tony, and Finn, Martin. "Millions of Men Have Dropped Out of the Workforce, Leaving Companies Struggling to Fill Jobs: It's 'a Matter of Our National Identity'." CBS News. 26 Jan. 2023.
17. Travis, Alan. "Public Services Face Real-Terms Spending Cuts of Up to 40% in Decade to 2020." *The Guardian.* 22 Nov. 2017.
18. Butler, Patrick, and WelfareTravis, Alan. "Public Services Face Real-Terms Spending for UK's Poorest Shrinks by £37bn Cuts of Up to 40% in Decade to 2020." *The Guardian.* 23 Sept. 2018, 22 Nov. 2017.
19. Soros, George. "Remarks Delivered at the World Economic Forum (2019, Jan. 24)." Retrieved from: https://www.georgesoros.com/2019/01/24/remarks-delivered-at-the-world-economic-forum-2/.
20. Brooks, David. "How China Brings Us Together." *The New York Times.* 14 Feb. 2019.
21. Friedman, Thomas L. "China Deserves Donald Trump." *The New York Times.* 22 May 2019; Friedman, Thomas L. *The World Is Flat: A Brief History of the Twenty-First Century.* Macmillan, 2005.

22. The Office of the President of the United States. *National Security Strategy of the United States of America*, 2017, pp. 2–3.
23. The actual number of United States military bases is controversial. The official statistics, which was used here, was released by Defense Department in 2018. Some argued that the number was underestimated. In 2011, Rep. Ron Paul claimed that U.S. has military personnel in 130 nations and 900 overseas bases in a Republican presidential debate. See: US Department of Defense. *Base Structure Report Fiscal Year 2018 Baseline*, 2018. p. 7; Jacobson, Louis. "Ron Paul Says US Has Military Personnel in 130 Nations and 900 Overseas Bases." *Politifact*. 14 Sept. 2011.
24. Data of GNI per capita retrieved from The World Bank in 2021: https://data.worldbank.org/indicator/NY.GNP.PCAP.CD?locati ons=CN-US&order=wbapi_data_value_2014+wbapi_data_value+ wbapi_data_value-last&sort=desc.
25. The last time the Chinese military engaged in combat was in a short border war with Vietnam in 1985.
26. Diamond, Larry, and Schell, Orville. *China's Influence & American Interests: Promoting Constructive Vigilance*. The Hoover Institution. 29 Nov. 2018.
27. Diamond, Larry. "Will China Rule The World?" *The American Interest*. 14 Dec. 2018.
28. Nye, S. Joseph. *Soft Power: The Means to Success in World Politics*. New York: Public Affairs Press, 2009.
29. Fukuyama, Francis. "The End of History?" *The National Interest*, vol. 16, 1989, pp. 3–18.
30. Dunn, John. *Breaking Democracy's Spell*. Yale UP, 2014.
31. Allison, Graham. "The Myth of the Liberal Order: From Historical Accident to Conventional Widsom." *Foreign Affairs*. Jul./Aug. 2018.
32. Campbell, Kurt M., and Ratner, Ely. "The China Reckoning: How Beijing Defied American Expectations." *Foreign Affairs*. Mar./Apr. 2018.
33. Li, Eric X. "Did America Get China Wrong: The Engagement Debate." *Foreign Affairs*. Jul./Aug. 2018; Kissinger, Henry. *White House Years*. Simon and Schuster, 2011.
34. During both crisis, China has been a driving force for the global economic recovery with its dynamic economic growth. China also helped other East Asian economies avoid a competitive devaluation

by maintaining renminbi's stability. See: Lin, Justin Yifu. "China and the Global Economy." *China Economic Journal*, vol. 4, no. 1, 2011, pp. 1–14.
35. Paulson, Henry. "America's China Policy Is Not Working." *Foreign Affairs*. 26 Jan. 2023.
36. Campbell, Kurt M., and Ratner, Ely. "The China Reckoning: How Beijing Defied American Expectations." *Foreign Affairs*. Mar./Apr. 2018.
37. Lind, Michael. "America vs. Russia and China: Welcome to Cold War II." *National Interests*. 15 Apr. 2018.
38. Allison, Graham. "The Myth of the Liberal Order: From Historical Accident to Conventional Widsom." *Foreign Affairs*. Jul./Aug. 2018.
39. Kennedy, John F. "Commencement Address at American University, Washington DC, June 10, 1963." Retrieved from: https://www.jfklibrary.org/archives/other-resources/john-f-kennedy-speeches/american-university-19630610.
40. Lind, Michael. "America vs. Russia and China: Welcome to Cold War II." *National Interests*. 15 Apr. 2018.
41. Summers, Lawrence H. "The Age of Secular Stagnation: What It Is and What to Do About It." *Foreign Affairs*. Mar./Apr. 2016.
42. Fukuyama, Francis. *Identity: The Demand for Dignity and the Politics of Resentment*. Farrar, Straus and Giroux, 2018. pp. 128–133, 151–152.
43. Mcdonald, Joe, and Lee, Youkyung. "AP IMPACT: China Surpasses US as Top Global Trader." *Associated Press*. 3 Dec. 2012.
44. Frankopan, Peter. *The New Silk Roads: The Present and Future of the World*. Knopf, 2019.
    Macaes, Bruno. *Belt and Road: A Chinese World Order*. Hurst. 2019.
45. For full member list of AIIB, see: https://www.aiib.org/en/about-aiib/governance/members-of-bank/index.html.
46. Lee, Jeong-ho. "Italy's Move to Join New Silk Road May See European Union Tighten Coordination on China." *South China Morning Post*. 24 Mar. 2019.
47. Maull, Hanns W. "Amid Much Controversy, German Chancellor Visits China." *The Diplomat*. 3 Nov. 2022.
48. Adler, David. "The West v Russia: Why the Global South Isn't Taking Sides." *The Guardian*. 28 Mar. 2022.

49. Gehrke, Joel. "FBI Director: Chinese Spies 'A Whole-of-Society' Threat to US." *Washington Examiner*. 13 Feb. 2018.
50. Perlez, Jane. "F.B.I. Bars Some China Scholars From Visiting U.S. Over Spying Fears." *The New York Times*. 14 Apr. 2019.
51. Gehrke, Joel. "State Department Preparing for Clash of Civilizations with China." *The Washington Examiner*. 30 April 2019.
52. Zakaria, Fareed. "Does a Trump Doctrine on Foreign Policy Exist? Ask John Bolton." *The Washington Post*. 2 May 2019.
53. In his State of the Union address in February 2023, Biden was nearly shouting when hurling a personal insult against Xi. See: Collinson, Stephen. "Biden's Dramatic Warning to China." *CNN*. 8 Feb. 2023.
54. "Xi to Biden: Knock Off the Democracy vs. Autocracy Talk." *Reuters*. 15 Nov. 2022.
55. Allison, Graham. "The Myth of the Liberal Order: From Historical Accident to Conventional Widsom." *Foreign Affairs*. Jul./Aug. 2018.
56. Kennedy, John F. "Commencement Address at American University." 1963.
57. Allison, Graham. "The Myth of the Liberal Order: From Historical Accident to Conventional Widsom." *Foreign Affairs*. Jul./Aug. 2018.
58. Pei, Minxin. "The China Threat Is Being Overhyped." Bloomberg. 28 May 2021.
59. Ferguson, Niall. "Niall Ferguson Says U.S.-China Cooperation Is Critical to Global Economic Health." *The Washington Post*. 17 Nov. 2008.
60. James, Paul, and Steger, Manfred B. "A Genealogy of 'Globalization': The Career of a Concept." *Globalizations*, vol. 11, no. 4, 2014, pp. 417–434.
61. Li, Eric X. "The End of Globalism." *Foreign Affairs*. 9 Dec. 2016.
62. Huntington, Samuel P. "Dead Souls: The Denationalization of the American Elite." *The National Interest*, vol. 75, 2004, pp. 5–18.
63. This section is adapted from the author's article in *Foreign Affairs*. See: Li, Eric X. "The End of Globalism." *Foreign Affairs*. 9 Dec. 2016.
64. "Transcript: Jeffrey Sachs' Speech at the U.N. Food Systems Pre-Summit." 27 Jul. 2021. Retrieved from: https://www.jeffsachs.org/recorded-lectures/5jf86pp5lxch35e6z3nct6xnmb8zy5.

65. Madhani, Aamer. "Biden Declares 'America Is Back' in Welcome Words to Allies." *AP.* 20 Feb. 2021.
66. Alden, Edward. "Biden's 'America First' Economic Policy Threatens Rift with Europe." Foreign Policy. 5 Dec. 2022.
67. Li, Eric X. "Xi Jinping's Guide to the Chinese Way of Globalisation." *Financial Times.* 19 Jan. 2017.
68. This section is adapted from the author's article in *American Affairs.* See: Li, Eric X. "China, America, and 'Nationalism'." *American Affairs.* Oct. 2017.
69. The Philippines is a good example of the various movements to counter globalism. After many years of "liberal" leadership, the Philippines had become a massive haven for drug lords. The conduct of Duterte's efforts to save the country run counter to liberalism's universal values. As a result, Western political and media establishments have turned him into a pariah.
70. Orbán, Viktor. "Viktor Orbán's Speech at the Conference 'China-CEE Political Parties Dialogue'." *Cabinet Office of the Prime Minister.* Retrieved from: http://www.miniszterelnok.hu/viktor-orbans-speech-at-the-conference-china-cee-political-parties-dialogue/.
71. "Italy Joins China's New Silk Road Project." *BBC News.* 23 Mar. 2019.
72. Li, Eric X. "China, America, and 'Nationalism'." *American Affairs.* Oct. 2017.
73. Trump, Donald. "Remarks by President Trump to the 72nd Session of the United Nations General Assembly." *The White House.* 19 Sept. 2017. Retrieved from: https://www.whitehouse.gov/briefings-statements/remarks-president-trump-72nd-session-united-nations-general-assembly/.
74. *Slava Ukraini.* Directed by Bernard-Henri Lévy. With in Features Story Production. 2023.
75. Winterer, Caroline. *American Enlightenments: Pursuing Happiness in the Age of Reason.* Yale University Press, 2016.
76. Winterer, Caroline. "Debunking the Myth of the American Enlightenment." *Yale University Press Blog.* 17 Oct. 2016. Retrieved from: https://blog.yalebooks.yale.educom/2016/10/27/debunking-the-myth-of-the-american-enlightenment/.
77. Baculinao, Eric. "Belt and Road Initiative: China Plans $1 Trillion New 'Silk Road'." *NBC News.* 12 May 2017.

78. Tweed, David. "China's New Silk Road." *Bloomberg*. 16 Apr.2019.
79. "Qin Gang: China Will Never Seek Hegemony or Engage in Expansionism, Nor Will It Bow to Any Hegemony [秦刚: 中国永不称霸, 也不向任何霸权低头]." *IFeng News*. 2 Feb. 2023.
80. Jin, Keyu. "Trans-Sovereign Networks China's Role in the New Global Order." *Revitalizing the Spirit of Bretton Woods*, 2019, pp. 92–100.
81. "China Keywords: Community with Shared Future for Mankind." *Xinhua Net*. 24 Jan. 2018.

CHAPTER 10

Epilogue: Xi Jinping and *Tian Xia*

It is now abundantly clear to the world that Xi Jinping, the party's general secretary and president of China since 2012 and 2013, respectively, is one of the most consequential leaders for the future of the world. Since assuming his top position, Xi has steadfastly consolidated his power and, with the constitutional amendment in 2018 and the confirmation of a third term as party secretary at the 20th party congress in October 2022, is expected to lead China as both party general secretary and president in the foreseeable future.

So, this epilogue serves only as an interim assessment, if that, of the Xi Jinping era and, perhaps, a prospectus, if only in broad strokes, of its meaning to China and the world.

AN INTERIM REPORT CARD

When Xi Jinping took over as general secretary of the CCP, China was capping off a 30 year stretch of breakneck economic growth. During that period, China's GDP had grown at an average annual rate of around 10%, making it the world's second-largest economy behind the United States. China had achieved significant progress in urbanization, and its urban population grew rapidly, from around 20% of the total population in 1978 to over 50% in 2012. In 2013, China surpassed the United States as the world's largest trading nation, helping increase its international influence and its role in the global economy.

But all these achievements were becoming overshadowed by three seemingly intractable society-wide problems: official corruption, environmental degradation, and economic inequality. By the time the party convened its 18th national congress in 2012, they were reaching near crisis levels.

In his report at the 18th party congress, Hu Jintao warned that failing to handle corruption could "prove fatal to the party and even cause the collapse of the party and the fall of the state." A survey conducted in 2013 showed that 71.5% of those polled had rated corruption as either a "very serious" or "extremely serious" problem.[1]

The level of environmental degradation in China was also alarming. According to a study published in *Science*, during the winter of 2012–2013, 70% of the nation's 74 largest cities logged pollution levels above the Chinese government's own air quality standards. In the winter of 2013, the harmful smog contributed to at least 90,000 deaths and sickening hundreds of thousands more.[2] Ministry of Supervision reported that there are almost 1700 water pollution accidents annually. And around 40% of China's rivers were seriously polluted in 2012.[3] And China was on course to becoming the largest carbon emitter in the world, although still far behind the United States in terms of per capita emissions.

At the party's 17th national congress in 2007, Xi was elevated to the standing committee of the Politburo as the successor in waiting to his predecessor Hu Jintao. The widely held expectations both domestically and internationally were that he would be a leader of continuity, not dramatic reforms. Well, big surprises were in store for them all.

In my essay for *Foreign Policy* in July 2021, I wrote that a key success factor of the party was self-reinvention—its ability over long duration to continuously adapt itself to changing times.[4] It turned out I was too modest in my choice of words. At the 20th party congress in October 2022, Xi Jinping used the term "self-revolution" to describe the party's determination to keep changing with the times. At the congress, self-revolution was placed into the amended party constitution itself.[5] Indeed, the past ten years have demonstrated in abundance that Xi is the most revolutionary Chinese leader since at least Deng Xiaoping, if not Mao.

The most breath-taking was the anti-corruption campaign, sustained to this day. The intensity, breath, and depth are unparalleled and, thus, makes it very difficult to make Western media's accusation of it being driven by a pure political agenda stick.[6] In the past, there were anti-corruption drives, though never as intense and far-reaching as this one, but they came and went like political movements. There are many signs that Xi's efforts to purify the party are being institutionalized to a significant degree. The party's central disciplinary commission has acquired much greater power than before and its regional and local agencies now operate with much more independence from party committees.[7] The establishment of the State Supervisory Commission through the State Supervisory Law in 2018 further expanded and institutionalized anti-corruption enforcement mechanisms throughout the entire Chinese state bureaucracy.[8]

If Xi's anti-corruption initiative is indeed institutionalized, both in terms of hard rules and behavioral patterns, Chinese politics could be cleansed of at least the most corrosive aspects brought on by corruption. This would also have significant implications for rule of law as a political concept.[9] Most importantly, the continuous purification of the party institution can ensure the CCP remains a vanguard force in Chinese society.

Xi has also been the most environmentalist leader in modern Chinese history. After the 18th party congress, when it became clear fixing the environment topped the government's agenda, many expressed doubts about the sincerity of the government's efforts to reverse the lax environmental protection policies of the past. Some were concerned the stringent rules could damage economic growth and therefore were unsustainable. Both were proven wrong. Xi's government really meant it and was willing to pay the economic price to sustain it. Ten years on, from Beijing's air[10] to the water of Erhai,[11] the country's ecological environment has seen the most tangible improvements in decades.

On the global policy front, China has made a gradual but unambiguous shift. For decades, it held to the principle of "common but differentiated responsibilities" for its obligations toward climate change. This position is justified by the fact that the effects of carbon emission are cumulative. Developed countries industrialized while emitting a large amount over the past century. China has just begun to industrialize and is still a developing country. In addition, even though China's total emission is becoming the largest in the world, on a per capita basis, it is still far behind developed countries. Therefore, China's obligations must be adjusted accordingly. To the general public, this position is morally beyond reproach. But it also made climate negotiations more difficult as the world faces the existential threat of global warming. During the Copenhagen climate conference in 2009, Chinese prime minister Wen Jiabao and U.S. President Obama famously got into a stalemate.[12]

While "common-but-differentiated-responsibilities" remains China's official position in climate negotiations, in the Xi era, China has clearly downplayed this concept. The world has noticed this shift and it could become an important force in helping global cooperation in confronting climate change.[13] This shift was surely not due to a change of mind of Chinese bureaucracy and industry or even public opinion. It is all but certain to have come from Xi's personal convictions. A *Tian Xia* outlook is emerging.[14]

The third, and perhaps the hardest, is inequality. More than thirty years of market economics brought about rather extreme income and wealth gaps.[15] Increasing general prosperity, in so far as all are better off than before when compared to themselves, has kept the country away from the kind of widespread dissatisfaction that led to excessive populism in many parts of the world.

Xi's approach to inequality has been two-prong: campaign and institutional reforms. To lift the very bottom, Xi took a drastic campaign style mobilization to eradicate absolute poverty in the country. In 2012, China still had 98.99 million people living below the absolute poverty line, defined as earning less than $1.69 per day. The campaign was unprecedented and dramatic.[16] The entire party apparatus was mobilized. To carry out this mission, millions of party cadres went to the frontlines of poverty in remote rural and mountainous regions under harsh conditions. More than 1800 party members lost their lives on duty.[17] On February 25, 2021, the country declared victory by achieving its goal of eradicating extreme poverty.[18] Although the standard of absolute poverty is still low, China is the very first developing country that has eliminated absolute poverty.

As with any market-driven economy, and China's economy certainly is one, inequality can be the most intractable problem. Furthermore, China's is a socialist market economy. Fundamental economic fairness guaranteed by socialism is central to the system's long-term legitimacy. The efforts to address this issue at institutional and structural levels began in earnest in 2017 at the 19th party congress.[19] The development of common prosperity was placed at the center of the party platform. The congress report also specified that the central contradiction in Chinese society has shifted from the lack of economic development to the need for more balanced development.[20] In the party political lexicon, this essentially declares a paradigm change in the party's overall governing agenda.

Longer term institutional and policy changes have also been implemented. The central government has pledged the building of 6.5 million low-cost rental homes between 2021 and 2025, accounting for 26% of the new housing supply.[21] Enlarging the percentage of middle-income groups as the share of total population has become the stated goals of many regional and local governments. Equalizing public services between social and economic classes and geographic regions is now a policy priority. Rural development is atop of most central, regional, and local government policy initiatives.[22]

As a contemporary example of experimental governance, common prosperity pilot zones have been launched. Zhejiang province, for instance, became such a policy experimentation zone in 2021 with specific goals to be reached by 2025. These include the increase of share of wages in GDP, increase of the share of the population earning middle income of between $15,500 and 77,300; increase of the percentage of pre-school aged children with access to free kindergartens; and decrease in the urban–rural income gap ratio.[23]

It is important to note that common prosperity is not just a political and moral proposition, it is an economic one as well. An economic and social structure where the few at the top get infinitely richer, while the majority in the middle and lower classes remain stagnant, is not going to deliver the long-term economic gains China needs to become a developed country. Only an olive-shaped society where economic benefits are widely shared can underwrite sustainable economic growth.[24] As Thomas Piketty's recent research shows, economic inequality remains a significant problem in China.[25] Common prosperity is still a goal far over the horizon. Whether Xi's new era can make substantial progress toward that goal will determine his place in history.

CAPITAL IN THE CHINESE CENTURY

As Liu He, China's vice premier and top economic policy maker, pointed out at Davos in January 2023, China will not, and cannot, return to the old days of a planned economy.[26] Market economics will certainly be a guiding framework of China's overall development far into the future. With all the improvement in the standard of living, China still faces real tests in this unique absorption of market economics into socialism. The challenges are manifold. Among all the major economies in the world, China stands out as the only one that is still without a property tax and inheritance tax, and the only socialist country led by a communist party. This seemingly glaring contradiction demonstrates the complexity of Chinese society and politics as a whole.[27] How does it lift the bottom quarter without making the middle feel insecure? How does it incentivize entrepreneurial drive and innovation but distribute the gains equitably?

The party's policies toward the roles of capital and entrepreneurship in the past several years is a case study in this challenging and far-reaching agenda. In the 20 years since China joined the WTO in 2000, private enterprises enjoyed perhaps the most sustained period of dramatic growth and preferential policy treatments in modern Chinese history. More billionaires were made in those years in China than any other country in the world.[28] It was the Chinese version of a "gilded age."

Signs were also emerging that some of the owners of this enormous new private wealth were no longer content with economic gains. The most prominent example was, of course, Alibaba founder Jack Ma's attempt at publicly influencing the central government's policymaking on financial regulations, to which his company, Ant Financial, is a major interested party.[29]

It is against this backdrop the political leadership launched a series of initiatives to rein in the power of concentrated private wealth. The two most notable sectors in which huge wealth—and also power—was accumulated in short order were real estate and consumer internet platforms.[30]

Ironically, both sectors relied heavily on state investments for their successes. Enormous private real estate companies were built on state bank lending and took on excessive risks to the financial system. Beginning in 2020, the government started to tighten bank lending and the real estate bubble began to burst. In the following years, more than a few real estate tycoons saw their ultra-wealth and social stature cut down in size.

Then there was the internet sector. I have borrowed the concept of the two 30 years of the People's Republic (historians divide the first 60 years of the PRC into the first 30 years under Mao and the second under Deng) and suggested that the Chinese new economy can be divided into the first and second 20 years.[31] The first 20 years was between 2000 and 2020 during which we saw the Chinese internet economy grew into the largest in the world. The Chinese internet sector became the most vibrantly entrepreneurial in the country and attracted a huge amount of venture capital both domestically and internationally. Virtually every leading Silicon Valley venture capital firm established funds in China. It seemed that the world was going to be dominated by internet giants from two countries, the U.S. and China. America has Amazon, China has Alibaba; America has Uber, China has Didi; the list of companies worth tens and hundreds of billions of dollars goes on.

Almost all of these companies, though, share some common attributes. They are mostly consumer-based platforms that innovated successfully with new business models. These business models are largely winner-take-call in nature. In other words, many companies race to become the largest scale and probably the only dominant player in the end. This required an enormous amount of financial capital to fund huge customer acquisition costs before one of them reaches the dominant position. And that dominant position, once reached, is a monopoly or a near-monopoly. This formula became the closed-loop financial process that bred a group of companies that are now known as the big-techs. Entrepreneurs developed business models that aimed to become monopolies. Once they become monopolies, they can collect rents and achieve huge returns on capital. This projected future-return story was used to raise large amounts of financial capital based on big net present values (NPV) for early and growth stage companies to fund many years of losses—what is commonly known as burning capital. The eventual winner became the monopoly.

The growth of the big-techs was tremendous for the Chinese economy and advanced many new business sectors and improved the lives of many millions of people. But, by the middle 2010s, the problems also became clear. These consumer platforms sucked in huge amounts of capital and innovated on business models; but there was very little real technology innovations. The ubiquitous QR code that powered e-commerce and social media companies, for instance, was invented in 1990s.[32] During those same 20 years, China was lagging behind on substantive technology innovations it badly needed in fields such as semiconductors, aerospace, and advanced manufacturing.

Then, of course, monopoly companies brought about the problems associated with monopolies. And in the case of consumer internet platforms, such as food delivery and ride-hailing, these issues were doubled because these companies are both monopolies and monopsonies.[33] They collect rents by squeezing both their downstream and upstream. Their dominance in their markets has led to the reduction of consumer choice and benefits downstream. Their market powers have also enabled them to exploit their upstream—suppliers and workers. Public outcries spread over poorly paid and overworked delivery workers without health benefits required by law (some big-techs classify them as independent contractors to avoid this).

What is also ironic is that the growth of the big-techs was to not-small-extent leveraged on state investments. 3G, 4G, and 5G were built by state companies that demanded low returns on capital to build these networks, which are the most extensive and advanced in the world. Physical infrastructures, such as roads, were built by the state and relied upon by platform companies to deliver e-commerce worth billions. While these companies used the positive externalities produced by the state for free, they generated negative externalities of which the costs have to be absorbed by the society as a whole—the lack of health benefits for workers, the effects on the environment, the displacements of bricks and mortar businesses. I called the first 20 years of the Chinese new economy an era of capital leveraging on the state.

There is another perhaps more important issue. Big-techs have become so dominant and so all-encompassing in our lives that they can effectively control our societies to serve their own interests.[34] Many big-techs around the world are doing exactly that by using their power to capture political systems. In the U.S. and Europe, these problems have become obvious and there have been many calls to rein in the big-techs.[35] But so far they have been to no avail.

Xi Jinping's China reined in the big-techs!

Beginning with suspending the IPO of Ant Financial in the fall of 2020, a series of anti-trust actions targeted at the big-techs shocked the financial world. The market caps of the top five big-techs were halved in the two years since.[36] From ride-hailing apps to online entertainment, tech giants that were used to a freewheeling empire building environment were forced, one by one, to comply with government regulations on market competition, labor practices, and data security.

To be sure, there are areas for improvements, mostly in terms of implementation and communication. Chinese policymaking process remains too opaque, especially to global capital markets. The tightening of regulatory enforcements against the big-techs from 2020 to 2022 came as a big surprise to investors. It incurred unnecessary financial market turmoil. In its efforts to manage macro-economic directions, the government needs to finetune the approaches.

THE ECONOMIC TRANSFORMATION

Many have pronounced the end of China's technology industry and even entrepreneurship itself. This is a gross misreading. On the contrary, China's technology industry is at a turning point and may very well be at the beginning of a new growth era. I call it the second 20 years of the Chinese new economy. The driver of it all is the new buzzword, high-quality development—a term coined by Xi Jinping to map out the new direction of the Chinese economy.

One of China's strongest assets, and a key competitive advantage in its global position, is its industrial capacity. China makes everything for the world. Its industrial capacity is larger than the United States, Japan, and Germany put together. China's industrial output is estimated at around US$ 5 trillion a year.[37] It is hard to imagine the gross quantitative size has too much room to grow. The problem is that the value-add of this industrial capacity is still relatively low. If China was a company, its revenue is already so large that it is near the ceiling of what the addressable market can take. Yet, the market value of the company is still way below potential. The gap is in gross margin. Much lower gross margins of China's manufacturing companies are the biggest inhibitor of the country's growth potential. No reliable statistics are available to get to an accurate accounting of this. But enough surveys have shown most of China's industrial companies operate at much lower profit margins than their peers in the developed world.[38]

This is precisely what China has neglected in its economic model. In its pursuit of growth, it has not done enough to develop technologies required to raise the value of its output. A ten to twenty percentage points gap between China's current profit margin on its industrial capacity and what it can produce with better technologies is a huge amount of economic value waiting to be created. Take semiconductors alone, China essentially gave up developing its own integrated circuit industry more than 20 years ago. It has been importing semiconductor chips of US$350 billion a year. This is larger than China's imports of crude oil and iron ore combined—both are imported by China in the largest quantities in human history![39] Gradually moving up the value chain in semiconductors would perhaps account for five to ten percentage points of the margins gap.

To be sure, Chinese industry has made strides. When Apple started producing iPhones in China in 2007, Chinese manufacturers only accounted for 3.6% of the total value of an iPhone. Now the number is 25%.[40] The new Chinese economic model needs to repeat the iPhone story in many more sectors.

Many mistook the downturn in China's internet companies and the bursting of the real estate bubble by government policy as evidence that the Chinese state is reasserting itself to contain private enterprises—the so-called "*guo jin min tui.*" This is false. While internet platforms and real estate giants have been cut down in size, private companies, such as CATL and BYD, that are in technology sectors important to China's future development are growing leaps and bounds.[41]

It is now clear that China's political leadership judged that this transformation of economic model could not happen by market forces alone. It needs to be engineered from top down. Capital needs to be redirected, by political initiative, away from real estate, consumer internet, low-end manufacturing to higher-quality development projects. I call it technology-enabled industrial capacity. The shock therapy of the past two years is showing some significant effects. Venture capital for consumer internet has dried up. But investments in hard technology innovations have increased substantially.[42] These include high-end manufacturing technologies such as robotics, artificial intelligence, supply chain technologies, life sciences, aerospace technologies, alternative energy, new industrial materials, and semiconductors. Local governments have gone back to aggressively relaunch their investment and policy initiatives to build clusters for these sectors, much in the same way as they did during the first phase of China's industrialization for low-end manufacturing 20–30 years ago. Technology entrepreneurs have also gotten the message and are building many startups in these sectors. No doubt, there will be much inefficient and wasted investments. On the other hand, China is attempting something no major developing economy has been able to do—to move up the value chain in large scale and achieve the kind of high value-add in its industries that only developed economies have been able to deliver. The second 20 years of the Chinese new economy might be an era of the state leveraging on capital.

This emphasis on technology advancements is also reflected at the highest political level. At the 20th party congress, an unprecedented number of techno-political leaders (officials with technology backgrounds) were promoted onto the new central committee—the party state's highest governing body.[43]

Can China succeed? It is not a foregone conclusion, and the Chinese economy will probably face headwinds for a number of years as it goes through with this drastic restructuring. But it is interesting to note that the U.S. is alarmed. America sees China as the only peer competitor that threatens its global dominance.[44] The Biden administration has gone so far as making it a criminal offense for U.S. citizens to work for certain Chinese technology companies.[45] If someone had predicted merely a few years ago that the U.S. would feel sufficiently fearful that it would legally takeaway its own citizens' employment rights, that person would have been laughed at.

The U.S. is now even trying to copy China's strategy. For decades, industrial policy was a dirty word in American policymaking circles. Now, industrial policies are flooding U.S. legislations.[46]

The technological race with China has become a top priority for US leaders, who have repeatedly stressed their commitment to maintaining US technological superiority. The Biden administration is beginning to restrict U.S. investments in China that could undermine U.S. competitiveness.[47] In a speech, Biden stated that China's aim to become the leading country in the world was not going to happen on his watch.[48] So the race is on.

Xi Jinping has no other choice. It is not about America. It is not even about China's desire to lead the world. It is about China itself. Although China's economy is now of comparable size to that of the U.S., its per capita income is only a quarter of the latter. To deliver on the party's promise to make China a prosperous developed country by the middle of this century, it must undertake this economic transformation on Xi's watch.

A New Ideological Era

After ten years at the helm, Xi Jinping has brought China into a new ideological framework. This is a new development, and in many ways unexpected. The Deng Xiaoping era, from 1979 to 2012, saw the downplaying of ideology in Chinese society. There were many reasons for that. To course-correct the ideological excesses of the late Mao years was certainly one. The single-minded focus on economic development also called for the relaxation of ideological controls to unleash individual initiatives.

Rapid economic development did happen. But in the same period, ideological vacuum in Chinese society also led to moral decay as manifested in official corruption, wealth worship, and disregard for the poor, as well as destruction of the environment for short-term gains at the expense of future generations. In those four decades, nearly two generations of Chinese grew up knowing only the market. Western liberal and neoliberal ideas infested Chinese society.

Since Xi Jinping became China's leader, *bu wang chu xin* has become the mantra of the party and society in general. It means to remain true to our heart—don't forget why we are doing all this, essentially. Many in the West have pointed to strengthened ideological oversight of Chinese media and universities and internet regulations as being backward attacks on freedom. They are right that Xi's China is indeed saying a resolute no to the West's liberalism. While China is deploying market economics for development, it does not want to become a Western liberal society in which private wealth can control politics and the individual reigns supreme at the expense of the community and the future.

However, none of this represents an attempt to go backwards to the days of the ideological rigidity of the Cultural Revolution. I'd give two significant pieces of evidence that Xi is not Mao reincarnate in this regard. While the Mao era's planned economy and centrally controlled politics decimated private enterprises and capital, Xi's China takes an inclusive approach toward capital both at practical and philosophical levels. In both party doctrines and policy implementations, the party has made it clear that state-owned enterprises and private companies are the twin forces to be supported.[49]

Central to the narration of the party's ideological doctrine is the official biweekly publication of the party central committee, *Qiushi*, or Seeking Truth. It is usually a collection of essays pronouncing what the party sees as the correct path and right answers. This is why it was unusual that Xi took to its pages in the May 2022 issue to instead pose a question. He stated that when socialism was first conceived by Marx and Engels, large scale industrial and financial capital was not a major factor. But in today's world, capital is a reality and it is upon the party's intellectual apparatus to explore new thinking to harness its productive power and define its boundaries.[50] Can Chinese society and politics be structured in ways that private interests operate productively for the collective good? (This is of course my own understanding and rephrasing of Xi's question.) We wait to see if Xi's question can yield answers for China's future. But by posing such a question, Xi is clearly indicating he is not intending to make the public sector overwhelm private enterprise as before the Deng era. The goal is to allow private capital to grow but contain its excesses. It is to be a process of evolution that involves continuous negotiations and compromises. But it is also clear that in a socialist China, capital can only achieve legitimate returns under the framework of the public realm. I would argue this is a fundamental difference with Western liberal (and neoliberal) societies in which private wealth is paramount and public interests are only given minimal power as necessary to keep societies functioning.

This exploration into the role of capital and how to manage it also has global implications. As political scientist Chu Yun-han wrote that despite significant gains brought about by globalization, dominated by neoliberal ideology, it has also introduced unprecedented social risks, with the most notable being globalized rent-seeking capitalism. The U.S.-led globalization empowered transnational capital and reduced state capacities around the world. Market forces driven by global capital now control the distribution of production resources and the formation of consumer desires. Global corporate leaders and the ultra-wealthy have obtained unparalleled political influence, wielding power across national borders, in other words, in the process of globalization, America has exported its neoliberal oligarchy to the world. This cannot be healthy for the future.[51] Xi Jinping's intellectual and political experiment may bear fruits for the world in the decades to come.

The second, and somewhat related, indication of the direction of Xi's leadership is the fact that, among all top Chinese leaders since the beginning of the People's Republic, Xi is the first and only one to place Chinese traditional culture front and center of the party's political platform. From literature to morality, from history to medicine, on numerous occasions, Xi has played the role of a leading proponent of reviving Chinese tradition.[52] This is in sharp contrast to the revolutionary character of Mao and the market orientation of the Deng era leaders. At the 20th party congress in 2022, traditional Chinese culture was for the first time placed in the party' constitution.[53] In numerous speeches and published writings, Xi has prioritized the so-called Sinicization of Marxism in the party's ideological work. The ideological linkage of modern Chinese socialism and the Confucian ideal of *tian xia wei gong*—all under heaven for the common good—is opening up a new phase in China's moral development.

Former Australian prime minister and a China hand Kevin Rudd lamented in Foreign Affairs that Xi was a true believer in Marxism and, therefore, is taking China backwards to dogmatism.[54] This is a misreading of both Xi and Marxism. If Rudd was right that Xi is a true Marxist (and I believe he is), then he is not taking China backwards. The application of Marxist dialectical materialism[55] would have him attempt to resolve the contradictions between the Mao and Deng eras by leading the country to a higher synthesis—a new era.

From corruption to the environment, from inequality to controlling capital, and many other areas of deep reforms, the past ten years were transformational. I Would like to remind my readers how extraordinarily difficult it was, and still is, to do all of the above, or any of the above. China is a highly complex and very large country. By the time of the 18th party congress in 2012, many special interest groups with huge stakes were entrenched in the country's bureaucracy, economy, and society. Many worried that China, just like the United States, were becoming ossified before reaching the status of a developed country. Just as Samuel Huntington, Mancur Olsen, and Francis Fukuyama studied and wrote, when such ossification happens, political decay sets in, and it is very difficult to break out short of violent revolution or war.[56] Xi Jinping's first ten years proved that the Chinese party-state remains capable of extraordinary self-correction—"self-revolution." It is able to break the ossifying forces of entrenched interests and make decisions based on collective and long-term goals. This is a major takeaway that can serve as an important data point in predicting the future.

The future is, of course, uncertain. But the vision is set. The blueprint for China's future in the Xi era is laid out in rather specific terms in the reports of the 19th and 20th party congresses. There is a set of milestones by 2035, and then the more comprehensive goals to be reached by 2049—at the 100 year anniversary of the PRC. I will try to put that vision in layman's terms. By the middle of this century, the Chinese people will live in a developed country with per capita income comparable to the developed West. Marxist ideals and socialist institutions combined with traditional Chinese values will frame the nation's moral character. Economic and social institutions are modernized to effectively use capital and entrepreneurial initiatives to drive technological innovations and economic development. The resulting prosperity will be equitably shared by all in an olive-shaped society with no one being below the poverty line. Socialism will be the political compass of Chinese society that places the collective—family, community, and nation—above the individual, but leaves enough room for the latter to flourish. The environment will be clean and China will be a net contributor to the world's ecological well-being.

TIAN XIA—A PROSPECTUS

In 2012, Professor Zhang Weiwei advanced the idea that China was a civilizational state, to be distinguished from a nation state.[57] Xi's elevation of Chinese traditional culture onto the nation's top agenda is perhaps the official initiation of this intellectual development. Perhaps no concept is more central to Chinese civilization than *Tian Xia*—all under heaven.

The concept of *Tian Xia* is so very present in Chinese thought and history since time immemorial that all Chinese sort of take it for granted. In this regard, it is not dissimilar to the concept of God in Western culture. It means the entire human world under heaven. Chinese scholar Wen Yang traced the first significant political conceptualization of *Tian Xia* to the historical and mythical political figure, Jiang Ziya, a founding father of the Zhou dynasty in 1000 BC.[58]

When the Zhou King asked Jiang to whom *Tian Xia* belongs, he answered: "*Tian Xia* does not belong to any one person, *Tian Xia* belongs to *Tian Xia*. Those who bring benefits to *Tian Xia* will rule *Tian Xia*; those who take benefits from *Tian Xia* will lose *Tian Xia*."[59]

Confucius further cemented this idea with *Tian Xia Wei Gong*—all under heaven for the common good. As Wen points out, Jiang's original conceptualization of Tian Xia 3000 years ago laid the groundwork for Chinese political philosophy and has defined the source of Chinese political legitimacy to this day. As the Zhou dynasty was at the beginning of Chinese political history, the concept of *Tian Xia* predated the existence of the state. It is all-encompassing and bigger than states and nations. Indeed, politically, there is nothing beyond *Tian Xia*.

To be understood from this perspective, a civilizational state is a political structure based on the political philosophy of *Tian Xia*. The first such political entity was the Qin dynasty. By abolishing landed aristocracy and establishing the *Jun Xian* system, Qin developed a state that serves *Tian Xia*.[60] Many in the West misunderstand the nature of centralization of political power in China as dictatorship. This is because they are comparing it to despotism in European feudal history. On the contrary, the Qin emperor used centralized political power to begin to abolish the feudal aristocratic system and design a political system with the *Tian Xia* philosophy. It was the emperor ruling on behalf of heaven for the commoners and for the common good. Confucian scholars in the centuries that followed affirmed the legitimacy of this process.[61]

Theorized from this basis, Chinese civilization, and its political state, became essentially egalitarian in ideal 2000 years ago. Western liberalism and capitalism, with their overt emphasis on the individual and private interests, theoretically are mere extensions of feudalism.

The party state of the People's Republic, in the same vein, is a modern reincarnation of China's millenniums-old political and moral tradition. And the Xi era is a contemporary affirmation of the same.

So, what does this all mean for the world?

In the past ten years, Xi Jinping has put forth many new ideas. The most relevant to the rest of the world, also perhaps the one that needs the most filling-in-the-blanks, is "human community of shared destiny"—*ren lei ming yun gong tong ti*.

I would like to suggest that it emanates from the concept of *Tian Xia*. And the all-encompassing nature of *Tian Xia* is the most relevant to our world today. Globalization has run aground; but all of its effects, economic, social, and political, have already happened and are not going away. Climate change has placed humanity before an existential threat and the current world order seems unable to effectively respond. Geopolitical tensions have now led to major military conflicts.

The so-called liberal international order is failing us. It is failing perhaps because the ideology upon which it is based, liberalism, is now the cause, not the solution, of our problems. The atomized individual with divinely endowed rights is corroding community everywhere. Private interests, in the form of oligarchical capital, have become Frankensteins whose avarice is infinite and will not stop until they devour everything. Nation states on the world stage interact as if they are individuals of the liberal doctrine in society, caring only about their own economic interests and their own security. Yet, at the same time, we are more interdependent than ever; the existential threat we face cannot be met without some form of worldwide solidarity.

Xi Jinping seems to be saying that we need a new outlook.

When he first put forth the idea of a human community of a shared destiny, he said:

> In our world, the degree of interconnectedness and interdependence among nations is unprecedented. Humanity lives in one global village, at

the meeting time and place of history and present. More than ever, I am within you, and you are within me. We are in a shared destiny.[62]

Chinese political philosopher Zhao Tingyang attempted to theorize Chinese *Tian Xia* in the modern context. As he points out, instead of a world based on the individual (the ontology of being), A *Tian Xia* outlook is based on the metaphysics of relations. And this ancient conceptualization now speaks to the very world we inhabit, a world of interconnectedness and interdependence. He wrote that "the concept of internationality is not suitable for dealing with worldwide political problems; worse still, it could even eclipse the real issues which need to be reorganized and solved."[63]

In a *Tian Xia* outlook, as Zhao puts it, every individual and every nation internalize the entire world's problems as their own, in a framework whereby "all problems in the world will be re-interpreted as problems of the world." And he calls for world-oriented political reforms to facilitate a rebirth of the world.[64]

So, what is the actual content of Xi's human community of a shared destiny? It is at early stage and sketchy. But he has proposed some broad outlines:

- Partnerships of equal and consultative nature among nations (as opposed to alliances that target and exclude others);
- Just and shared security among nations (as opposed to one's own security—even absolute security[65]—at the expense of others' security);
- Open and inclusive development among nations (as opposed to protective "kicking away the ladder' models");
- Inclusive cultural interchanges that accommodate differences among nations (as opposed to universal values that exclude other moral values[66]); and
- Green development that constructs a healthy ecology (as opposed to economic gains at all costs).[67]

The above are Xi's words, with those in parathesis my own to show how his ideas differ from the worldview we have been living under. *Tian Xia*, in its original conception, has always been pluralistic. Accommodation of differences is central to this outlook. This characteristic distinguishes it from the liberal universal outlook that claims a singular set of values for all.[68]

Western elites are largely ignoring this. It is a mistake. Although the idea needs much further development, it is already resonating around the world. Since Xi coined the term, a majority of China's neighboring countries have signed bilateral documents with China in support of the concept. It is increasingly playing a leading role in China-ASEAN, China-Africa, China-Arabia, China-Africa, and other regional cooperation. The idea of a human community of shared destiny has also been included in resolutions or declarations of international organizations such as the United Nations and the BRICS.[69]

It would be erroneous to see this as an attempt to overturn the current world order. On numerous occasions, Chinese political leaders have acknowledged the fact that China has been a great beneficiary of globalization and their desire to prevent de-globalization.[70] Xi himself said, when describing the concept of human community of a shared destiny, that it was not intended to abandon the current world system and start a new one (*ling qi lu zao*), but an effort to reform and supplement the current order.[71]

The current form of globalization is undoubtedly deteriorating and in reverse. Yet, the world needs a globalized outlook more than ever. Could *Tian Xia* offer such an outlook for the future of globalization?

If the Xi era delivers the China that is envisioned by the party, can China help birth a new *Tian Xia* for the world?

It is here, Xi Jinping may yet prove to be the most consequential leader in the twenty-first century.

Notes

1. Li, Hui. "To Tackle Corruption, Start With Inequality." *The Six Tone*. 20 Sept. 2018.
2. Kintisch, Eli. "Why Is China's Smog So Bad? Researchers Point Far Away to a Melting Arctic." *Science*. 15 Mar. 2017.
3. Economy, Elizabeth. "China's Water Pollution Crisis." *The Diplomat*. 22 Jan. 2013.
4. Li, Eric X. "The CCP's Greatest Strength Is 'Self-Reinvention'." *Foreign Policy*. 2 July. 2021.

5. "'Party's Self-Reform Being a Journey to Which There Is No End' Added to Amended CPC Constitution." *Global Times.* 2 Oct. 2022.
6. See: Chapter Seven, Section "Corruption—Saints or Thieves" for more details.
7. See: Chapter Four, Section "Three Phases of the Chinese Party-State and the New Era" for more details.
8. "CPC Proposes Listing Supervisory Commissions as State Organs in Constitution." *Xinhua.* 25 Feb. 2018.
9. See: Chapter Seven, Section "On the Rule of Law" for more details.
10. See: Chapter Seven, "Revolution (Almost) in the Air—Wumai and Celebrity."
11. Erhai Lake, one of China's largest fresh water lakes located in Yunnan province, was nearly destroyed by rapid development with unregulated tourism and agricultural activities. In 2016, after a visit by President Xi Jinping, the government initiated a large-scale restoration project named "Seven Major Actions (七大行动)". Actions included the forced removals of a large number of environmentally unsound commercial establishments and the building of one of the largest waste water treatment systems in the country. In a span of three years, the restoration project achieved significant success, resulting in a return of Erhai's ecological health and an upgrade of the local tourism industry. See: Cao, Desheng. "Erhai Lake Cleans Up Its Act in Pollution Fight." *China Daily.* 13 Feb. 2019.
12. Goldenberg, Suzanne, and Stratton, John. "From Dinner to Desperation: The 24-Hour Race for a Deal in Copenhagen." The Guardian. 18 Dec. 2009.
13. Geall, Sam. "Clear Waters and Green Mountains: Will Xi Jinping Take the Lead on Climate Change?" Lowy Institute. 16 Nov. 2017; Lai, Hongyi. "The Evolution of China's Climate Change Policy: International and Domestic Political Economy and a Strategy for Working with China." *Journal of the British Academy*, vol. 9, no. 10, 2021, pp. 69–98.
14. According to political philosopher Zhao Tingyang, tianxia, literally meaning "all under heaven," is an alternative philosophy of world order, emphasizing harmonious reciprocal dependence and ruled by virtue as a means for lasting peace.

15. Sicular, Terry. "The Challenge of High Inequality in China." *Inequality in Focus*, vol. 2, no. 2, 2013, pp. 1–5.
16. "China's Xi Declares Victory in Ending Extreme Poverty." BBC. 25 Feb. 2021.
17. State Council Information Office of the People's Republic of China. "Poverty Alleviation: China's Experience and Contribution." 2021.
18. "China's Xi Declares Victory in Ending Extreme Poverty." BBC. 25 Feb. 2021.
19. "Full Text of Xi Jinping's Report at 19th CPC National Congress." *Xinhua*. 3 Nov. 2017.
20. Ibid.
21. "China Plans Millions of Low-Cost Rental Homes in Equality Push." Bloomberg. 11 Jan. 2022.
22. Gupta, Sourabh. "China's 'Common Prosperity' Pathway to Socialist Modernization." ICAS. 14 Dec. 2022.
23. "Xi Tests 'Common Prosperity' Policies in Alibaba's Home Province." Bloomberg. 1 Sept. 2021.
24. Xi, Jinping. "Making Solid Progress Toward Common Prosperity." *Qiushi*. 18 Jan. 2022.
25. Piketty, Thomas, Li Yang, and Gabriel Zucman. "Capital Accumulation, Private Property, and Rising Inequality in China, 1978–2015." *American Economic Review*, vol. 109, no. 7, 2019, pp. 2469–2496.
26. "Davos 2023: Special Address by Liu He, Vice-Premier of the People's Republic of China." World Economic Forum. 17 Jan. 2023.
27. In the past 40 years, China's middle-income group has grown tremendously. As of end 2021, the urbanization rate of China had reached 64.7%, more than 80% of households own their homes. The politics of redistribution must balance many interests.
28. According to Rupert Hoogewerf, founder of *Hurun Report*, China first surpassed the US in the number of billionaires in 2015. In 2020 alone, China created 257 billionaires in US dollar terms.
29. Mr. Ma's speech at the Bund forum was largely seen as an attempt at publicly pressuring the government to change course of impending financial regulations that could be negative to the interests of his company Alipay. See: "Jack Ma Blasts Global Financial Regulators' Curbs on Innovation." *Bloomberg*. 25 Oct. 2020.

30. In 2020, among the top ten richest Chinese billionaires, four came from real estate and four from consumer internet. See: https://www.forbeschina.com/lists/1734.
31. Li, Eric X. "China's New Economy: The First Twenty Years and The Second." Guancha. 19 Jun. 2022.
32. "Japan-Invented QR Code Wins Award for Global Impact in Electronics." *The Japan Times*. 18 Oct. 2020.
33. Monopoly refers to companies that monopolize the market and, thereby, take away market choices by customers. This is downstream. Monopsony refers companies that monopolize their supply side, making them the only customers to their suppliers, including labor. This is upstream.
34. See: Wu, Tim. *The Age of Surveillance Capitalism: The Fight for a Human Future at the New Frontier of Power*; Zuboff, Shoshana. *The Age of Surveillance Capitalism: The Fight for a Human Future at the New Frontier of Power*; Foer, Franklin. *World Without Mind: The Existential Threat of Big Tech*.
35. See: Bouie, Jamelle. "Facebook Has Been a Disaster for the World." *The New York Times*. 18 Sept. 2020; Manjoo, Forhad. "Can Washington Stop Big Tech Companies? Don't Bet on It." *The New York Times*. 25 Oct. 2017; Bartlett, Jamie. *The People Vs Tech: How the Internet Is Killing Democracy (and How We Save It)*.
36. Lee, Emma. "Top 5 Chinese Tech Firms Have Lost Nearly Half of Combined Market Cap in 2 Years." *TechNode*. 9 May 2022.
37. China's manufacturing value added (in current US$) was 4.87 trillion in 2021, according to World Bank.
38. In 2021, profit margin of operating income of China's industrial enterprises above designated size was 6.81%. In the United States, the BEA data showed the profit margin for nonfinancial corporate business after tax was approximately 15%. See: "The Profit of Industrial Enterprises above Designated Size in 2021," *National Bureau of Statistics of China*; Boesler, Matthew. "Profits Soar as U.S. Corporations Have Best Year Since 1950." *Bloomberg*. 31 Mar. 2022.
39. Zhang, Dan. "China May Raise Imports of Chipmaking Machines to Expedite Localization: Analysts." *Global Times*. 3 Feb. 2021.
40. Mickle, Tripp. "How China Has Added to Its Influence Over the iPhone." *The New York Times*. 6 Sept. 2022.

41. CATL (Contemporary Amperex Technology Limited) and BYD are two leading Chinese companies in the electric vehicle (EV) battery and electric vehicle manufacturing industries. They are at the forefront of China's efforts to promote the development and adoption of electric vehicles and clean energy technologies.
42. Feng, Coco. "China Technology Funding Hits Record High on Boom in Semiconductors, Health Care Amid Tech War, Covid-19." *South China Morning Post*. 14 Jan. 2022.
43. Huang, Ruihan, and Henderson, Joshua. "The Return of the Technocrats in Chinese Politics." *Macro Polo*. 3 May 2022.
44. Tiron, Roxana, and Jacobs, Jennifer. "US Sees China as Only Other Nation Capable of Reshaping Global Order." *Bloomberg*. 13 Oct. 2022.
45. Cox, Chelsey. "U.S. Commerce Secretary Raimondo Doubles Down on Biden Plan to Restrict American Companies, and Citizens, from Helping China Make Semiconductor Chips." CNBC. 3 Nov. 2022.
46. For Instance, the recent *Infrastructure Investment and Jobs Act*, *Inflation Reduction Act* and the *CHIPS and Science Act*.
47. "Remarks by President Biden on the CHIPS and Science Act at IBM Poughkeepsie." *The White House*. 6 Oct. 2022.
48. Dalaney, Robert. "Biden Pledges to Prevent China from Becoming the World's 'Leading' Country." *South China Morning Post*. 26 Mar. 2021.
49. The 19th Party Congress established "two Unwaverings," meaning unwavering support for private companies, as well as state-owned ones, as a basic strategy of socialism with Chinese characteristics. See: *Xi's Report to the 19th CPC National Congress*.
50. Xi, Jinping. "The Correct Understanding of Major Theoretical and Practical Problems of China's Development [正确认识和把握我国发展重大理论和实践问题]." *Qiushi*. 15 May 2022.
51. Chu, Yun-Han. *Globalization's Fracturing and Re-integration [全球化的裂解与再融合]*. Beijing: CITIC Publishing Group. 2021.
52. "Xi Focus: Xi and the Power of Chinese Culture." *Xinhua*. 3 Jan. 2022; Xie, Echo. "Xi Jinping Puts Culture, Heritage at Heart of His Chinese Dream." *South China Morning Post*. 15 Oct. 2020.
53. "Full Text of Resolution on Party Constitution Amendment." Xinhua. 22 Oct. 2022.

54. Rudd, Kevin. "The World According to Xi Jinping: What China's Ideologue in Chief Really Believes." *Foreign Affairs*. 10 Oct. 2022.
55. Xi, Jinping. "Dialectical Materialism Is the Worldview and Methodology of the Chinese Communists [辩证唯物主义是中国共产党人的世界观和方法论]." *Qiushi*. 31 Dec. 2018.
56. See: Chapter One, "'Hotel Liberalism—Check-Out Time'."
57. Zhang, Weiwei. *The China Wave: Rise of a Civilizational State*. World Scientific, 2012.
58. Wen, Yang. *The Logic of Civilization [文明的逻辑]*, 2021, pp. 90–97.
59. From "King Wen's Teacher [文师]" in Six Secret Teachings [六韬]. Origional text: 天下非一人之天下, 乃天下之天下也。同天下之利者, 则得天下; 擅天下之利者, 则失天下. See: Sawyer, Ralph D. *The Seven Military Classics of Ancient China*. Basic Books, 1993. p. 41.
60. Ibid.
61. The most authoritative theory on this was written by Confucian scholar Liu Zongyuan (773–819 AD) in the Tang dynasty in his work *On Feudalism*. Wang Fuzhi, a thinker of the late Ming and early Qing dynasties, theorized the same in *Comments after reading the Tongjian* [读通鉴论].
62. On March 23, 2013, visiting Chinese President Xi Jinping delivered a speech entitled "Keeping up with the Trend of the Times and Promoting World Peace and Development[顺应时代前进潮流促进世界和平发展]" at the Moscow State Institute of International Relations, firstly bringing the notion of "a community with a shared future for mankind" to the world's attention.
63. Tingyang, Zhao. "A Political World Philosophy in terms of All-under-heaven (Tian-xia)." Diogenes, vol. 56, no. 1, 2009, pp. 5–18.
64. Ibid.
65. Luxner, Larry. "How the US Can Deal with China from a Position of Strength, According to Dan Sullivan." *Atlantic Council*. 24 Mar. 2021.
66. Scholars have made the distinction between *tian xia* and universal values. As Zhao Tingyang put it, the tolerance of cultural diversity associated with monotheism is not a way of truly respecting other cultures, but rather merely represents a means of placing

other cultures into a fringe or periphery position vis-à-vis the self-avowed dominant culture. A tian xia system, as a compatibilist universalism, would recognize cultural "pluralism" that is different from this derogatory sense of "diversity." See: Zhao, Tingyang. *All Under Heaven: The Tianxia System for a Possible World Order.* Vol. 3. University of California Press, 2021, pp. 242–243.
67. See: Xi Jinping's speech at the United Nations Office at Geneva in 18 January 2017, entitled "Work Together to Build a Community of Shared Future for Mankind."
68. Zhao, Tingyang. *All Under Heaven: The Tianxia System For A Possible World Order.* Vol. 3. University of California Press, 2021, pp. 242–243.
69. Deng, Wenke, and Jiang, Yuechun. "How China Can Help Build an Asia–Pacific Community with a Shared Future." *China Daily.* 19 Jul. 2022.
70. See: Parker, Ceri. "China's Xi Jinping Defends Globalization from the Davos Stage." *World Economic Forum.* 17 Jan. 2017. "President Xi Jinping Stresses the Need to Advance Economic Globalization." *CGTN.* 18 Jun. 2022. "Full Text: Remarks by Chinese President Xi Jinping at the Opening Ceremony of the Fifth China International Import Expo." *China Daily.* 4 Nov. 2022.
71. "Full Text: Xi's Speech at B20 Summit Opening Ceremony." *China.org.cn.* 5 Sept. 2016.

Index

A
AAC Technologies, 34
Afghanistan, 5, 9
Alibaba, 32–34, 218, 219
Allison, Graham, xiii, 54, 189, 192
Andropov, Yuri, 6
Anti-Rightist Campaign, 79
Arab Spring, 12, 86, 152, 155
Aristotle, 162, 164, 166, 170
Articles of Confederation, 15
Artprice, 37
Asian Infrastructure Investment Bank (AIIB), 56, 190, 194
Australia, 38

B
Bangladesh, 13
Belt and Road Initiative (BRI), ix, 38, 39, 190, 194, 201, 205, 206, 230
Berlin Wall, 1, 10, 77
Biden, Joseph, 14, 57, 223
Bolshevik, 73
Brazil, 38
Brexit, 17
Brezhnev, Leonid, 2
BRICS, 29
Brown, Jerry, x
Brunei, 38
Bush, George H.W., 2, 7, 47, 48
Bush, George W., 108
ByteDance, 33

C
Campbell, Kurt M., 189–191
Central Committee Politics and Law Commission, 170, 171
Central Disciplinary Inspection Commission (CDIC), 82
Central Organizational Department (COD), 111, 112
Chai Jing, 158
Chang, Gordon, 50
Chernenko, Konstantin, 6
Chiang Kai-shek, 71
China
  art and creativity, 36
  Belt and Road initiatives, 37–39
  Confucianism and, 74–77
  culture revolution and, 4, 7

economic growth, 29, 31
entrepreneurial governance and, 129, 130, 132
experimental governance and, 122–127, 129
from feudalism to republic, 67–73
globalization and, 185
internet and, 152–156, 158–160
market reforms, 40
poverty alleviation, 31
private capital and, 216–219, 221–223
rule of law and, 160, 161, 163, 166–172
strategic governance and, 133–136, 138, 139
technology and innovation, 32–35
the development model of, xi, xii, 1, 4, 7, 16, 27–29, 63, 64, 66
the United States and, 47–49, 53, 54, 57–60
western perspectives of, 50–53
Chinese Soviet Republic, 72
Christopher, Warren, 47–49
Chu Yun-han, 225
Clinton, Bill, 8, 14, 47, 48, 51, 102
Clinton, Hillary, 53
Cold War
the world after, xi
color revolution, 9
common prosperity, 52, 83, 216, 217
Confucianism, xi, 74, 76, 168–170
Confucius, 69, 74, 75, 101, 167, 227
cooperative medical systems (CMS), 124, 125
Covid-19, 17, 58, 172–174, 181, 204
Cox Report, 51
Cuba, 48, 135
Cultural Revolution, 4, 7, 79, 81, 86, 197
Czech Republic, 11

D
Davos, 187
Deng visit to Singapore, 39
Deng Xiaoping
COD and, 111
party-government separation and, 115
political transformation and, 79
pragmatism and, 40
reform and opening-up, ix, 27, 28, 52
special economic zones and, 122
visit to Japan, 133
De Tocqueville, Alexis, 15
Diamond, Larry, 13, 187
diaoyan, 138
Dicey, A.V., 166
Douyin, 33
Dunn, John, 188
Duterte, Rodrigo, 58, 201
Dworkin, Ronald, 161, 169, 171

E
Enlightenment, 14, 15, 64
Eryuehe, 145
European Union, 9

F
Fairbank, John K., 68
Fan Zhongyan, 148
Farage, Nigel, 58
Federalists, 15
Fei Xiaotong, 131
Ferguson, Niall, 121, 198
First United Front, 72
Five-Year Plan, 135–138
Four Cardinal Principles, 80
Fourth Plenum
of 18th Central Committee, 164
Freedom House, 9, 10, 13
Friedman, Thomas, 187

Fukuyama, Francis
  on bad emperor problem, 114
  on China's reform, 29
  on determinism, 8
  on evolution of human history, 3
  on identity politics, 151, 157
  on political decay, 18
  on the "End of History", 8, 192

G
Galli, W.B., 167
Gingrich, Newt, 51
globalism, 198–201, 203, 205
Goldman, Marshall, 4
Gomulka, Wladislaw, 5
Gorbachev, Mikhail
  rising to power, 6, 7
  Soviet dissolution and, 2, 6
  Soviet reform and, 4, 6, 7
Great Firewall, 33, 151–153
Great Leap Forward, 81
Greece, 38
Griffiths, Daniel, 145
Grishin, Viktor, 6
Guangming Daily, 40
Gu Weijun, 70
Gwadar Port, 39

H
Hayek, Friedrich, 121
Hegel, Frederich
  determinism and, 3
Heilmann, Sebastian, 122
Heritage Foundation, 9, 10
high quality development, 83, 221
high-speed rail, ix, x, 33, 39, 133–135, 155–157
Hong Kong, 68, 86, 152
Hu Angang, 136
Huang Yukon, 149
Huawei, 35, 36

Hu Jintao
  his career, 107, 108
  his leadership, 214
Hungarian uprising, 5
Hungary, 11, 201
Huntington, Samuel, 12, 17, 195
Hurd, Douglas, 2

I
India
  corruption and, 149
  infrastructure of, ix
  internet and, 160
Indonesia, 8, 39
iPhone, 185, 221
Iran, 12
Iraq, 9, 13

J
Japan, 29, 55, 69, 133
Jenks, Edward, 162
Jiang Zemin
  Clinton and, 14
  his career, 102–104
Jiawu War, 68, 69
jiefangqu, 72, 73, 78
Jin Keyu, 206
Judt, Tony, 7

K
Kaplan, David, 165
Kazakhstan, 8
Kennan, George, 2, 7, 59
Kennedy, John F., 196
Khrushev, Nikita, 5
Kim Jong-un, 58
Korean war, 80
Kuhn, Thomas, xi
Kuomintang (the KMT), 71, 72

L
Lake, Anthony, 8, 48
Larry, Diamond, 14
Latin America, 8
Lee Kuan Yew, 63, 130
Legalism, 168, 170
Levy, Bernard-Henri, 203
Liang Qichao, 70
liberal democracy, 14
Ligachev, Yegor, 6, 7
Li Hongzhang, 69
Lincoln, Abraham, 189
Lind, Michael, 191
Linz, Juan, 14
Liu Bang, 73
Liu Shaoqi, 75, 76, 82, 111
Locke, John, 162
Luther, Martin, 65
Lyotard, Jean-François, 3

M
MacIntyre, Andrew, 147
Madison, James, 15
Magna Carta, 162, 163
maidanocracy, 86
Ma, Jack, 218
Mali, 38
Mandate of Heaven, 168
Mao Zedong
    Anti-Rightist Campaign and, 79
    Culture Revolution and, 76, 77
    experimental governance and, 122
    first 30 years of PRC and, 82
    involvement in KMT, 72
    national independence and, 80
    political ideas in early years, 69
    state building and, 78
Marshall Plan, 38
Marx, Karl, 3, 101
May Fourth Movement, 70
Mearsheimer, John, 54

Mei Ciqi, 125
Mencius, 74, 78, 169
Merkel, Angela, 186
Millennium Challenge Corporation (MCC), 10
Mill, John Stuart, 15, 101
Ministry of Supervision, 214
Modi, Narendra, ix
Montesquieu, 15
Most Favored Nation (the MFN), 48
Mounk-Foa, 19

N
Nasr, Vali, 110
National Congress of the Chinese Communist Party
    1st, 70
    14th, 144
    15th, 144, 160
    16th, 144
    17th, 144, 214
    18th, 77, 81, 144, 214
    19th, 41, 113, 143, 144, 167
    20th, 83, 173, 214, 222, 225
National People's Congress (NPC), 81
National Supervisory Commission, 115
NATO, 9, 59
New Community Medical System (NCMS), 126
Nietzsche, 64
Nigeria, 13
Nixon, Richard, 47, 189–191
North Korea, 48, 58, 135
Nye, Joseph, 188

O
Obama, Barack
    election campaign, x
    his career, 108–110

INDEX 257

pivot to Asia and, 53, 189
stalemate in the Copenhagen climate conference, 216
the quasi-containment, 55, 56
Oi, Jean, 133
Olson, Mancur, 17
Omicron, 173
Opium War
  the first, 68
  the second, 68, 69
Orban, Viktor, 11, 201

P
Pakistan, 39
Parekh, Bhikhu, 15
Paulson, Henry, 27, 190
Peerenboom, Randall, 172
Pei, Minxin, 196
perestroika and *glasnost*, 7
Philippines, 19, 55
Pillsbury, Michael, 50, 54
Piraeus Port, 38
pivot to Asia, 53
Plato, 64, 101
Poland, 11
Polish United Workers Party, 5
poverty reduction, 31
Putin, Vladimir, 5, 12, 58
Pye, Lucian, 76

Q
Qianlong, 67–70
Qin Gang, 206
Qing dynasty, 68, 69
Qiushi, 224

R
RAND Corporation, 125
Ratner, Ely, 189–191
Reagan, Ronald, 135, 196

Reif, Rafael, 184
Roberts, John, 184
Rudd, Kevin, 225
Runciman, David, 14
Russia
  post-Soviet era, 12

S
Sachs, Jeffrey, 199
Saez, Emmanuel, 16
Schell, Orville, 28, 187
Schmitt, Carl, 163
Scholz, Olaf, 194
self-revolution, 214, 226
shidafu, 74–77, 169
Shklar, Judith, 162
Singapore, 39
Smith, Adam, 121
Smith, Jean Edward, 108
Solomon, Richard, 77
Soros, George, 187
Southern Tour, ix, 144
South Korea, 11
Soviet Union
  dogmatism of, 4
  invasion of Afghanistan, 5
  national economy during the Cold War, 2
  political model, 3, 4
  the dissolution, 2
  the reform model of, 1
  the unrest of, 5
  the world order and, 191
Special Economic Zone, 122
Spence, Michael, 16
Stalin, Joseph, 4, 5, 72, 73
Su Nan model, 131
Sun-Joffe Declaration, 71
Sunny Optics, 132
Sun Yat-sen, 71
Suzhou Industrial Park, 131

T

Taiwan, 11, 59, 68, 132
Tamanaha, Brian, 163, 164, 170
Temburong Bridge, 38
Tencent, 32
te qu, 122, 123
Thailand, 14
The End of History, 8
Third Plenum
  of 18th Central Committee, 81–83
Third Wave, 12
Thucydides' Trap, 54
Tiananmen Square incident, 48, 83, 85, 87, 88, 191
Tian Xia, 216, 227–230
TikTok, 33
Tito, Josip, 5
town and village enterprises (TVE), 131, 132
Trans-Pacific Partnership (TPP), 55
Trump, Donald
  America First and, 59
  China and, 58
  China policy, 56
  his 2016 election, 19
  his career, 110
  recession of democracy and, 14
  worries about China, x

U

Ukraine, 11, 13, 59, 86, 102, 152, 155, 194, 195, 203, 204
United Kingdom, 29
United Nations, 39, 59, 190, 202, 230
United States
  cold war and, 191, 192
  corruption and, 147
  de facto alliance with China, 81, 189, 190
  economic growth, 29
  globalism and, 199
  globalization and, 185
  global order and, 191
  high-speed rail and, x
  infrastrucrture and, 135
  liberal democracy and, 16, 101, 191, 202
  liberalism enlargement and, 8–10, 14, 48
  national economy during the Cold War, 2
  nuclear arsenal, 57
  perceptions of the political system, x
  pivot to Asia and, 189
  quasi-containment, 54–57
  regulations on telecommunications and, 151
  rule of law and, 160–163
  sanctions against China, 48
  the liberal model and, 1
  the new cold war and, 193–195
  trade with China, 48
  vetocracy and, 18

V

Venezuela, 14
vetocracy, 18, 138
Vietnam, 48, 56

W

Wang Qishan, 145, 148
Wang Shaoguang, 123, 138
Washington Consensus, 8–11, 13, 52, 58, 198, 203
Weber, Max, 121
WeChat, 33
Weibo, 155, 157
Weiner, Norbert, 153
Wen Jiabao, 216
Whampoa Military Academy, 72
Williamson, John, 8

Winterer, Caroline, 204
World Trade Organization, 49, 189, 207
Wuhan, 103, 172, 173
wumai, 157, 158

X
Xiao Yang, 165
Xi Jinping
  anti-corruption drive and, 145, 148, 150, 215
  Biden and, 195, 196
  common prosperity and, 167, 216, 217, 220
  ecological civilization and, 215, 216
  globalization and, 200, 206
  high-quality development and, 167, 221
  his career, 108–111, 113
  his leadership, 82, 114–116, 143, 213
  his political thought, 223–230
  rule of law and, 160
  self-revolution and, 214
  the new era and, 41, 81, 83
Xinhai Revolution, 69, 71

Y
Yangwu Movement, 69
Yan Yilong, 138
Yeltsin, Boris, 2
Yeo, George, 153
YGZ reform, 126, 127, 129
Yugoslavia, 5

Z
Zakaria, Fareed, 18, 195
Zhang Weiwei, 116, 227
Zhang Xinsheng, 129
Zhao Dingxin, 168
Zhao Tingyang, 229, 231
Zhao Ziyang, 84, 85
Zheng Yongnian, 77
Zhou Enlai, 67, 75, 111
Zhu Rongji
  Chinese economic reform and, ix
  his career, 105, 106
Zhu Yuanzhang, 73
Zubok, Vladislav, 2, 6
Zucman, Gabriel, 16

Printed by Printforce, the Netherlands